Stanley Jackson is a successful businessman and self-described compulsive entrepreneur, his current business being the third that he has started in a career spanning more than fifty years. He is Chairman of Performing Artistes that he set up twenty-two years ago and which has grown from modest beginnings into one of the UK's leading international speaker agencies. He is the author of two previous books plus a musical based on *A Tale of Two Cities* by Charles Dickens.

Gavin Jackson BA (Hons), PG Dip graduated from Manchester University with a degree in Philosophy in the nineties and from Sheffield Hallam University with a postgraduate diploma in Technical Writing in the noughties. For over twenty years his day job has been as a technical author for various IT giants, and he has been published in the *BBC Education* magazine. He is a self-confessed bookaholic and passionate film lover.

Both authors are members of the Decamot collective.

Book of
DECAMOT

Stanley Jackson
and
Gavin Jackson

Library of Congress Control Number: 2015913889
ISBN: Hardcover   978-1-5144-6271-3
               Softcover   978-1-5144-6270-6
               eBook   978-1-5144-6269-0

Print information available on the last page.

Rev. date: 09/07/2015

To order additional copies of this book, contact:
Xlibris
800-056-3182
www.Xlibrispublishing.co.uk
Orders@Xlibrispublishing.co.uk
714987

CONTENTS

PREFACE

When we first came up with the name Decamot for our innocent family word game, we had no idea that we might be continuing a literary tradition stretching back to the Greek historian Herodotus (c480–c425 BCE), whose work inspired a host of subsequent writers including such literary luminaries as Geoffrey Chaucer and William Shakespeare.

Decamot (pronounced decker-mow) started as a Christmas parlour game in which each player writes a short story containing ten given words. Each participant is given the same set of ten words and, once completed, invited to read out their story to the assembled group of fellow competitors who vote on which one they consider to be the most entertaining and original. Needless to say, a contestant is not able to vote for his or her own entry.

As we continued to play Decamot at a distance (by email), rules evolved to protect the identity of an individual author to ensure that each offering is treated with equal reverence and that the story itself is judged purely on its own merits. Only when the winner is announced is the author revealed. How many literary awards might be spiced up, one wonders, if they were conducted according to similar rules? So far we have spent the best part of fifteen years playing and developing Decamot from a simple competitive short story writing game to a device for writing novellas and screenplays for cinema and television.

A few years ago we stumbled across an entry in *The Oxford Companion* to English Literature (OCEL) for *The Decameron*, a collection of tales from many sources gathered and retold by Giovanni Boccaccio, the Italian writer and humanist, between 1349 and 1351. In Boccaccio's *Decameron* three young males and seven young females leave Florence in 1348 to escape the plague and visit neighbouring villas. They spend part of each of ten days in amusing one another with stories, each person telling one tale on each day so that there are 100 tales in all. The accent would seem to have been on entertainment rather than literary merit.

Boccaccio's masterpiece is one of a number of translations into English by William Painter (c1525–c1595) in *Palace of Pleasure*. Painter's book became a storehouse of plots for Elizabethan writers and dramatists. According to the OCEL, Shakespeare probably used it for *The Rape of Lucrece* and *All's Well that Ends Well* and John Webster (c1578–c1632) for *The Duchess of Malfi*.

Painter's other sources included Herodotus, Bandello and Marguerite of Navarre (1492–1549) whose tales were based on the fiction that the narrators are travellers trapped at an inn during a flood. There were meant to be 100 tales but only 72 were completed. As a consequence, the collection was named *The Heptameron* (seven days) in 1559 echoing Boccaccio's *The Decameron*.

So other people have had similar ideas to ours in the past. Where our idea differs is the way in which we stimulate the initial ideas for the story. The Decamot writing process doesn't just suggest that storytelling is a satisfying and worthwhile pastime; it also suggests how to find that initial spark and then how to develop an idea into a story. The largest obstacle to inspiration is often the blank page; the Decamot writing process takes away that obstacle.

This book tells the tale of how our simple Christmas pastime became the Decamot method of short story writing. Along the way, it looks at the secrets of what makes a successful short story and provides plenty of samples written by the authors. Essentially, this is a story about story writing, a story-writing process, and the stories written using that process.

STANLEY JACKSON AND GAVIN JACKSON

Included in this book is a chapter that discusses how the Decamot writing process was applied to develop a simple story into something more substantial. Initially, a set of Decamot words inspired two short, but related stories. At a later date, rereading the two stories suggested a third longer story that contained the first two and new material that bridged the gap between the two. Ultimately, we turned the story into the screenplay for a movie. At this point in time we realised that we had transformed Decamot from a game into a writing process.

All the stories included in this book were written between 2000 and 2015 by various members of the Jackson Decamot Collective using the principles of the Decamot writing process. They have been edited a little during the preparation of this book but only really to address typos, grammar issues, and in some places problems with the logic of the story. Every effort has been made to maintain the character and spirit of the original stories. We hope you enjoy them all and feel inspired to write your own!

The Jackson Decamot Collective, April 2015

CHAPTER 1

The Decamot Writing Game

A Simple Parlour Game

Before it had a name, Decamot was a game with a single simple rule: Take a set of ten ordinary, but totally disconnected words, and put them together within a single coherent story. Our first Decamots were far from literary masterpieces. To be brutally honest, they were often little more than linguistic tongue-twisters, perhaps an extension to the Victorian game of similes.

But what we were quick to recognise was that the basic Decamot concept provides a starting point for a story. A blank sheet of paper and no direction at all quite often leads to a blank mind. But given ten initial disparate words, a little time, and the element of competition, something magical happens: Two or three of the words can suddenly combine to give you an unexpected idea from which a story can slowly (or sometimes suddenly) emerge. The remaining Decamot words can then help you to discover where the story might next go. Interestingly, when two or more people are given the same set of words, they invariably come up with radically different stories.

Some Decamot stories, if left for a while to settle once initially written, mature, like a fine wine. These may have taken many hours to write over several weeks. Returning to them, editing them, and collaborating on them to produce an improved version have proven to provide a certain intellectual satisfaction.

Inspiration

The creation of the game stems from our love of playing with words whether in regular letter writing, joking in puns, or simply playing board games. Scrabble is naturally a favourite, providing endless hours of competitive fun. It must rank among the most inventive of board games ever devised. Each game is different, and the margin between winning and losing is often reduced to a few points for evenly matched opponents. We have also had periods of making up our own crosswords with admittedly mixed results. How appropriate or fair a cryptic clue is can be a bone of contention.

During the Christmas holiday of 1999, we were playing another family favourite: our version of *Call My Bluff* which we based on the TV programme of the 1970s and 1980s hosted by Robert Robinson. It featured Frank Muir and Arthur Marshall as team captains. In our version, each team prepares in advance a set of possible definitions for a selection of rare or obscure words but, in each set of definitions, only one is genuine, the others are 'bluffs'. Team members take it in turns to read the definitions, each reading the definition that they wrote; the opposing team then has to guess which of the definitions is correct.

Call My Bluff had its limitations. Firstly, writing the bluffs could be fun if the chosen obscure word inspired a good idea, but after you'd written a few bluffs, the writing process became formulaic, and the resultant bluffs less satisfying to both construct and to listen to. Secondly, there was always a possibility that a member of the opposing team might already know the word for which you were attempting to concoct spurious definitions. So how best to improve the game?

We had a brainwave: Rather than trying to compose a set of fake definitions for an obscure word, why not take a set of ordinary, but totally disconnected, words and let each person attempt to put them together in a single coherent story? Keeping in the spirit of *Call My Bluff*, each person in turn would read out their own work, but this time their work would be a short story rather than a *Call My Bluff* definition. The winner of this new game would be the person adjudged by their fellow players to have written the most satisfying story.

We handed round scraps of paper and pens, came up with a set of words to work with, and allowed ourselves thirty minutes. Some pretty daft stories emerged, but it was fun.

Exchanging Stories

After the Christmas holidays ended we decided to continue playing the game by email. To do so, we picked ten words or phrases at random; each person wrote a short story containing all ten items, then emailed that story to a central point. Thanks to Internet technology, we managed to add an element of anonymity; because we set up and shared a story competition email account, it was possible to play the game of Decamot without the identity of the individual authors being immediately apparent. Each participant would later retrieve the entries, read them all, and vote for the story (other than their own) that they thought was the best. The winner of each game would then select ten items for the next short story. This marked the genesis of the Decamot writing process, although it would be many months before the game morphed into a process. For now, it was still just a game.

We exchanged our first stories in January 2000, but as a family we've always loved reading and performing aloud. The works of Roald Dahl were a particular favourite, first the Charlie Bucket novels, *Fantastic Mr Fox, and Danny the Champion of the World*; then Dahl's books of short stories, books written for adults, but dynamite for young imaginative minds. When TV adaptations of Dahl's work were made under the title *Tales of the Unexpected*, we quickly became avid fans.

The whole family fell in love with *The Hitch-Hiker's Guide to the Galaxy*, firstly on the radio, then when it came out as a sequence of novels. But that's just the tip of the iceberg. The family bookshelves are stacked with books of many genres and styles, including collections of short stories for when time is limited. It's fascinating to discover short stories by authors who you generally associate with novels: Charles Dickens, H.G. Wells, Stephen King, Lawrence Block, Salman Rushdie, Ian Rankin, Neil Gaiman, and Terry Prachett have all written corking short stories. However, it wasn't until we devised the Decamot game that we considered writing short stories of our own for fun. The Decamot game got us writing short stories on a monthly basis. The number we've written is well into three figures.

It's quite interesting to see how a single set of ten items can often inspire several radically different stories. We've included in this book five chapters each of which contain two Decamots, both of which were inspired by the same set of ten Decamot items.

How Long Is a Yarn?

Our very first Decamot attempts were simple exercises in word-play and not much else. How best to squeeze the ten unrelated items into one coherent story containing as few words as possible?

We are fans of the moderately cryptic crossword puzzle, those that conform to the cryptic pattern but are not totally obscure. The *Radio Times* Prize, the *Guardian* Quiptic, and, when time permits, the *London Evening Standard* Cryptic crossword are good examples. We've also been known to compile the odd crossword for fun at family get-togethers.

Although writing short stories and ultra-short stories was good fun, it tended to become a little samey and their writing, formulaic. It's rather like limerick writing: It loses its freshness after you've written a dozen or so, as the late Ronnie Barker discovered when he set about trying to improve upon Edward Lear's book of nonsense verse by providing an alternative last line to each of the famous poet's somewhat circular ditties. Barker's own inscription to the completed work describes his worthy endeavour:

> There was an old fossil called Lear,
> Whose verses were boring and drear,
> His last lines were worst,
> just the same as the first;
> So I've tried to improve on them here!

For example, in the following limerick:

> There was a Young Lady of Turkey,
> Who wept when the weather was murky;

When the day turned out fine,
she ceased to repine,
That capricious Young Lady of Turkey.

Barker changed the last line to the much more amusing:

In fact, she became rather perky!

But by the end, Barker had clearly had enough; the final limerick he
enhanced became:

There was a Young Lady of Clare,
Who was sadly pursued by a bear;
When she found she was tired,
she abruptly expired.
As do these rhymes—in despair!

The end product of the economically written Decamots had limited
appeal to readers not party to our Decamot writing game. The following
entry is the most extreme example of Decamot concision. It was inspired
by the following Decamot Items: *world's longest maze, Marble Arch, Internet,
bus, piano, Plasticine chicken, remote Scottish island, hidden treasure, off-duty
policeman, black taxi.*

Self-Centred

'Surfing the Internet is like navigating the World's longest maze,'
announced the bald-headed man from his seat on the red bus.

'I am not sure I agree,' replied an off-duty policeman, his temporary
companion, from the seat opposite. 'More like finding a Plasticine
chicken on a remote Scottish island, if you ask me.'

'Or playing piano in the back of a black taxi,' chimed in the conductor
as he exchanged tickets for money.

'Three more breaths wasted by the lower classes,' thought Will Self as
he steered the bus round Marble Arch. 'O the hidden treasures one

finds on public transport, must credit them in my next Booker Prize *losing* opus.'

* * *

We knew that if we were going to continue writing Decamots on a monthly basis, they would have to be more satisfying to write and would have to appeal to a more general readership; so we changed the rules. We lifted the limit on word length. Instead, we allowed the stories to be as long as they needed to be to tell a satisfying story. We also revisited stories after a short period had elapsed since their writing to see how well they worked, and to improve them if any part did not appear to work as well as they might.

We found the more open-ended nature of the story length liberating. The satisfaction in writing Decamots increased immediately, and never abated. We still write Decamots and use the Decamot writing process to get and to keep the inspiration flowing.

What's in a Name?

Names are an important feature of any story, long or short. Some names are brilliantly chosen and stick in the memory long after the details of the story itself have been forgotten. Others are less successful. Sheridan's Mrs Malaprop, Shelly's Frankenstein, Doyle's Holmes, Dickens's Scrooge, Bronte's Heathcliff, Wodehouse's Jeeves, Edgar Rice Burroughs's Tarzan, F. Scot Fitzgerald's Gatsby, and J.K. Rowling's Harry Potter are names widely known by most people whether or not they've read any works in which they appear.

Ian Rankin chose well with Inspector Rebus (a crime solver named for a type of puzzle). Ian Fleming was the king of the double entendre when naming his Bond 'girls': Pussy Galore, Honey Ryder, Plenty O'Toole, Mary Goodnight, names that were curiously out of character in his otherwise serious novels. The central character of James Clavell's novel King Rat couldn't be better named. Corporal King truly is a king rat; he profits at the expense of his fellow prisoners in the Changi POW camp at the tail end of World War II, and is left at the end of the novel being sent home in disgrace to face trial.

Joseph Heller's World War II profiteer in *Catch 22* is the brilliantly named Milo Minderbinder. Attempting to contemplate some of his antics really does bind your mind. He manages to persuade everyone to invest with him (including the Germans); he starts off with relatively small deals: he buys eggs for his unit for 8c each, then sells them to other units for 6c each, and somehow still makes a profit; by the end of the war, in perhaps his most audacious business transaction, he contracts out a German bombing raid of American supplies to his own American bombing unit; a task that they do superbly, with no loss of life to either side, which of course shortens supply and thereby increases profit potential for Minderbinder Enterprises.

Jasper Fforde's novels are peopled with an army of well-named characters: Landen Park-Laine, Harris Tweed, Millon de Floss, Red Herring, and of course, the Cheshire Cat, who, due to boundary changes, is referred to as the Unitary Authority of Warrington Cat. Our favourite Jasper Fforde name though appears in the first of his Nursery Crimes novels, and is the name of an institution, not a person, St Cerebellum's; a great name for a psychiatric hospital! Jasper Fforde is so well known for his love of word play and whacky naming that the annual fan conference that meets in Swindon (the epicentre of Fforde's fictional universe) is called the *Fforde Ffiesta*.

In our stories names do often have a habit of being recycled, so where the same name crops up in two stories, they're not necessarily the same person. For example, Jake Gaston crops up a few times, but always as a different character; but the Willem Schmidt and Erik Friedheimer, who appear in **A Tale of One City**, **German Graffiti**, and **The Wall,** are the same characters in all three. Other names have been selected very carefully for their character's role in a particular story, for example, Milo Dimas in **The Wishing Well** TV screenplay.

Decamot, Jackson Decamot

The name *Decamot* was a collaborative effort. It is a portmanteau word that we came up with after several months of playing our create-a-story-with-ten-perfectly-ordinary-but-totally-disconnected-words game. We decided we needed a new catchier name and thought it would be fun to create a new word that appeared to have a mixed linguistic root. We gave it hints of Greek (influenced by words like decathlon) and French (influenced by the phrase *le mot juste* meaning 'the right word').

We may have been inspired in part by *The Decalogue*, a cycle of ten films by the Polish director Krzysztof Kieslowski. The stories are set round the same Warsaw apartment block and focus on the complexities of human relationships. The themes are the universal ones of love, marriage, infidelity, parenthood, guilt, faith and compassion – all excellent themes for short stories too!

The fact that the name *Decamot* bears a similarity to the Italian Decameron is a genuine coincidence. It was a fact of which we were blissfully unaware until many years later. It is helpful to draw a distinction between the two: *Decameron* is an anthology of stories; *Decamot* is a methodology, a way of generating and developing story ideas.

We now use the word *Decamot* in four ways:

- **Decamot writing process:** the process that originated with the game whereby you select ten words or phrases and use them to inspire a story
- **Decamot:** the story that emerges from the **Decamot writing process**
- **Decamot items:** the list of ten words or phrases that must be included in the **Decamot**
- **Jackson Decamot Collective:** members of the Jackson family who write **Decamots**

We sometimes refer to some of the stories as being by Jackson Decamot: our family name *is* Jackson and they *are* Decamots. The first draft of any given story is the work of any one of us, but subsequent edits are often a collective effort.

Over time, Decamot has taken on a life of its own. So much so that in one of our Decamot writing competitions we received a surprise entry from one Jackson Decamot. The entry was biographical in nature and provided a fictitious account of the origins of the name Decamot taken from the inside jacket of a hypothetical book of short stories written by the non-existent Jackson Decamot. The account contained each of that month's Decamot items and was entitled **Inside the Jacket**. In a later story, **An Invisible Man**, a certain Mr Jackson Decamot appears as a non-existent employee that the protagonist invents for his own nefarious purposes.

Choosing Decamot Items

If you enter a short story competition in a magazine, the more prescriptive the rules, the less satisfying is the writing of that story and the more predictable the outcome. There was recently a competition in a travel magazine with the following instructions: Write a story that describes your best ever holiday . . . in the sun . . . in Turkey! Naturally, you could have sent in a tale about how you spent one summer teaching a troupe of penguins how to tango in the Antarctic sunshine, but your entry would probably not have made the final cut. The travel magazine obviously wanted to publish a very specific type of stories, and weren't really interested in whether it was actually *your* best ever holiday.

In a similar way, if you allow a set of Decamot items to be connected, or to have a theme, the nature of the stories that emerge tend to be predictable. For example, for the following Decamot items *white bearded old man, North Pole, present, red nose, turkey, sleigh, hanging stockings, mince, little helper, Holly* you might be inspired to write a story about Holly, the aging, pot-smoking, transvestite from Gdansk, taking a budget holiday in Bodram, hanging out his laundry on the balcony, before getting sunburn while floating in the swimming pool on an inflatable sleigh, a quirky tale that might satisfy that travel magazine's prescription. But it would be hard to overlook the option of writing about a traditional family Christmas.

For one of our monthly Decamot games, the Decamot word-setter clearly had something in mind when the first five items given were

Starship Enterprise, moonscapes, nuclear warhead, leaky pen, and a bluish tinge. Unsurprisingly, that setter is a science fiction aficionado with a scientific bent. Curiously, the remaining five items in the list were: *Kama Sutra, rubber glove, a lampshade, faggots,* and *breast pocket.* As a result, the stories that emerged were either sci-fi in nature or somewhat saucy. One entry, **Space: The Final Full Frontal**, was both. It was a cheeky parody of a certain sci-fi series; the dialogue was as close to a typical episode as possible with the speech patterns and mannerisms of the main characters being as close to the original as possible.

Competitive Edge

The game aspect of Decamot writing has always been an important element with a positive influence on the quality of the stories that we produce. All games need winners, and the Jackson Decamot Collective is a competitive bunch. We all want to be the one who wins a round and sets the Decamot items for the next round. How we determine a winner for each of our monthly rounds of Decamot has changed over time. Initially, we all simply emailed the stories to each other and voted on which story we thought was the best. Now we rank each of the stories (other than one's own) giving our least favourite one point, next least favourite two points, and so on. We then email the votes to each other, aggregate the scores, and declare the winner to be the story with the highest score.

Winning

Voting and assigning a winner helped to determine what was good, what was not, what worked, what didn't. Since writing the first Decamots, we've added an element of anonymity to the sending and receiving of the stories. We set up a Web address from which we could email the entries, which meant we could no longer automatically identify authorship. When we started to use the anonymous Web address it was still obvious who wrote which stories. There's no point in sending entries anonymously if your writing style gives you away. If Dick Francis had written a novel using a pseudonym, but included a preface that started: 'I can't remember when I first learnt to ride', his identity as the author would have been rumbled instantly.

Anonymity helped to encourage variety and experimentation. In time, in order to outwit each other, we would experiment with style, content, and format. Apart from quality and variety, an interesting aspect of this experimentation came when selecting stories for inclusion in this book: It was often hard (if not impossible) to remember who wrote the original story, especially if two or more of us had later collaborated to produce an improved version.

Deadlines

In *The Salmon of Doubt*, Douglas Adams claims to love deadlines especially 'the whooshing sound they make as they fly by'. Unlike Mr Adams, we've found deadlines valuable. We generally impose a time limit on ourselves of two weeks for each Decamot contest. We find this helps to concentrate the mind and get the story written. We're all busy people, we all have full-time jobs, so without the deadline, it would always be possible to put off the writing. With the deadline, you find yourself squeezing in the writing whenever and wherever you can: Breakfast at work, coffee shop for elevenses, or an evening burst in lieu of the TV. We've also found that a two-week time frame is long enough to sketch out enough of the story to determine whether it's worth developing the story further at a later date.

Rules of Engagement

Just as we improved the way we submitted entries and determined winners, we also gradually refined the way we selected the ten Decamot items. We now use the following five rules:

1. The words or phrases should be as unrelated to each other as possible.
2. 1–3 items should indicate people (they should be in the form of a name, profession, or description).
3. 1–2 items should indicate locations (they should be a specific place or a geographic description).
4. 4–6 items should be inanimate objects of varying sizes (anything from a thimble to a nuclear warhead).
5. 0–1 items should be a saying or metaphor.

The rationale for these rules was twofold: to guarantee a level of consistency of the Decamot item lists and to make the selection process as easy as possible. Plans are afoot to go one step further and generate Decamot item lists automatically using a computer, a database, and an appropriate algorithm.

Surprising Connections

The random nature of the words and their unconnectedness is the key to the success of the Decamot writing process. The juxtaposition of two or more of the Decamot items quite often throws up something funny or surprising. One approach is to start by trying to find a novel idea by considering just two of the items, attempting to think about as many meanings of those two items as possible, and then seeing what combinations of those meanings evoke.

For example, consider the words 'game' and 'killer', perfectly reasonable candidates for a Decamot. Taken literally, there are many types of game: board games, card games, ball games, team games, etc. 'Game' could just as easily refer to the world's oldest profession. Sherlock Holmes refers to 'game' metaphorically when exclaiming: 'The game is afoot.' On TV, the schedules are often padded out with game shows. And of course, 'game' can refer animals being hunted. As for the word 'killer', it could be taken as either a noun or an adjective, or used colloquially as a superlative.

Putting 'killer' and 'game' together might then make you start thinking about one of the following:

- Murderball, also known as wheelchair rugby
- Russian roulette
- A murderous prostitute wreaking revenge on abusive clients
- A grouse shoot on the glorious twelfth
- A chess grandmaster playing his best ever match
- Holmes and Moriarty toppling over the Reichenbach Falls and plunging into the icy waters below.

Which of these you'd choose as a starting point and where the story would then move would of course depend on the remaining list, your state of mind, what odd or quirky fact or event you most recently read or heard about, and a whole host of other things. One thing is for sure though; you have immediately got rid of that blank page. It would be great to think of Suzanne Collins starting with 'killer' and 'game', and also having in a Decamot list: *mockingjay, sister, tribute, Sunday best, sponsorship, a mound of food, chat show host,* and *a thickly wooded forest,* then being inspired to write *The Hunger Games!* Fanciful perhaps, but not inconceivable.

According to his biographer, Roald Dhal would do his writing sitting all alone at his desk in the shed at the bottom of his garden, armed only with sheets of paper and a clutch of sharpened pencils waiting for inspiration. For Charles Dickens, with weekly instalments being constantly demanded, and a huge number of mouths to feed, inspiration was borne out of necessity. Perhaps for either of these writers Decamots could have been of assistance. Or perhaps they juggled words and ideas automatically all the time; for them the process of capturing them on paper might simply have been agonising over which particular words to choose from their vast personal lexicons.

For us, Decamots have been a boon. Once you've completed and submitted a Decamot, it's always fascinating to see what other paths you might have taken, paths which become apparent when you read the entries of your fellow combatants.

Playing the Game

Over the years, we have devised various different ways of playing Decamot. The one you choose depends on the number of people involved, the type of people involve, the rationale for playing, the physical location of each of the combatants, and the time frames that you have at your disposal. Playing a basic round of Decamot can be summarised in the following ten steps:

1) Decide how long you've got to play the game.
2) Decide how long you long you want the story to be.

3) Select 10 Decamot items.
4) Develop the Decamot items into a story of the chosen length.
5) Submit your completed story before the deadline.
6) Inform your fellow Decamot competitors that the story is available.
7) Read your fellow Decamot competitors' stories.
8) Rank your fellow Decamot competitors' stories.
9) Aggregate the scores for each story.
10) Inform the Decamot competitors who the winner was.

Step 3, *Select 10 Decamot items*, is one that can be performed in many ways. The way you choose will largely be determined by your rationale for playing the game and the people at your disposal, but you should adhere to the following guide for selecting the Decamot items:

1. The words or phrases should be as unrelated to each other as possible.
2. 1–3 items should indicate **People**.
3. 1–2 items should indicate **Location**.
4. 4–6 items should be **Objects**.
5. 0–1 items should be a **Saying** or **Metaphor**.

It's a good idea to come up with more than ten Decamot items to begin with, then select the ten that are the most disparate.

Ways of Playing

The following list of Decamot writing situations and methods of playing is included for inspiration and is certainly not intended to be an exhaustive list:

- **Party game:** Suppose a group of friends want to use Decamot as an alternative to party games like charades and Pictionary, Decamot could be used as follows:

  1. Allow a maximum of thirty minutes to write the stories.
  2. Restrict the word length to about 100 to 200 words.

3. Get the whole group of players collectively to suggest words to use for the Decamots.
4. Organise the words suggested into the three categories: People, Location, Objects.
5. From the words suggested, select a list that adheres to the Decamot item selection criteria.
6. Selecting a phrase or metaphor in a party setting can be quite useful to generate story ideas quickly.
7. Write the stories quickly in isolation from each other.
8. Gather together for each person to read out their effort in turn.
9. Each person votes on the winner (the story other than their own that they think is the most satisfying).

- **Correspondence:** Suppose a group of friends enjoyed playing Decamot as a party game, but want to continue playing at a more serious and leisurely pace via email correspondence, Decamot could be used as follows:

1. Allow two weeks to write the stories.
2. Initially set a limit of 1,000 to 2,000 words.
3. Take it in turns to decide upon the words to use for the Decamots.
4. Select a list that adheres to the Decamot item selection criteria.
5. If there are more than two participants, to introduce an element of anonymity, set up a shared email account.
6. Write the stories.
7. Exchange the completed stories using the shared email account on the target completion date.
8. After the target completion date, each person accesses and reads all the stories.
9. Each participant ranks all the entries (other than their own) awarding the least satisfying one point, the next most satisfying two points, and so on.
10. Nominate a participant to be responsible for aggregating the scores and announcing a round winner.

- **Teaching aid:** Suppose a school wants the pupils in a particular class or year to develop a school play collaboratively, Decamot could be used as follows:

  1. Allow one week's homework to write the initial stories.
  2. It's worth imposing no restriction on the word length.
  3. Get the whole group of students collectively to suggest the words to use for the Decamots.
     This can best be done by the teacher encouraging pupils to brainstorm words ideas.
  4. The teacher uses whiteboards or flipcharts to organise the words suggested by the students into three categories: People, Location, Objects.
  5. From the words suggested, the teacher gets the students to vote on the words suggested so that they can collectively generate a list that adheres to the Decamot item selection criteria.
  6. Selecting a phrase or metaphor as one of the Decamot items in a teaching setting can be quite useful if specifying a theme is desirable.
  7. Set the writing of the stories as a homework task.
  8. In a subsequent lesson, get each of the students to read out their entries in turn.
  9. Each student votes on the winner (the story other than their own that they think is the most satisfying).
  10. Consider allowing a lesson a week for half a term to continue to develop the winning story into a class/school play (see later chapter).

- **Book club:** Suppose, for variety, a book club want to write a set of short stories so that during one meeting they can discuss their own work rather than that of an established writer, Decamot could be used as follows:

  1. Each club member considers their favourite book.
  2. They think about the aspects of that book that make it memorable to them.

3. From those aspects, they derive a set of ten Decamot items that the author could have used to inspire that book.
4. Each club member swaps their set of Decamot items with that of another member without telling the other member which book they were considering.
5. Each club member writes a Decamot story using the items that their fellow club member derived.
6. Discuss the completed Decamots at the end of the next meeting.
7. Identify the source of the Decamot items at the end of the meeting.

- **Magazine competition:** Suppose a magazine wants to prompt their readership to write short stories for inclusion in an edition of the magazine, Decamot could be used as follows:

  1. Allow sufficient time for your readers to notice and act on the competition notification.
  2. Limit story entries to 500 words (that should be sufficient to fill a magazine page).
  3. Select a list that adheres to the Decamot item selection criteria.
  4. Try to avoid being too prescriptive in your choice of Decamot items.
  5. Announce in the magazine the story competition, stipulating the rule that all entries must contain the Decamot items chosen in Step 3.
  6. Set a target deadline.
  7. Judge the entries based on what you thing makes a satisfying story.
  8. Publish the winning story and details of the winner in a later magazine.

Sample Decamots 1

The two sample Decamots in this chapter were inspired by the following Decamot items: *oak tree, Covent Garden, gendarme, wooden cross, boots, fence, gypsy, mobile phone, rope, cards.*

Caught in the Act

In **Caught in the Act** a sneak thief gets his comeuppance when he takes what he thinks will be a short cut.

Caught in the Act

Paul stood casually in the crowded train pretending to read the *Evening Standard.* He was surreptitiously watching his fellow passengers. He was disappointed with what he saw: a scruffy woman with equally scruffy waif, possibly a displaced Romanian gypsy begging for money; an old man using a tattered rope as a belt; a nun wearing a habit, wooden cross, training shoes and an iPod; a young man dressed as a French gendarme, possibly on his way to a fancy dress party or maybe just into power games with his boyfriend. Colourful they may be, but certainly not what Paul was looking for.

He was more fortunate at the next stop: An elegant lady was one of the last people to squeeze on to the train before the doors closed. She was well dressed, probably ready for a night out and carrying a Gucci handbag. As Paul discreetly moved closer, he noticed she was wearing Chanel No. 5. She would do nicely.

As the train pulled into the next station, Paul made his move. He quickly grabbed the expensive handbag, stuffed it inside his coat, and dashed out of the door and along the platform. To his annoyance, there was a mass of people waiting for the lifts to take them back to the surface, and he could not see an escalator. Getting out of this station without someone stopping him was not going to be easy.

'Stop thief!' A loud and well-modulated voice shouted out behind him. A few people's heads turned to look around with mild interest.

Don't panic, he said to himself. *There's got to be another way out*. And there it was – the emergency stairs. He started running up them at full speed, two at a time, passing the few people who'd also decided to avoid the queue for the lift. If he had not been in such a hurry he might have thought it odd that there were so few people who had decided to take the stairs and that the staircase was spiral.

As he rounded the first bend in the stairs, his hands were already searching through the Gucci handbag. He quickly found and removed her mobile phone, credit cards, fifty pounds in cash, and two tickets for *The Graduate*. As he climbed his fortieth step he dumped the handbag, having stashed the valuable items. Should he risk touting the ticket himself or just sell it to his fence with the rest of the loot? He'd decide later when he got to the top of the stairs.

His legs were really beginning to ache when he reached the one hundredth step. Next time he'd have to find an escalator, any more of this and he would have legs the size of oak trees. One-hundred-and-one, one-hundred-and-two, one-hundred-and-three . . .

Can't be many more to go, surely? He needed to rest but knew he would have to wait until he was out of the station and sitting calmly in a cafe before he could.

One-hundred-and-eleven, one-hundred-and-twelve, one-hundred-and-thirteen . . .

He was passing fewer people on the stairs now, not because there were fewer people, but because he was no longer the fastest ascender. Fortunately, no one had tried to stop him for at least a seventy steps, he was glad that there was so little in the way of community spirit these days; he had got away with a mugging in broad daylight with hundreds of witnesses none of whom had attempted to hinder his escape.

One-hundred-and-eighty-one, one-hundred-and-eighty-two, one-hundred-and-eighty-three . . .

At last he could see daylight at the top. Ten stairs to go. Just before going through the turnstile and out of the station to freedom, Paul paused to catch his breath. As he was bending over double with sweat cascading off his brow, a pair of highly polished boots came into view, and he felt a hand tap him gently on the shoulder.

'Paul Bannister?'

'Yes?' he gasped, bemused.

'You are under arrest for the mugging of Penelope Forster-Young. You have the right to remain silent, but anything you do say will be taken down and may be used against you in a court of law. You also have the right to know that Covent Garden tube station (this one) has 193 stairs to the surface, fifteen security cameras, and an alarm straight through to the police station on The Strand. We've been watching your progress for the last five minutes; you were doing reasonably well until step number 175, but your posture was too upright, which gave you that cramp in your left thigh. But don't worry, lad, you'll have plenty of time to improve your fitness at Her Majesty's pleasure; Pentonville Prison has an excellent running machine!'

The Gypsy's Curse

The Gypsy's Curse is a chilling tale from pre-Soviet Russia which proves that truth really can challenge fiction for strangeness.

The Gypsy's Curse

On a cold December night in St Petersburg, two men were struggling along the side of the river Neva holding between them a large rolled-up carpet bound in the middle by a stout rope. They stopped to catch their breaths; they had about another hundred yards to go before they reached the ancient oak tree that marked their intended destination.

Between them they heaved the carpet and its contents over the fence and into the middle of the river and tossed a wooden cross after it. Neither man knew, nor cared, what or who they had just disposed of;

they were dutifully following the orders of their masters. Judging by the mayhem they had observed when summoned to the palace, they both assumed it was a corpse, but neither wanted to confirm their thoughts.

But the carpet did not contain a corpse. The freezing water of the Neva woke Gregory with a start. His sharp mind immediately went back to the treacherous events earlier that evening: He was greeted eagerly at the gate by Felix, and they had gone inside for dinner. They had chatted cheerfully as they walked through the magnificent hallway adorned with *objects d'art* collected from as near as St Basil's in Moscow to as far as Covent Garden in London. Even when they were joined by Dimitri instead of Felix's wife, Gregory had suspected nothing.

Then the mood changed. They accused him of gaining the family's trust by deception, of abusing that trust by abusing their daughters, of being an untrustworthy lecher and a sinister joker in a political pack of cards. As their tirade continued, Gregory began to feel increasingly drowsy and finally fell unconscious. Felix and Dimitri had drugged him. They dragged him down into the basement where they took it in turns to beat him with clubs and kick him with their heavy boots. Finally, they shot him, assumed him dead, and called for their servants.

And now in the icy waters he was conscious again, but unable to move or to see. So tightly bound was he that struggling was useless. He knew that he would surely die without assistance, and he knew also that no assistance would come even if he shouted out; and so he decided to save his remaining energy for one final task: to utter the most powerful gypsy curse on those who had betrayed him, one last sin to commit and confess, a confession that might still save his soul.

Three days later, Gregory's frozen and now-lifeless body was found under the thick ice of the river Neva. Even without mobile phones or other modern communication systems, news of his death spread through Russia like wildfire. Three months later, the whole family who had betrayed him had lost their wealth and power. Eighteen months later, they too were dead; twenty people executed by gendarmes, the gypsy's curse fulfilled.

Sample Decamots 2

The two sample Decamots in this chapter were inspired by the following Decamot items: *broken cup, poltergeist, mask, skeleton, record collection, bus pass, fourteenth-century church, wood chopper, fox, priest.*

More Tea, Vicar?

One member of the Jackson Decamot Collective decided to take the opportunity to confront an irrational fear of poltergeists and demon possession. Not being a fan of horror films, particularly those that include the supernatural, and who even managed to find the tame, temporary ride *The Chiller* at Thorpe Park's Halloween Fright Night (designed to be little scary for young teenagers and a mild diversion for everyone else) absolutely unnerving, he treated writing a Decamot with a poltergeist theme as a form of cathartic therapy. The result was **More Tea, Vicar?** in which a Man of the Cloth learns to live in harmony with his poltergeist.

More Tea, Vicar?

Steve pulled into the vicarage, parked his white van under the yew tree, walked up the gravel path to the front door, and pulled on the handle of the doorbell. After a few minutes the heavy oak door slowly swung open.

'Hello, Steve,' Reverend Chesterton said. 'Please, come in. I think you'll be busy for a few hours this afternoon.'

The vicar turned on his heel and walked back into his house with Steve following closely behind. They walked through the long hallway until they reached the last doorway.

'Over to you, my boy,' said the vicar ushering him into the grand dining room. It was an impressive room measuring twenty feet by forty, with walls clad in oak panelling and adorned with picture rails. A huge table dominated the room surrounded by twenty-four sturdy oak chairs upholstered in leather. The overall effect was that of a Tudor country mansion.

The most notable thing about the room today though was its chaotic state. The pictures on the walls were draped with a plastic sheet, and the table was covered in thick tarpaulin. Both the plastic sheet and the tarpaulin were flecked liberally with the remnants of an earlier repast. Several of the chairs were overturned, and picnic-style crockery lay strewn in various places around the room.

As Steve surveyed the carnage he noticed some cake trodden into the carpet, jelly stuck to the ceiling, and some blancmange hanging from the curtains.

'I think they've surpassed themselves this time,' said Steve, handing a broken cup to the vicar. 'I best get my equipment from the van.'

Steve owned his own company, Steve's Premier Industrial Cleaning Kwik (SPICK), and he was its sole employee. He did everything from answering the phone, through driving the van, to office cleaning. He had even painted the company name on the side of the van and added the legend: Putting the SPICK in Spick and Span, a slogan of which he was particularly proud. He was here in a professional capacity to clean up after the annual children's tea party.

These events were always a source of great amusement. For years there had been rumours that the old vicarage was haunted, rumours that many of Reverend Chesterton's predecessors had denied vehemently, but that had increasingly dissuaded people from attending church.

When he took over the parish, Reverend Chesterton did not seem to mind about the tales of ghosts inhabiting his fourteenth-century church, nor of forgotten skeletons locked away in darkened cupboards. In fact, within weeks of moving in, bringing with him not much more than an eclectic record collection and a bus pass, the vicar had invited the boys and girls of the local cub pack and brownie troop to attend the first annual Charity Poltergeist Tea Party, each child had to collect sponsorship pledges before attending the haunted meal and all the proceeds went to the local old people's home.

The first Charity Poltergeist Tea Party had been a huge success with all the children leaving in high spirits with tales of flying fondant fancies, cascading cucumber sandwiches, and self-propelled china teapots. The annual tea party quickly became a tradition, a tradition now ten years old.

It took Steve until the early evening before he had tidied up after this year's party. Once completed, he went in search of the vicar to inform him that the dining room had been restored to its former glory. He found Reverend Chesterton in the parlour putting the finishing touches to a balloon animal.

'It's supposed to be a fox. What do you think?'

'Not at all bad,' said Steve, sitting down at the table across from the vicar and helping himself to a cup of tea. 'Do you ever regret giving up your old profession?'

'I thoroughly enjoyed my many years as a children's entertainer, but in the end I couldn't ignore my true calling. I still have fun with Sunday school, and of course I've got the kid's tea party to enjoy each year.'

'About these parties, there's something I've wanted to ask you ever since I attended the first one. How do you manage to make the tables and chairs move, and the plates and the sandwiches levitate? Do you use hidden strings and mirrors, or is it a trade secret?'

'Oh, it's no secret. I put Jacob on to the case.'

'Jacob?'

'Jacob's my poltergeist. The original occupant of the church, over seven hundred years ago, was a Catholic priest, and Jacob was his wood-chopper. Jacob had a beautiful daughter, the spitting image of his late wife, and the priest took rather a shine to her. He took her in as his housekeeper, and as it transpired, a little more besides,' the vicar said, tapping the side of his nose.

'Before long Jacob's daughter discovered that she was with child. The priest had to take drastic action to avert a scandal and excommunication. So he accused Jacob's daughter of being a witch and of using her evil powers of enchantment to seduce him into committing sins of the flesh. He got the villagers on his side, and they agreed to burn her.

'After his daughter's death, Jacob never went outside again for fear of encountering any of the villagers who had been responsible for the callous murder of his only child. By the time he died, his face had become like a mask, devoid of all emotions.

'After his own death, Jacob returned to the priest's house as a poltergeist. He slammed doors, moved tables, knocked over lamps, spilt the priest's bath water, and tore his vestments. Jacob was so good at his new job that the priest died of a heart attack less than a year later.

'Every year on the anniversary of the priest's death Jacob likes to let off steam. Previous incumbents were frightened by these sporadic outbursts, but I sensed the presence of a tortured soul. I was the first person to take the time to talk to him since his daughter's death. He said that what he despised the priest for most was denying him the enjoyment of having grandchildren and watching them grow up.

'I came up with the idea of the children's parties so we could make the most of his excess energy and so that he could enjoy making them laugh. They are his surrogate children. The rest of the time Jacob likes to occupy himself as my valet.'

When the vicar had finished his story Steve gave him an appreciative laugh. Naturally, he did not believe a word of it, but one of the things he like most about the vicar was his ability to tell a good yarn.

Just then he noticed the teapot in the middle of the table move a little. As he watched, it slowly rose six inches into the air, hovered over his companion's cup and tilted ever so slightly.

Then a deep, disembodied voiced asked: 'More tea, Vicar?'

Illusions

Illusions is likely to send a shiver running down your spine when you get right to the end, especially if you recall the real-life physician mentioned who was very much in the news at the time of writing the story, as were his victims.

Illusions

When Father Frank O'Reilly died on the anniversary of the death of St Francis of Assisi, the people of Edenbridge took this as a sign from God himself. His funeral, followed three days later by a memorial service, sparked an unofficial week of mourning among the faithful. Such was his popularity in the local area that the period of mourning eventually stretched to one month and might have continued indefinitely had it not been for the intervention of the BBC and the West Sussex Coroner's Office.

The fourteenth-century church of St Francis in the Sanctuary had been the unlikely epicentre of radical Catholicism since the Middle Ages. Father O'Reilly embraced that tradition with unbridled enthusiasm from the start. During his tenure as parish priest, which lasted fully sixty years, Father Frank managed to uncover a huge amount of hitherto unknown facts about the Franciscan Order and their migration from Assisi in Italy via France and Spain to Canterbury in Kent and ultimately on to Edenbridge.

As a young scholar attached to the Holy See within the Vatican itself, Frank's early researches into established shibboleths imbued him with a heightened appreciation of the value of true belief. On taking up his first parish appointment, he had immediately felt at home and uniquely well prepared for ministering to the needs of the sophisticated parishioners of Edenbridge, to whom he subsequently dedicated his life.

On entering the deserted church for the very first time, the young priest had been overwhelmed by a sense of majesty. He stood at the lectern ornately carved in the shape of an eagle on whose outstretched wings an ancient Bible rested. Off to the left stood a latticed choir screen, and looking down from the pulpit he saw rows of pews stretching out in front of him.

He turned back to gaze in wonder at the high altar twenty-five yards further back. Even higher, above the altar, looking down was a truly magnificent figure of Christ, nailed to a massive and impressive solid oak cross.

He was humbled by his physical position, standing midway between his flock in front and the Son of God looking over his shoulder from behind. The nature of his vocation was crystal clear to him: to act as interpreter and guide, a kind of earthly go-between, someone who could throw light on the more arcane rituals; he was on a mission to explain the very mysteries of Catholicism.

Above all else, the youthful cleric was seized by a sense of theatre. The acoustics were unbelievable, the lighting dramatic. Even on a dull day, shafts of light would force their way through the stained glass windows stretching up to the roof behind the altar. A storm raging outside would rattle the windows like a poltergeist. The director of a Hollywood movie could not have had a better set of special effects at his disposal.

At that moment, Father Frank also realised that his covert membership of the Magic Circle might be put to divine use. His lifelong fascination with sleight of hand and magic illusions were so well practised that he could easily have earned a lucrative living as a professional magician. Early on in his ministry at St Francis he began putting these privately acquired skills to good use, illustrating his sermons to dazzling effect. Adults and children alike all sat enraptured as he wove an intricate pattern of fact and fiction before their very eyes. He regularly performed his own minor miracles. When asked whether they were performed by the hand of God or were magic tricks, he would reply enigmatically: 'I am but a mere flawed mortal. My broken cup doth runneth over.'

His special monthly sermons consistently attracted huge congregations. The car park was often full to overflowing with the very latest models in fashionable transport. Rover 2000s in the sixties, Porsche 911s in the seventies, BMW M3s in the eighties, Renault Scénics in the nineties, and Toyota Priuses in the new millennium.

Father Frank's easy Irish eloquence meant his stories were invariably laced with humour. He always seemed able to polish up and enliven the most obscure parables. Blowing away the dry dust of ecclesiastical history was his métier. If the Catholic hierarchy ever harboured doubts about the authenticity of his version of events, they were well hidden. No one could deny the popularity of his ministry and the growing number of converts who were joining the church.

Frequent appearances on *Any Questions* and *Thought for The Day* on the BBC added to his celebrity. But it was his dramatic demonstrations of early religious experiences that firmly established him as a presentational genius. His telling of the little-known medieval story of the wood-chopper, the fox, and the chicken, in which all three make common cause to defeat the black plague, was a typical example of his technique: He created a spectacular illusion using smoke and a glass coffin-shaped box. As the box rose, it rotated, as if on an invisible vertical axis. On its first revolution, a live chicken appeared within; on its second, a red fox; and a third revolution revealed a hooded monk-like figure in a white mask. As the box picked up speed, all three appeared together in apparent harmony. At its climax, to the astonishment of the captivated congregation, the box exploded, showering the choir with feathers.

On another occasion, a devout Catholic friar from the French Order of Capuchin visited Father Frank seeking spiritual guidance. A ghost-like figure in a coarse grey cloth habit with pointed cowl, under-tunic, drawers, and waist cord appeared to him during midnight prayers. Frank was able to explain the true intellectual significance of the visitation to him and offered to use it as a basis for his Sunday sermon. This he did by dressing a skeleton in the garb of an early Franciscan monk and suspending it above the alternative pulpit to the right of the choir screen directly opposite the pulpit from which Father Frank delivered his sermons. One of his parishioners, known for the pride he took in his record collection, said it was like listening to an address in stereo.

His flock were held spellbound as Father Frank explained that the very concept of 'life' was an illusion of Man's own invention, a creation to cover his obvious insecurity before the might of eternal God. 'If you strip away every scientific discovery, every scientific proof and empirical fact, every experience, every fad, and every fashion, what is there left to explain? Only the inexplicable!'

Each sentence that Father Frank uttered was accompanied by a single solemn tolling of the church bell and echoed by his brother monk who cast aside one item of clothing after another, in time with the chimes, until he was completely disrobed before the congregation.

'It is then you come face to face with absolute faith,' implored Father Frank. 'True faith! It is only by stripping away layer after layer after layer of your own prejudices that you can reveal the skeleton of true belief.'

By the time of his death, Father Frank had acquired a cult status, without ever rising above the station of parish priest. Modesty was his watchword. As he once told Sue Lawley on Desert Island Discs, his most prized possession was his bus pass as this had enabled him to avoid having to learn to drive.

* * *

The West Sussex Coroner's Office thought long and hard before granting permission to exhume Father Frank's body so soon after his death. But they had no real alternative. Dr Harold Shipman had visited Father Frank the afternoon of his death, and they were now convinced that he had been one of his victims.

The grave was opened at 3 p.m. in full view of the BBC TV News outside broadcast team. The coffin was lifted from the ground and carefully transferred to the local morgue. Here it was opened in the presence of the Roman Catholic Archbishop of Westminster.

Inside, they found a wood-chopper's axe wrapped in a monk's habit, a leather bag full of bones, and a bus pass. The bones were later identified as those of a fox and a chicken and carbon dated to 1665, the year of the last Great Plague of London. The bus pass had expired. There was no sign of Father Frank O'Reilly's body.

CHAPTER 2

The Decamot Writing Process

Decamot started as a game with a single simple rule: Take a set of ordinary, but totally disconnected, words and put them together in a single coherent story. From this modest start we've made various modifications and evolved the game into a writing process.

The initial Decamot game gave us a way of getting past that initial blank page. Stories started with two or three items combining to generate a flash of inspiration. By adding a few more items, a direction of travel emerged. Then the remaining items were added for a sight of the final destination. The ultimate motivation was the creation of a satisfying story that had sufficient peer support to win the round.

After playing many rounds of Decamot, and having invested a lot of time on various entries, quite often many hours over a period of a fortnight or so, we devised a further development to Decamot. We thought it might be interesting to try to improve and polish some of our better stories. We didn't have any greater motive in mind beyond the intellectual satisfaction of producing something well crafted. So peer review, collaboration and editing became a part of the Decamot writing process.

Collaboration

In his book *On Writing*, Stephen King claims, 'My basic belief about the making of stories is that they pretty much make themselves . . . [they]

are relics, part of a pre-existing world. The writer's job is to use the tools in his or her toolbox to get as much of each one out of the ground intact as possible.' King is probably referring to fossils (the remains of long-dead creatures) rather than what you might normally think of as relics (the remains of long-dead Catholic saints). If that is the case, this is something that we found with our Decamots.

The initial shape of our story appears when we submit them. The image of the author then leaning over the emerging story, using soft, archaeologists' brushes to gently remove more and more of the debris obscuring it is an appealing one, and it certainly describes well how the Decamot writing process works when we subsequently discuss ways of improving the story.

The very process of writing has a liberating effect on one's vocabulary. It can be frustrating when grasping for the right word, but nothing that a trip to the OED can't resolve. And then there's the escapism. You very quickly find yourself taken to unexpected places, writing a story that you would never have thought of otherwise. The Decamot writing process has helped us to write everything from a short historical mystery to a whimsical tale of good fortune set in Central Park, New York, via the murder of a tyrannical boss. An oft-quoted dictum for budding authors is 'Write what you know'; but what if you want to write about encounters with a bug-eyed alien in deep space? H. G. Wells, Jules Verne, and Isaac Asimov clearly did not comply with that advice. In the non-science fiction world, Yann Martell, Jasper Fforde, Ellis Peters, Robert Harris, and Anthony Horrowitz were happy to write well outside of their first-hand knowledge.

As the story emerges, we've found the way it should be told also emerges, as does its ultimate, natural length. First person, third person; narrative, descriptive, driven by dialogue; light-hearted or serious; pithy, witty, profane, or profound. We've found time and again that our two-week time limit for the Decamot writing game is generally sufficient to uncover enough of the story to know how the story starts and finishes, how it should be told, and whether there's more under the surface that's

STANLEY JACKSON AND GAVIN JACKSON

worth continuing to unearth. The collaboration element has played a vital part in producing stories of much higher quality.

The Editing Process

We've done a certain amount of editing of the short stories that we've included in this book, in places reworking sections, and in a number of cases rewriting the story, but always basing the edited story on the original concept or central theme, and always trying to keep the Decamot items intact.

With all the edits we start off by checking the logic of the story. Does the story go from A (at the beginning of the story) to Z (at the end of the story) in logical steps, and does each step make sense and lead logically to the next? This is something akin to confirming the solution to a cryptic crossword clue. You're never absolutely convinced of a cryptic solution until you can account for all elements in its clue. Logic checking, and where necessary flaw fixing, can be the hardest part of the editing task for two reasons: Firstly, we never want to stray too far from the original story, and secondly, the more familiar with a story you are, the easier it is to overlook an omission in the logic because you know by now what the ultimate outcome will be.

After the logic of the story, we move on to the internal consistency. This is no less important than the logic of the story, but it's easier to do because it's more mechanical. If a name has changed at any point, have we changed it consistently throughout? If we've removed a person or an object, have we also removed all references to him/her/it? Is a stated colour, number, name, or anything else consistent (and consistently spelled) all the way through?

We then move on to the sound of the dialogue. It's often necessary in stories to have characters speak more than they might otherwise so that the story can be moved along without constantly relying on lengthy narrative, but at the same time, it's essential that the dialogue is believable. In ordinary speech, people rarely speak in complete, well-formed sentences, so this should be reflected in the story; but at the same time, the dialogue does have to be intelligible. We've found that one of the best ways to work on the dialogue is to read it aloud and, if possible, with different people taking different parts as if reading through a play. That way you can quickly identify bits that aren't natural and adjust them accordingly.

Where necessary, we add descriptions for clarity and we also remove things that are not essential to the story; sometimes we find a phrase has been kept in simply because of the sound of it, or it was funny or clever, but have to admit that it doesn't actually move the story along. At this stage in the editing process, we try to be ruthless and remove the superfluous. Finally, for each of the story edits we finish off with a grammar, spelling, and punctuation check.

The Decamot Writing Process in Practice

The rest of this chapter provides a worked example of the Decamot Writing Process starting from the initial ten Decamot items, which led to the submission of two related stories and the receipt of comments from reviewers, which in turn led to the writing of a single, but longer story, then to a further collaboration that finally led to the writing of a complete film screenplay.

The original two stories, **A Tale of One City** and **German Graffiti**, were inspired by the following Decamot items: *skinny ankle, apricot slice, satchel, thong, appendage, lever, saucepan, Berlin, foundations, wife*. Both stories featured the same two leading characters, but separated by a thirty- year gap during which they were unable to meet as they were on different sides of the Berlin Wall.

The two key items from the Decamot list were *Berlin* and *foundations*, which brought to mind the Berlin Wall. The inspiration for one of the stories came from a university encounter with a West Berliner and some photographs that he had of his home city which depicted extraordinary graffiti on the West side of the Berlin Wall. The quality and wit of much of it was arresting, including a piece that depicts an East German Trebant motor car driving through the Wall. It's painted on the West side, but because you see the front of the car, it looks as though it has been driven through the Wall from the East. The inspiration for the other story came from witnessing the moving scenes of East and West Berliners shaking hands across the Wall when it was finally demolished. People from the East and people from the West had gathered spontaneously after the collapse of the Soviet Union. They were united by a single objective: to bring down the Wall. The stories follow:

A Tale of One City

Two boys stood in the shadows of a ruined cottage. They were waiting for the border guard to complete his circuit before dashing for the front door. They had been watching his movements carefully for the last two nights attempting to gauge when it would be safe to make a move. Tonight they had decided was the night that they were going in for the first time. This was not the only derelict property in their city, nor was it the first that they had broken into, but it was the most complete, the most securely boarded up and so the most challenging the young housebreakers had yet come up against.

The taller of the two absent-mindedly checked for the leather thong of his satchel. Naturally, it was over his shoulder as it had been all summer; his mother had joked earlier that day that it had become like an extra appendage so often was he seen with it. He reached into the bag and withdrew a tyre lever.

'Now,' he whispered quietly.

As one, they dashed to the front door. While his partner in crime, shorter but more solid than he, leant heavily against the door, he jammed one end of the lever into the crack that opened. That done, they both shoved with all their might. The door gave with surprising ease, spilling both boys noisily into the dark and dusty hallway, its first visitors for almost two decades. They lay there for a few moments catching their breaths, their hearts bounding in their breasts, giggling silently. When they had calmed down, they ventured deeper into the house.

Together they made their way down the darkened corridor and into the kitchen at the end. They gasped at the completeness they beheld. A table was laid for four people – there was even a saucepan on the hob. It was as if the occupants had left the room for a few minutes, not eighteen years ago, except of course, where there should have been food, there was just a thick layer of dust. Erik sat down at the table and wrote his name with his finger. Willem added the name 'Anna' and drew a heart around them both. Erik blushed.

'So it's true,' he teased. 'You do fancy her! Although I don't know why. She's like a boy she's so thin. She's even got skinny ankles!'

Erik half-heartedly threw a punch that Willem parried easily. The two friends fell to the floor again, this time in a mock fight, exchanging blows that contained no malice. Their brawl ended when Willem offered to share the remains of his tea: a dried sandwich and an apricot slice. He had been carrying these items in his satchel along with his makeshift door key, so they were somewhat the worse for wear. They sat back at the table to eat nonetheless.

Their meagre meal was disturbed by the sounds of the curfew sirens. Both were amazed that so much time had passed so quickly; now they had to move quickly, Willem had to get back to Schöneberg before the border was closed for the night. But tomorrow they would return, they had so much more to discover about the former occupants of the abandoned home.

Early next morning Erik was woken by the sounds of drilling. He looked at the clock on his bedside table; it was only four in the morning. He hurried over to the window and peered through the curtain. In the half-light he saw a group of soldiers armed not with guns but with spades and jackhammers. They were clearing the ruined buildings and appeared to be laying foundations that stretched onwards for an eternity. He spotted another group of soldiers further up Ebert Street hastily erecting a sturdy fence topped with a barbed wire entanglement.

Erik watched in horror as he realised that they were working with a ferocious industry to construct a makeshift barrier before daybreak. How would he and Willem ever meet again? What would he do now that they had taken his playground away? For him, Berlin would never be the same again.

German Graffiti

Erik raised the binoculars to his eyes and looked out across the no man's land to the Wall and the checkpoint on the other side. He saw looking back at him through similar, but more modern binoculars, another soldier, dressed in a uniform similar to his own and also with a gun permanently slung over his shoulder like an extra appendage. He wondered, not for the first time, if it was Willem on the other side of the Wall looking back at him. And just as quickly he dismissed the thought. Willem was too intelligent to have joined the army.

He cast his mind back twenty-eight years to that last summer they spent together as young lads, breaking into abandoned houses, not to loot them you understand, just to see them. It had been Willem's idea. 'If you want to understand the past, you have to experience it. And to experience the past, you must experience people's lives. We have a unique opportunity in our city. It would be a crime not to exploit it.' Well, that was the justification of a juvenile mind, and he had been happy to go along with it.

Those days were long gone, as were those houses, whose very foundations were used to build this wall, now in its fourth incarnation. He missed those days and he missed Willem. And Anna, of course. *Whatever happened to her,* he wondered. Anna with the skinny ankles. Anna and Willem had been locked into a prison of his country's making, and now he, Captain Erik Friedheimer, was helping to defend it.

No, that soldier wasn't Willem. He'd have a good job and a pretty wife to come home to. He'd drive a nice car to a nice house each night, and she'd have dinner on its way – a chicken breast roasting in the oven, perhaps, and fresh vegetables boiling in a saucepan on the hob. No doubt they enjoyed the bounty of the West, not sparing a thought for the past. Whereas he had guard duty, a dirty two-stroke Trabant and an empty house. That, and memories. Memories of a once-happy marriage and a teenage son, the end of the first being caused by the death of the second.

His son had been shot two years earlier as he attempted to escape to the West. His wife hated the system for causing her such pain, and as her husband was part of that system, she hated him too.

*   *   *

Erik was right, at least in part. Willem had gained a doctorate before he was twenty-five and had become head of the Political Science faculty at the city's Technical University before he was thirty. But he did not enjoy the bounty of the West, not while it was still at the expense of the East. No day went by when he did not feel the guilt. He longed for the day when the wall that divided his native city would be brought down and when his beloved Europe was no longer fragmented. Many feared the inevitable reintegration of the East, prophesising economic ruin, but he knew that after a period of readjustment the economy would prosper.

Professor Willem Schmidt glanced over at the ancient satchel that lay on the chair on the other side of the desk. Anna, his wife, had attempted on many occasions to replace this relic from their past with a briefcase or something equally fitting, but he had declined. He claimed it help to keep fresh in his mind the city of his youth that he remembered. He allowed himself to cast his mind back to his boyhood twenty-eight years before: He thought of Erik: *What was he up to now? No doubt Erik was campaigning about the Wall as vehemently as was he and demanding its removal.* With communist states falling throughout Europe, Willem felt sure that Erik would be eagerly awaiting its demise so that their city could once again be whole.

Outside in the shadows, not more than 500 metres away, stood a tall, slender youth known to a select few within the city as 'Phizz'. He was holding a plastic bag containing several spray cans of varying colours. Phizz was a familiar and unmistakable sight in the city with his ripped clothing and long, unwashed hair tied back with a tattered leather thong. Equally well known, but not generally attributed to him, was his artwork: Adorning much of the Western side of the Wall were his incredible works of graffiti.

He was waiting for a gap in the crowd so that he could hurry to the Wall unseen and produce this evening's masterpiece. His hurried nocturnal improvisations filled him with as much excitement now as they had four years ago when he'd written on the Wall for the first time. Back then all he'd managed was a humble 'Max Schmidt woz 'ere'. He had progressed on to simple monochromatic doodles, then larger and larger multicoloured images. He painted large stylised figures, creatures of all descriptions, stunning abstracts, and psychedelic landscapes. And of course, he had long since abandoned signing them with his real name, preferring instead the tag 'Phizz'. There was nothing essentially illegal about adorning his side of the Wall, but he enjoyed the anonymity that a pseudonym provides.

Throughout his adolescence this Wall had been his playground. His favourite times were just after a piece of the Wall had been repaired and he would be presented with a virgin expanse; it was like being given a pristine canvas on which to produce something new and exciting. On one such occasion, within twenty-four hours of replacement, a new section was sporting a vast apricot slice, fully thirty-foot in width and covering the whole twelve-foot height; this piece he proudly referred to as his *still life*.

Tonight he was in for a long wait for passers-by to pass by. The crowd he was watching was not dissipating; in fact, from his vantage point it appeared to be growing. During the day he had vaguely noticed more people than usual arriving in the city but had not paid it much heed.

At about midnight a burly man approached the Wall. Phizz looked on in horror as he produced a tyre lever from inside his long overcoat and started to attack the concrete, sending chippings of one of his masterpieces flying through the air. Spontaneously the crowd joined in the destruction, using anything that came to hand. For over two hours they tore into the Wall with a ferocious industry. By 3 a.m., holes started to appear, and soon people were able to shake hands with each other through the Wall.

The mood of the crowd was jubilant, the mood of Phizz was not. How would he produce his artwork now that they had destroyed his studio? For him Berlin would never be the same again.

Characters with a Life of Their Own

Some writers claim that the very act of putting a character on paper gives them a life of their own. The fascination with what a fictional character might get up to presents the writer with endless potential. The classic Italian play by Luigi Pirandello *Six Characters in Search of an Author* features a whole family of fictional characters who have been created by the author, but whose story he has since abandoned. When he tries to write a new play, they turn up demanding to have their story told.

Similarly, we felt that Erik Friedheimer and Willem Schmidt, the two leading characters in **A Tale of One City** and **German Graffiti**, also had parts of their story still to be told. Having written those short stories, the obvious questions were: What did they both get up to in the years between the rise and fall of the Wall? And, what would happen if they met up again sometime after November 1989? As a consequence, we wrote the longer short story **The Wall**:

The Wall

The queue stretched around the block. Erik Friedheimer peered at them from the safety of the bookshop's interior with a mixture of pride and apprehension. On the orders of his publisher, he was going to meet his adoring public for the first time. They had been arriving since six on a November morning that was cold even by Berlin's standards. Some had now been waiting patiently for almost three hours to catch the first glimpse of their hero, a man who even now could walk the full length of the line of expectant fans without being recognised. But that anonymity was about to change forever.

So many people, he thought to himself. *I just can't believe they've all turned out so early on such a cold morning just to see me.*

Ever since his school days in Mitte, he had been a compulsive scribbler: poems, plays, short stories, essays, sketches, he had no particular preference. The form mattered little to him; it was the idea that was important. He smiled to himself as he recalled the rather pompous line that he had given one of the characters in an early play: *The truth will always find its own outlet.* He consoled himself with the thought that he was only twelve years old when he wrote it.

The truth was that once an idea popped into his head, he felt compelled to jot it down, develop it to a certain point immediately, and then file it away for more considered expansion later whenever time permitted. He had always written for private pleasure, not for publication, although a small group of close friends had often asked him to share his literary efforts with them, requests that he seldom fulfilled and only when they plied him with enough vodka.

He could trace the start of his incessant jottings and note-takings to a single event that took place in 1961. On that day a friendship had been taken away from him, one that he had kept alive in his heart through his writing. Erik took a copy of his *Collected Works* off a pile in the table in front of him and found himself reliving the very eve of that momentous occasion through his own words:

* * *

Two boys stood in the shadows of a ruined cottage. They were waiting for the border guard to complete his circuit before dashing for the front door. They had been watching his movements carefully for the last two nights attempting to gauge when it would be safe to make a move. Tonight, they had decided, was the night that they were going in for the first time. This was not the only derelict property in their city, nor was it the first one they had broken into, but it was the most complete, the most securely boarded up, and so the most challenging the young housebreakers had yet come up against.

The taller of the two absent-mindedly checked for the leather thong of his satchel. Naturally it was over his shoulder as it had been all summer – his mother had joked earlier that day that it had become like an extra appendage, so often was he seen with it. He reached into the bag and withdrew a tyre lever.

'Now,' he whispered quietly.

As one, they dashed to the front door. While his partner in crime, shorter but more solid than him, leant heavily against the door, he jammed one end of the tyre lever into the crack that opened. That done, they both shoved with all their might. The door gave with surprising ease spilling both boys noisily into the dark, dusty hallway, its first visitors for almost two decades. They lay there for a few moments catching their breaths, their hearts bounding in their breasts, giggling silently. When they had calmed down they ventured deeper into the house.

Together, they made their way down the darkened corridor and into the kitchen at the far end. They were overawed by the sight which confronted them. A table was laid for four people; there was even a saucepan on the hob. It was as if the occupants had just left the room for a few minutes, not abandoned it eighteen years ago. Except, of course, where there should have been food on the plates, there was just a thick layer of dust.

Erik sat down at the table and wrote his name with his finger. Willem added the name 'Anna' and drew a heart around them both.

Erik blushed.

'So it's true,' he teased. 'You do fancy her! Although I don't know why. She's like a boy; she's so thin: flat-chested, thin-hipped. She's even got skinny ankles!'

Erik half-heartedly threw a punch that Willem parried easily. The two friends fell to the floor again, this time in a mock fight, exchanging pretend blows that contained no malice. Their theatrical brawl ended when Willem offered to share the remains of his tea: a dried sandwich and an apricot slice. He had been carrying them in his satchel along with his improvised door key. As a result, they were less than appetising, but they sat back at the table to eat nonetheless.

Their meagre meal was interrupted by the sounds of the curfew sirens. Both were amazed that so much time had flown by; now they had to move quickly, Willem especially, as he had to get back to Schöneberg before the border was closed for the night. But tomorrow they would return, they had so much more to discover about the former occupants of this abandoned home.

STANLEY JACKSON AND GAVIN JACKSON

Early next morning, Erik was woken by the sound of drilling. He looked at the clock on his bedside table – it was four in the morning. He hurried over to the window and peered through the curtain. In the half- light, he saw a group of soldiers armed, not with guns, but with spades and jackhammers. They were clearing the ruined buildings and appeared to be laying foundations that stretched onwards for an eternity. He spotted another group of soldiers, further up Ebert Street, hastily erecting a sturdy fence topped with a barbed wire entanglement.

Erik watched in horror as he slowly realised that they were working with a dedicated industry to construct a makeshift barrier before daybreak. How would he and Willem ever meet again? What would he do now that they had taken his playground away? For him, Berlin would never be the same again.

*   *   *

Those're the truest words I've ever written, Erik thought to himself as he carefully placed the book back on the table. *Berlin never was the same without you. I only hope that you heard my thoughts as I wrote them, Willem, because I wrote them for you. You've been my muse all these years, I owe it all to you. How different it all might have been.*

He looked at his watch for the tenth time that morning. It was 8.45; quarter of an hour to go before the doors opened and the masses started marching in. He had not seen so many people on the streets of Berlin since the fall of the Wall exactly ten years before.

Just as all Americans can remember where they were when Kennedy was shot, so all Berliners know where they were on 9 November 1989. Erik was no exception. On that night he had been a duty officer for the Brandenburg district. He remembered raising his binoculars to his eyes and looking across the no man's land to the Wall, and to the checkpoint on the other side. There, he had seen looking back at him through similar, but more modern binoculars, another soldier, dressed in a uniform similar to his own, also with a gun permanently slung over his shoulder. He had wondered, not for the first time, if it was Willem on the other side of the Wall looking back. And, just as quickly, he had dismissed the thought, because Willem was too intelligent to have joined the army.

Of course Willem could not have been that soldier. He would have landed a good job and would have married a pretty wife. He would have driven a nice car to a nice house each night and his wife would have had his dinner on its way; a chicken breast roasting in the oven, perhaps and fresh vegetables boiling in a saucepan on the hob. Willem would have had the good sense to enjoy the bounties of the West.

On that historic night, all Erik had were guard duty, a dirty two-stroke Trabant, and an empty house. That and his memories: Memories of a once-happy marriage and a teenage son, the end of the first being caused by the death of the second. His only son had been shot two years earlier as he attempted an escape to the West. His wife had hated the system for causing her such pain. As her husband had been part of that system, she had turned her hate on him too. Eventually she had left him, finally tiring of his acquiescence in the system and his writing that she described as 'futile scribbles from an impotent mind'.

*   *   *

Erik Friedheimer had been right about Willem, at least in part. His friend had not joined the army but had instead gained a doctorate before he was twenty-five and had become head of the Political Science faculty at the West Berlin Technical University before he was thirty. And he had married a pretty woman and they lived in a comfortable suburb. But he had not allowed himself to enjoy the bounty of the West. He had been wracked with guilt about how the West's success had been at the expense of the East. He had spent every available hour writing document after document, pamphlet after pamphlet about and against the Wall, hoping that someone, somewhere, would eventually take notice. He had lived for the day when the wall that divided his native city would be brought down and his beloved Europe reunited. Whilst many feared the potential reintegration of the East, prophesising economic ruin, Willem knew that, after a period of readjustment, an enlarged Germany would lead Europe to lasting prosperity.

Professor Willem Schmidt certainly remembered where he was on 9 November 1989. He had been in his office working late; he had glanced over at the ancient satchel that lay on the chair on the other side of the desk. On many occasions, Anna, his wife, had attempted to replace this relic from their past with a new briefcase or something equally in keeping with his position as a leading academic; but he had always declined, claiming it helped to keep fresh in his mind, the city of his youth. On that night, as on so many others, he had thought of Erik and had wondered what had happened to him. With communist states falling throughout Europe, Willem could picture Erik campaigning as vehemently on the Eastern side of the Wall as he had been on the Western side. He had felt sure that Erik would have been eagerly anticipating its demise, sharing his vision of a dynamically revitalised economy.

*   *   *

Unbeknown to Willem, at that very moment back in 1989, outside in the shadows, not more than 500 metres away, stood a tall, slender youth known to a select few within the city as 'Phizz'. And he too would remember where he as on that dramatic night. He had been holding in his hands a plastic bag containing several spray cans of various colours. Phizz had been a familiar and unmistakable sight in the city with his ripped clothing and long, unwashed hair tied back with a tattered thong. Equally well known at the time, but not generally attributed to him, was his artwork, which had adorned much of the Western side of the Wall: his incredible works of graffiti.

On that day in 1989 Phizz had been waiting for a gap in the crowd so that he could hurry to the Wall unseen and produce that evening's masterpiece. His hurried nocturnal improvisations had filled him with as much excitement then as they had four years previously when he'd written on the Wall for the first time. Back then, all he'd managed was a humble 'Max Schmidt woz 'ere'. Shortly after, he had progressed to simple monochromatic doodles, then larger and larger multicoloured images. He had painted huge stylised figures, creatures of all descriptions, stunning abstracts, and psychedelic landscapes. And, of course, he had long since abandoned signing them with his real name, preferring instead the tag 'Phizz'. There was nothing actually illegal about decorating his side of the Wall, but he rather enjoyed the anonymity of a pseudonym.

Throughout his adolescence this Wall had been his playground. His favourite times were just after a piece of the Wall had been repaired when he would be presented with a virgin expanse; it was like being given a pristine canvas on which to produce something new and exciting. On one famous occasion, within twenty-four hours a new section of wall had sported a vast apricot slice, fully thirty foot in width and covering the whole twelve-foot height: a piece he proudly referred to thereafter as his *still life*.

On the night of 9 November 1989, though, Phizz waited an eternity for a sufficient gap in the passers- by. The crowd failed to dissipate; in fact, from his vantage point, it had appeared to grow. During the day he had vaguely noticed more people than usual arriving in the city but had not thought anything of it. Eventually the crowd had grown to thousands. It was as if they were responding to a subliminal homing signal.

* * *

As the gathering grew louder Professor Schmidt closed his window and turned up the volume on his hi-fi to drown out the sounds that were distracting him from completing his latest treatise on the evil of the Wall.

Outside, at about midnight, a burly man approached the Wall. Phizz looked on in horror as he produced a hammer from inside his long overcoat and started to attack the concrete, sending chippings of one of his creations flying through the air. Spontaneously, the crowd joined in the destruction, using anything that came to hand. For over two hours they tore into the Wall with a ferocious industry. By 3 a.m., holes started to appear, and soon people were able to shake hands with each other through the Wall: East and West organically reuniting. The mood of the crowd was jubilant, but Phizz became increasingly morose. How would he produce his artwork in the future? For him, Berlin would never be the same again.

* * *

The destruction of the hated Wall left Erik without gainful employment for the first time in his life. But, with time on his hands and encouraged by his close circle of admirers, Erik wrote a novel based loosely on his experiences as a trusted member of the East German politburo. It was a brilliant political satire full of insightful material which could only have come from someone on the inside.

'One of the funniest, most poignant, anti-establishment novels since *Catch-22*' was Clive James verdict for the *New Yorker.* 'I laughed until I cried.'

'A post cold war comic masterpiece which will finally put James Bond into retirement' was the view of *The Guardian.*

Sales exceeded all expectations. The hardback version stayed in the best-sellers list for nearly thirty-six consecutive weeks, and the paperback went through reprint after reprint. Erik was rumoured to have sold the film rights for over £2 million. The name Erik Friedheimer was known everywhere, even if the man was not.

In six short years since the publication of his first book, Erik had become a literary sensation. His second novel was another enormous success; hence the mammoth queue was now snaking its way around the Berlin offices of Lehmanns. Interest in this one-time East German border guard was so intense that his second novel was being published together with the author's *Collected Works.* These accumulated observations of life on the 'wrong' side of the Wall, in the form of poems, short stories, essays, and diary notes formed a unique autobiography that was both pacey and profound. Parts of this work had caused a diplomatic and literary sensation even before its official publication when they appeared on the Internet, courtesy of some enterprising fans of Erik. Now the full printed version of the same work was the number one best-selling non-fiction book, and simultaneously, his novel was the number one best-selling fiction book.

Not all readers were convinced by the honesty of Erik's account of East Germany before, during, and after the Wall. One of those was Professor Willem Schmidt, who was now waiting patiently in the queue for an audience with his erstwhile school friend and fellow housebreaker.

'Airport thriller novels' were not to Willem's taste, so the runaway commercial success of Erik's first book had passed him by. What had alerted Willem to Erik's true identity was the peremptory publication of his *Collected Works* on the Internet. They had caused a sensation at the university. The phenomenon was so widely spoken about that even Professor Schmidt could not ignore the 'Collected Works' of Erik Friedheimer.

His initial reaction was that Erik's words were a distortion of the truth and nothing short of betrayal. When published, Willem bought the 'Collected Works' and read every poem, every play, every short story, and every essay over and over again. He readily acknowledged Erik's skill with language, his ear for dialogue, the subtleties of his humour, even his candour; but the more he read, the angrier he became. He was increasingly outraged because, nowhere in Erik's 'Collected Works', could he find a single reference to the two different economic systems under which they lived. Damn it, there was hardly a single reference to the bloody Wall, for so long the outward and visible sign of economic injustice! Worst of all, there was barely a passing reference to his own son's heroic death.

Willem, on the other hand, had devoted his whole life to bringing down the Wall. He had eschewed the profitable business career his superior intelligence entitled him to in order to remain in the vanguard of the intellectual protest movement. He even blamed his son's delinquent behaviour on the forbidding presence of the Wall. Now, fully ten years on from the Wall's destruction, what did he, Willem, have to show for twenty-eight years of passionate professional protest? A working lifetime of self-denial for absolutely nothing. No social standing. No respect. No thanks. In fact, almost the reverse. Many of his compatriots from East Berlin were openly sceptical, even scathing, about the merits of free enterprise. Even worse, there were those like Erik who seemed happy to exploit their good fortune, never once even questioning their right to do so. The *Collected Works* was absolute proof, if you really needed it, that Erik had never suffered on his side of the Wall.

*   *   *

STANLEY JACKSON AND GAVIN JACKSON

The doors finally opened, and the crowd surged into the bookstore. In front of them was a signing table, two members of staff, and the famous author. For an uncomfortable moment no one knew which of the three to approach. But one person recognised Friedheimer immediately, even after thirty-eight years.

'Erik,' he called out as he broke rank and hurried along the side of the queue. 'Remember me?'

Erik looked up to see Professor Willem Schmidt virtually running towards him. As he approached he saw him reach into his pocket and bring something out that reflected in the light. As he raised it to shoulder height and pointed it in Erik's direction, he saw that it was an old Luger. When the shot rang out, the awaiting crowd gasped as they watched their favourite author collapsing on to the table in front of him, spilling copies of his latest bestsellers on to the floor in front of him. Before those closest to Erik could take in what had happened, a second shot rang out in the bookstore. Professor Willem Schmidt fell forwards on the pile of books, having turned the still-smoking gun on himself.

The Full Story

A dramatic death occurs in **The Wall** that has proven to be something of a bone of contention with some of the Jackson Decamot Collective. 'But why?' was the oft repeated question.

To answer that question, and also to fill in the gaps that still existed in **The Wall** (namely, what did Erik do during the twenty-eight years of the Wall, how did he get from being a border guard to a novelist, and what did Phizz do when he no longer had the Wall to decorate), we wrote an even longer piece in the form of a film screenplay called **The Border Guard** that appears at the end of this book. In the screenplay we tried to expand on Willem's sense of betrayal and we explored how differently Erik, Willem, and Phizz coped with the demise of the Wall.

After writing the preferred ending for the film, we also came up with four alternative endings. If a film of the screenplay were ever made and it got to DVD, it would be amusing to include the different endings as a 'special feature', thus allowing the squeamish or the sentimental to choose their preferred resolution. The choices would be:

Author's preferred ending: Willem goes to the book signing armed with a loaded Luger stolen from a house they had looted together as boys. Erik fails to recognise Willem. Willem shoots Erik, is arrested, and faces a possible death penalty.

Hollywood ending: Erik not only recognises Willem, but has read Willem's academic papers. He invites him to join him in New York, where perhaps they can work out a deal with his publisher for Willem's story to be published.

Greek tragedy ending: Willem has brought the World War II Luger with him not to shoot Erik, but to reminisce; it was one of the items that they found together on one of their many adventures in the ruins of East Berlin before the Wall. Erik recognises both Willem and the Luger. As Erik moves around the table with his arms held wide to embrace his childhood friend, the security guard sees the gun in Willem's hand, assumes Erik's life is in danger, and shoots and kills Willem. The Luger turns out not to be loaded.

Reichenbach Falls ending: Erik sees the gun as Willem raises his hand to shoot him. Erik leaps over the table spilling books everywhere. They grapple on the floor in a way reminiscent of their childhood tussle in the ruins of Berlin in 1961. Ultimately the gun is fired and Willem ends up dying on the floor in the bookstore. Erik is also injured, recovers in hospital, but does not re-emerge in public for several years.

The anti-climax: Erik looks up, sees, but does not recognise Willem. Willem gets cold feet and fails to take the weapon from his satchel. Instead, he gets Erik to sign his copy of *The Collective* and departs meekly.

Sample Decamots 3

The two sample Decamots in this chapter were inspired by the following Decamot items:

Peter Piper, sandwich, ivy league, helter skelter, peach melba, fireworks, radioactive, young wife, rocket launcher, stadium.

Helter Skelter

On the one hand **Helter Skelter** is a very heart-warming story where two men are helped to recover from a tragedy by the altruistic act of a young teenager, but it also has the spooky aspects of a classic ghost story.

When the final version of **Helter Skelter** was read outside of the Jackson Decamot Collective, one reviewer commented that it was in the style of a story from the *Tales of the Unexpected* TV series from the 1970s. Originally based on short stories by Roald Dahl, the series consisted of weekly thirty-minute dramas, each of which had an eerie theme and an unexpected twist. This inspired us to produce a second version of the story in the form of a script for a thirty-minute TV drama, effectively, our 'tale of the unexpected'. The script appears later in this book in the chapter **Decamot TV Screenplays**.

Helter Skelter

'Why don't we get Peter Piper to open the fair?' asked Emma Ford, who had been co-opted on to the Holmbury Village Committee to represent the youth of the village, somewhat against her will.

'I'm sorry, my dear, but I've never heard of him, outside the nursery rhyme that is. Who, or what, is Peter Piper?' asked Colonel Worthington-Smythe (retired), the chairman of the committee.

'He's a DJ on Radio Active. Most people at school think he'll be the next Chris Evans. He's huge with students. And I think he may live near St Holmbury.'

'Oh, I see,' replied the Colonel as he offered a plate of the turkey sandwiches around the table. 'I must defer to your greater knowledge of these matters, young Emma. All those in favour of Emma approaching Mr Piper, please raise your hand.'

All twenty people sitting round the table raised their hands.

'Motion carried . . . and if we can rely on Mrs Ormskirk, as ever, to supply the ornamental flourishes . . . ?' The Colonel looked over to a plump little woman of about fifty.

Mrs Ormskirk thought it heartless to even consider suggesting anybody else to perform the irksome task of preparing hundreds of stems into dozens of bunches, and so kept her own counsel . . . as ever.

'And of course, I'll supply the fireworks. I've got a new rocket launcher that I want to try out.'

'Boys will be boys,' said Miss Bennett, a fearsome-looking spinster who was renowned in the village for complaining about the noise, any noise.

'And finally, any other business. Is there any?' asked the Colonel, ignoring Miss Bennett's comment.

Unexpectedly, there was. Emma asked: 'Why don't we ask Mr Henderson to put up his helter skelter for the fair?'

No one replied. The entire room was silent for the first time that evening. Several people around the table exchanged glances.

'My parents told me how great it was in the old days.' Emma looked around the table. Some of the committee members avoided eye contact; some looked down at their empty plates; Mrs Ormskirk started to play with her peach melba. Emma continued, sounding less confident than before: 'My American cousin, Jed, is coming over to visit soon . . . he mentioned sliding down the helter skelter as a kid . . . and I just thought it'd be kinda nice to . . .'

The awkward silence stretched. The hitherto voluble participants were suddenly struck dumb and all seemed reluctant to comment. After two agonising minutes, the Colonel said quietly: 'Frankly, Emma, nothing would give us greater pleasure than to have Mr Henderson participate again. But since the tragedy of forty years ago, he has shut himself away and is very rarely to be seen out and about. My wife has tried many times to shake him out of his crippling despair, but nothing seems to work.'

'Perhaps rebuilding the helter skelter would help take his mind off his problems.'

'Emma does have a point,' said Edward Masters, who ran the village shop. 'Working on Henderson's Helter Skelter could be therapeutic.'

'That's very true,' said Mary Jones, a nurse at the local hospital. 'And pride of place in our village fair always used to be the fifty-foot multi-coloured marvel that was Henderson's Helter Skelter.'

'Put St Holmbury's Village Fair on the map,' Masters agreed. 'Made us a nationally renowned event. We even used to stock a postcard of it in the village shop. Hugely popular with tourists.'

'But what about the tragedy?' asked Barbara Davis, Chairwoman of the Holmbury WI. 'We can hardly overlook that now can we?'

'What did happen?' asked Emma. 'I know it had something to do with Mrs Henderson and their son, but I don't know what.'

The other members of the Holmbury Village Committee fell silent again. And again it was the Colonel who broke the silence, this time to tell the story of the tragedy that had occurred so many years before.

The old-fashioned fairs that St Holmbury's typified were uniquely English, and St Holmbury's was justifiably celebrated; it had all the expected major attractions from coconut shies to kiddies' roundabouts to roll-a-penny tables to catch-the-rat to the impossible bicycle to the white-elephant raffle to throw-a-wet-sponge-at-the-mayor, and to the exquisitely made, skilfully operated, politically incorrect, Punch and Judy booth. They were all homemade devices lovingly designed and expertly constructed by the villagers themselves, a veritable triumph of craft over commercialisation.

For ten years the centrepiece of the fair had been Henderson's Helter Skelter. Made entirely of wood salvaged from an ancient shipwreck, it was an ingenious design. You entered by a small door and climbed up the inside via a winding circular wooden staircase. Emerging at the top, the rider put down a coconut mat and slid down a highly polished wooden slide which circled the outside of the structure two and a half times before being deposited in a heap at the bottom. It would take Mr Henderson a whole day to erect the helter skelter with the help of the local scout troop and several hundredweight of assorted bolts and nails and guy pegs and other paraphernalia. By nine o'clock in the evening the structure would be complete and ready for use the next day.

By tradition, whoever opened the fair did so by first climbing up the helter skelter, sliding down and cutting a red-and-white finishing tape at the bottom. Over the years various celebrities had suffered minor indignities as they landed, but it was all conducted with a good community spirit and all caught on camera by the photographer from *The Cotswold Guardian*, the local newspaper.

But tragedy struck at 8.30 p.m. on the evening of Saturday, 27 April 1968, a tragedy that had even made the national newspapers. Sally Henderson and her five-year-old son Mark were crossing the road from the shop to the village green, Sally meaning to witness the final preparations of the helter skelter and Mark looking forward to his first ever slide down it the next day, when a white BMW Alpina 2000 came hurtling round the corner. Max Henderson saw everything from his vantage point atop the helter skelter. He screamed out a warning, but his young wife and son were struck and killed instantly before his very eyes. The driver, whose own six-month-old son was a passenger in a carrycot in the back of the BMW, was subsequently convicted of manslaughter, served six months' imprisonment, and was banned from driving for two years.

The entire village turned out for the Hendersons' funeral three days later at St Holmbury's Church. The graves of Sally Henderson and her son had been tended by a grief-stricken Max Henderson ever since.

1968 was the last year the helter skelter was seen, and as far as most people knew, it remained packed away in Mr Henderson's garage.

The Colonel completed the story by saying: 'Grief's a personal thing, and we should respect Mr Henderson's privacy.'

'Oh, come on, Percy,' said Masters. 'Grief's one thing, but his has been going on for decades.'

The Colonel felt affronted at the usage of his first name and started to say something about it but was cut off by Mary Jones. 'Perhaps we'd be better neighbours to Max if we stopped pussyfooting around and helped him to confront his loss and perhaps he'd able to move on. I think we'd be doing him a favour.'

Several people around the table started nodding.

'So can I do it? Can I go talk to Mr Henderson?' Emma asked eagerly.

With great reluctance, the Colonel said: 'All those in favour of Emma approaching Mr Henderson, please raise your hand.'

This second motion of the evening was carried by a slender majority. Many members of the committee left the meeting with a sense of foreboding. Was it really sensible to encourage a fifteen-year-old girl to intrude on Mr Henderson's private grief, even after forty years?

* * *

Despite their reservations, Emma set about her two tasks with a passion over the month that preceded the annual fair and with surprising success on both counts. The harder of the two was tackling Mr Henderson: How can a teenager gain the confidence of a semi-reclusive septuagenarian?

Emma hit upon a brilliant idea: Emma's school heavily encouraged all of its students to participate in the Duke of Edinburgh Award Scheme. In the school's prospectus, and on their web site, the school described the scheme as providing a vital part of 'a holistic education'. Most kids were happy to join the scheme because they associated it solely with hiking and camping and didn't realise that it had other components as well, including an element of community service. Emma's brainwave was to approach Mr Henderson, tell him about the Duke of Edinburgh Award Scheme and how helping an older member of the village would help her to satisfy the community service aspect of it, get chatting to him, gain his trust and eventually broach the subject of the helter skelter.

Emma's first meeting with Mr Henderson did not get off to a good start, but they unexpectedly discovered a mutual interest. Mr Henderson was adamant that he had nothing that needed doing about the house and really didn't need Emma's help. After a little persistence, he finally found a task for her to help him with. He'd recently gone up into the attic for the first time in years. There, amongst a host of boxes and long-forgotten furniture, toys and clothes, he'd found several canteens of silverware that his late wife had inherited. He normally couldn't bear to get rid of anything, particularly things that made him think of the long-departed love of his life, but he realised that items hidden away in the attic for years on end were items he really could do without, and the money he could get from selling them would be a useful supplement to his pension. So perhaps Emma could help him to shine up the silverware and then take it down to the antique shop in the village to sell for him. Would that satisfy the Duke of Edinburgh Award Scheme's criteria for community service? Emma was sure that it would.

And so Emma found herself standing in Mr Henderson's hallway waiting for him to fetch several boxes of silverware from the attic. It was a very large space, bigger almost than her parents' living room. There was an old-fashioned hat stand near the main front door, an oak table under the window, an ancient cupboard, and several bookshelves filled to overflowing. But one item that really caught Emma's attention was sitting in one corner: a piano. It was nothing fancy, just a simple, upright piano with a long piano stool in front of it with a booklet of sheet music placed on the stand above the keyboard. What really made it stand out was how well looked after it appeared. Most of the hallway looked a little worn: the wallpaper looked a little faded, the painting on the skirting boards looked a little scuffed, and the parquet flooring had lost its sheen. Nothing was dirty, just a little dusty in places. But by contrast, the woodwork on the piano had been polished to a high shine.

Having been standing just inside the hallway for what a felt like an age, Emma finally walked over to the piano. The lid over the keyboard was closed. Emma looked at the page to which the booklet of sheet music was opened and smiled. It was Beethoven's *Für Elise*, a piece that she'd learnt to play at school during the previous term.

Emma looked over her shoulder and called out to Mr Henderson. There was no response. She figured that he was thoroughly engrossed in his attic visit; perhaps he'd been side-tracked by some item or other; attics were like that: her mother would often go up to find something in their attic and then lose all sense of time, returning ages later often with something other than the item she'd gone to look for.

Eventually, Emma sat down on the piano stool and opened the lid of the piano to reveal the keyboard. She hesitated for a few moments, then started to play the right hand part of the piece very quietly. Her playing was a little tentative at first, but increased in confidence, getting louder as she progressed through the piece. Having played the first page with her right hand, she stopped and went back to the beginning, this time playing both the left and right hand parts together. When she reached the bottom of the page, she turned the page over and continued.

Just as she was reaching the bottom of the third page, she heard a noise behind her. She stopped suddenly and turned round. Mr Henderson was standing in the doorway to the kitchen holding a large cardboard box filled with assorted silverware. He had a tear rolling down his cheek. Emma leapt to her feet.

'I'm so sorry,' she said. 'I shouldn't've done that. I just couldn't stop myself. I'm . . . I'm . . . I'm so sorry.'

'Don't be,' replied Mr Henderson.

'Thing is, I just saw the piece open on the piano and . . . well, it's something I've learnt recently . . . and it . . .'

'And it needs finishing.'

'What?' asked Emma.

'It needs finishing. You've got about twenty bars to go. Why don't you take it from the low A with the left hand, just before the four-bar flourish with the right hand, and play it to the end?'

Stunned, Emma sat back down on the piano stool. She hesitated for a few minutes and then started playing again. Mr Henderson remained standing in the doorway still holding the box. Finally Emma finished the piece and laid her hands in her lap, too embarrassed at first to face Mr Henderson.

'That was very good,' Mr Henderson said gently.

'But it could sound better.'

'I know. I'm not very good. I've not been playing very long.'

'Not you. The piano could sound better. The E-flat is too flat, and the notes around middle-C are all a little strained. The top-end keys sound a little clicky. And I can see you working the sustain pedal, but it's not releasing fully enough, so the notes are running on for a little too long. But these things are easily fixable.'

Mr Henderson's whole demeanour had lightened. He put the box down on the oak table and walked over to the cupboard next to the front door. He opened the cupboard door and carefully removed a huge toolbox and placed it on the table next to the cardboard box and opened it out.

Inside the toolbox was an array of pliers and small screwdrivers. There were also rolls of piano wire of different thicknesses, offcuts of felt, some small lengths of wood, several round wooden pegs, a tube of superglue, a small oil can, and several tuning forks.

'Are you a piano tuner?' asked Emma, watching in fascination.

'Used to be. Or should I say, piano tuning's one of the things I used to do. In fact, that's how I met Sally, my late wife.'

'Really?'

'She was eighteen at the time, and still living at home. This home, in fact, she inherited it a few years later when her father died. On the day we met, she was playing when I got here. Her father let me in. I waited just here and listened until she'd got to the end of the piece before getting started with the tuning.'

Mr Henderson selected two pairs of pliers and walked around to the back of the piano and removed the panel protecting the strings.

'What was she playing when you got here?' Emma asked.

'It was another Beethoven piece: Moonlight Sonata, very calming, very dreamy.' 'I know that one. Mum's got it on CD.'

'You can't beat hearing it in person. Now, play a scale with two flats in it for me. Just the right hand.'

Emma did so.

'Could you hear that? B-flat was fine, but the E-flat not quite so.'

'I think so.'

Mr Henderson used the pliers to make some adjusts to one of the strings.

'And again please.'

Emma played the same notes again. Mr Henderson made another small adjustment and then tightened two other strings.

'One more time please.'

Emma played the notes again.

'Much better. Now let's see what we can do with that pedal. Play the first eight bars, pressing the sustain pedal as you're playing the left-hand triplets, releasing it as the right hand takes over each time.'

Emma played the first eight bars while Mr Henderson bent low and looked long the line of strings. He then walked round to the front of the piano and crouched down into the foot well.

'First eight bars again please.'

Emma played the first eight bars again.

'Got it.'

Mr Henderson hurried over to the toolbox, selected a screwdriver, picked up the small oil can, and hurried back. He crouched into the foot well again, removed one of the levers, and squeezed a few drops of oil on to it. He then replaced the lever.

'One last time with the eight bars,' said Mr Henderson.

Emma played the first eight bars for a third time.

'Much better. Can you hear the difference?'

'I think so,' Emma replied.

'The sustained notes stop much more quickly now when I lift the pedal.'

'Exactly. Now let's hear the whole thing, but without the repeats.'

Emma played the whole piece through without stopping. This time round her playing was much more confident. She felt totally relaxed and made no errors. When she reached the bottom of each sheet, she deftly turned the page with her right hand and smoothly continued. The whole time Emma played, Mr Henderson watched from the doorway as he had before, but this time he was smiling broadly, and as Emma came to the end, he clapped enthusiastically.

'Much better.'

Now that the ice was broken, Emma and Mr Henderson got on very well together. They spent the afternoon polishing the first of the silver. The task took a lot longer than they had thought it would, and they had not even finished the first box before Emma had to go home for dinner.

*   *   *

Emma returned several times over the next week to continue the job. On her fourth visit, she finally managed to ask Mr Henderson about the helter skelter. They were sitting at the kitchen table, both polishing silver plates. In the middle of the table was a stack of plates that had been polished to a high sheen, and on the kitchen counter was the last of the cardboard boxes that Mr Henderson had retrieved from the attic.

'What did you do apart from piano tuning?'

'General woodworking: anything from cabinet making, to fitting the wooden seating in the local football stadium, to boat building.'

'Boat building? But we're miles from the coast.'
'True. But we do have thirty-six miles of canals in the Cotswolds, sixty odd miles of the Thames not far off. Lichfield's not far away, and there's miles of canal that way too. I had plenty of work over the years. Still do the odd job if it's nearby.'

Emma spotted an opportunity to steer the conversation and asked nervously, 'Is that er . . . is that how you came to build the helter skelter? Being the master carpenter in the village?'

'You know about the helter skelter?'

'Yeah. My parents mentioned it, and I've seen a postcard it was on.'

'I don't remember whose idea it was, but yes, that's why I was asked to build it. We put it up each year for ten years, until . . .' Mr Henderson fell silent. He stared at the plate he'd been polishing and sighed, but said no more.

'Until the car crash?' Emma eventually asked in a very quiet voice.

'Yes. Yes, until the car crash.'

'It must have been terrible,' Emma said in almost a whisper, feeling terrible, and suddenly regretting having mentioned it.

'It was. I was depressed for the longest time. The next year I couldn't face rebuilding the helter skelter. Nor the next year, nor the next. In the end the village committee stopped asking me, and I shut myself away more and more.'

Emma walked over to the dresser. There were several photographs in frames, including one of a young woman and a small boy. She'd seen them the first time she'd come into Mr Henderson's kitchen. One thing she'd noticed was how similar the woman was to herself: she had the same long, thick, near-black hair, pale skin, and green eyes. Also like Emma, she looked quite slim without being skinny. Emma felt it was like looking at an older sister.

'Is this them?' Emma asked, although she knew what the answer would be. 'Yes. That was taken on Mark's third birthday.'

'He's a real cutie.' 'Yes, he *was*.'

'Yes, of course, *was*. Sorry.'

'Don't be,' said Mr Henderson surprisingly brightly. 'To be honest, I'm sick of people treading on eggshells around me. It was sweet at first,

STANLEY JACKSON AND GAVIN JACKSON

and I'm sure they all meant well, but it's got to the point where I don't feel I can walk around the village any more. It's nice to be able to talk about them with someone.'

Emma and Mr Henderson were silent for a few minutes before Emma asked, 'Do you still have the helter skelter?'

'Yes, I do,' he replied. 'I could never quite bring myself to get rid of it. It's taking up half of my garage; it's probably not up to much anymore. Do you want to see it?' 'I'd love to,' said Emma.

Five minutes later, Emma and Mr Henderson were in the garage, and Mr Henderson had removed several dust sheets that had been covering various piles of planks, panels, and struts.

'This is it,' said Mr Henderson. 'Henderson's Helter Skelter. Those long straight panels make up the bulk of the ride. That pile of struts make up the framework. Those curved pieces make up the slide. And that last pile makes up the turret.'

'Wow, all the pieces look in pretty good nick.'

'This garage is completely weatherproof, so there's been no water damage or anything like that.' 'Do you think it could be put up again?'

'I should think so, there might be the odd strut that needs replacing, and the panels need a good repainting, but I think it could.'

Emma paused awhile before asking her next question; the big one: 'Would you be prepared to build it one last time? For the fair? This year?'

'No, I don't think so.'

'What!' said Emma, dismayed. 'Why not?'

'Who'd be interested in a helter skelter these days?'

'Loads of people would. It's historic.'

'It was old-fashioned when I first made it. That was nearly fifty years ago. Kids like theme parks nowadays. My helter skelter is somewhat tame.'

'But it's famous.'

Mr Henderson scratched his head and looked over all the piles in front of him tutting quietly. 'No! It'll be a lot of effort, and I really don't think it's worth it.'

'Why did you keep it all these years if you had no intention of ever putting it back up?' Emma asked sadly, disappointed that all her efforts may have been in vain.

'It's like everything else round here, Sally . . . er sorry, Emma. It's just one more thing that I've been meaning to get rid of, but just couldn't quite get round to.'

'How about giving it one last go? Then you can get rid of it for good.'

Mr Henderson sighed. He said nothing for a while. He walked over to the pile of panels. He picked up a panel and leant it against the side wall of the garage. He took a few steps backwards to look at it, and shook his head. The paint was flaking, but the words 'Henderson's Helter Skelter' were still just about visible. Emma feared the worst, and so was amazed when Mr Henderson suddenly said:

'Oh, what the hell, why not? Although I think I'll need some help to put it up. I'm not as young as I used to be.'

'Oh thanks, Mr Henderson,' said Emma. And before she could stop herself, she threw her arms around Mr Henderson's neck and kissed him gently on the cheek.

*　　*　　*

Having got Mr Henderson on board, Emma set about the task of persuading Peter Piper to open the fair. This turned out to be a lot more straightforward. Emma knew that Peter Piper did a request show on the radio on a Friday morning and took live calls from listeners. If she could get on the show and ask him on-air if he'd like to open the fair, he might find it impossible to say no. Emma was not only lucky enough to get through to the radio show on the Friday two weeks before the fair, but was also selected by the producer to appear on the show.

'That was *I Can't Explain* by The Who,' Peter Piper announced on his show. 'And now we have our Friday Request. Who do we have lined up Jo?'

'On line one, we have an Emma Ford from St Holmbury,' replied Jo Nicks, Peter Piper's producer. 'That's your neck of the woods, isn't it?'

'That's right. I'm just a few miles down the road. Hi Emma, what's your request?'

'I've got a request,' said Emma, not quite believing that she'd got on the air. 'But it's not a musical request.'

'This is Friday's song request slot, Emma,' Peter Piper replied. 'No exceptions, sorry.'

'I think you could at least listen to Emma's request, Peter,' said Jo.

'Oh, go on then. What did you have in mind, Emma?'

'Will you come open St Holmbury's Fair?' Emma asked nervously.

'I'm afraid that really is something that I can't . . .'

Emma quickly cut across Peter Piper, gabbling slightly: 'We're reopening the helter skelter.'

'You mean the one and only Henderson's Helter Skelter?' asked Jo, sounding genuinely amazed.

'That's right.'

'I remember hearing about that,' said Jo. 'It's been out of action for years, hasn't it?'

'That's right, but Mr Henderson himself has agreed to put it up again.'

'Wow,' said Jo. 'Didn't realise he was still alive. This is truly historic, Peter. You don't really want to miss out on this one, do you?'

'Well, it's er . . . well, not really the sort of thing that I'd, er . . . normally do. But I . . . er . . . Henderson's Helter Skelter eh?!' Peter Piper paused for a few seconds; then he said more confidently, 'You know what? I think I might make an exception on this occasion.'

'Thanks, Peter,' said Emma hardly believing her luck. 'You're sick.'

'Er thanks, I think,' said Peter Piper. 'Listen, Emma, stay on the line and let Jo take your details while I play some more music . . . this little-played single is a personal favourite of mine. It got to number 3 in 1965. It's *Tossing and Turning* by the Ivy League.'

*   *   *

By the time Emma's cousin arrived, posters festooned the neighbourhood announcing the opening of the annual fair by Radio Active's famous DJ and that the fair would be 'featuring the one and only Henderson's Helter Skelter'. Such was the interest sparked by the reappearance of the fair's famous centrepiece that the local TV station sent a camera crew to cover the event.

Jed was really impressed. He'd spent the previous week in Oxford revisiting the Alice in Wonderland haunts that he'd enjoyed on his first visit to England as a boy and was delighted to be returning to St Holmbury to meet up with Emma and her parents. On the Saturday evening at nine o'clock, it really was just like old times. Mr Henderson had just put the finishing touches to his newly painted structure and had retired to the pub for a well-earned rest. He had clearly been rejuvenated by the experience, and his fellow villagers marvelled at the miracle of his re-emergence. Meanwhile, Jed was trying to persuade Emma to let him be the first down the helter skelter. He had had a great time reliving his previous trip to England, and being the first down the helter skelter would be the icing on the cake.

'Cool. So shall we have quick go on the slide while no one's around?' 'Absolutely not. The first person to go down has to be Peter Piper!'

'Why?' asked Jed.

'Village tradition. Whoever opens the fair has the first ride on the slide. That's how they always used to do it.'

'Shame. Look, I picked up this vintage, pre-digital camera on my travels. It would have been the latest thing when I was last here in England.'

Jed removed a camera from his rucksack and showed it to Emma. It was an old SLR 35 mm camera about four times the size of a digital camera and made of sturdy black plastic. On its upper side it was a huge flash.

'It's a Nikon F, made in 1960. You even have to load it with film and get someone to develop it for you; something you've never had to worry about!'

'Hmm, very nice,' said Emma. 'But what's that got to do with the helter skelter?'

'Well, look at this bit here.' Jed pointed to a small lever on top of the camera's casing. 'That's the timer control, it's the only gimmick that the camera's got. You get a delay of about fifteen seconds, so you have to set up the shot, set the camera, run round to the other side, and then . . . BOOM, you can take a shot of yourself.'

'Still not seeing where you're going with this,' said Emma.

'I just thought it would be a bit of fun to give it a whirl in the old-fashioned way. I thought I could set up the camera at the bottom of the helter skelter near the landing area. We could run up the inside and get caught on camera as we land. Then get the film developed, have several weeks' anticipation without knowing how well it will turn out, you know, the whole sixties thing.'

'Sounds like fun. I'm up for that. But why can't this wait 'til tomorrow?'

'Well,' said Jed. 'In the heat of the moment would we really get a chance to set up the camera? People will be too keen to clamber up the famous helter skelter to wait for us messing around. Do it now, and we can take as long as we like setting up the shot. Maybe you can be waiting at the top of the slide already, so only one of us has to run up to the top.'

'You do have a point, I s'pose.'

'So shall we go for it then? No one will know.' 'Yeah, go on then!'

Emma climbed to the top of the helter skelter while Jed set up the camera on a box and activated the timer by pushing the small silver lever. He then rushed up the winding inside staircase. At the top, they both squeezed on to one mat and came swirling down the slide, barely able to contain their excitement. As they landed the camera flashed. Several seconds later the camera flashed a second time.

'Brilliant,' said Jed. 'Not sure why it flashed again, but I'm fairly sure we were spot on with the first flash. Thank you so much. I'll send you a copy of the photo when I get back to the States.'

*　　*　　*

The next day was a triumph from beginning to end. It was estimated that 5,000 people squeezed on to the village square, all eagerly awaiting the opening of the fair.

On the centre of the green the giant helter skelter towered over the crowd. The woodwork was shiny and looked well-polished, the paintwork on the lettering on the side of the helter skelter was newly done by Mr Henderson, and the entire structure was covered in red, white, and blue bunting. There was a ribbon tied across the riders' entrance to the helter skelter.

STANLEY JACKSON AND GAVIN JACKSON

In the centre of the crowd the Vicar of St Holmbury's Church and his wife Marjorie were waiting to get proceedings underway. Next to them stood the local Mayor dressed in his ceremonial gown topped off with the chains of office, and on the other side of the Vicar, dressed in a very smart suit, was Peter Piper, and next to him, equally smartly dressed, stood Max Henderson.

At last they were joined by a man dressed as an old-fashioned town crier. In one hand he held a hand bell and in the other an oversized pair of scissors. The town crier rang the bell, and the crowd fell silent.

'Oyez, Oyez! Oyez, Oyez! People of St Holmbury, welcome to our annual fair. Please show your appreciation for Mr Peter Piper.'

The crowd cheered. The town crier handed the oversized scissors to Peter Piper who cut the ribbon. Peter Piper then turned to wave at the crowd, who cheered even louder. He then disappeared inside the helter skelter. After a few moments, he emerged at the top of the slide holding a large coconut hair mat.

After riding the helter skelter without mishap, Peter Piper took the microphone to officially declare the Annual St Holmbury's Fair open. He went on to make an emotional speech that the villagers would never forget.

'You can probably guess that Peter Piper is only my professional name. My real family name would have been known for the very worst of reasons to any of you who were living in the village forty years ago. It was my father's car that caused a fatal accident near this very village green. I was a passenger in that car. He had been drinking, and we took the bend much too fast.

'Of course, I was far too young to know anything about it at the time, but as a young reporter, I read the cuttings and knew what devastation it had caused Max Henderson and his family. I have never been able to drive through this lovely village without feeling the shame of what my father had done. Emma Ford somehow found all this out and introduced me to Max.

'Today, thanks to the marvellous generosity of spirit shown to me by Max Henderson, I have been able to atone. Sir, I will be eternally grateful to you, and I believe that today we have both achieved closure.'

The two men embraced in front of 5,000 cheering people, tears filling both their eyes.

*   *   *

Several weeks later Emma received an airmail package with a US postage stamp. Sitting on the sofa Emma opened the package and emptied its contents on to the coffee table in front of her. There was a letter and a small envelope. She unfolded and read the letter.

She then opened the envelope and removed two photographs. She looked at the first one. It showed Emma and Jed tumbling on to the landing mat together at the bottom of Henderson's Helter Skelter grinning like Cheshire cats.

She then picked up and looked at the second photograph. She gasped and dropped it on to the coffee table face up. It was of two people: a young woman and a small boy. She recognised them immediately from the picture she'd seen on the dresser in Mr Henderson's kitchen: they were Mrs Sally Henderson and her five-year-old son Mark; both were sliding down Henderson's Helter Skelter, and both were waving and smiling at the camera.

The Endowment Dinner

The inspiration for **The Endowment Dinner** came entirely from the name Peter Piper: What would life be like for a kid called Peter Piper who stuttered on the letter 'P'? How much would he be ridiculed by his puerile pre-pubescent peers at school? How would that experience affect his outlook on life? How might he settle the score if one day he were in a position of power?

The Endowment Dinner

Hors d'oeuvres

'. . . and several hundredweight of Ammonium Nitrate . . . Yes, that's right, all to be sent to my home in Baltimore . . . as soon as p-p-p-possible . . . Thank you.' The man replaced the handset of the telephone and spun round on his chair to face the young woman sitting on the other side of his vast mahogany desk.

'So you like your parties to go with a bang!' she observed before she could stop herself. She had been sitting quietly for the better part of thirty minutes listening to his half of a conversation discussing the arrangements for a forthcoming party, a conversation that culminated in him dictating a shopping list containing items that ranged from enough cold turkey to feed an army and enough explosives to destroy one.

She had arrived promptly at 5 p.m. for a job interview and had been shown into his office by the receptionist. He had been rocking back on his leather-upholstered chair with his feet on the desk, puffing out great clouds of bluish cigar smoke. He had indicated the chair on the opposite side of the desk. She was not sure what to make of this treatment. Had he staged the telephone call to assess how she would react? If nothing else, he was certainly living up to his reputation as the oil industry's most eccentric CEO.

During her wait her feelings had gone from mild amusement to annoyance. She had decided to wait patiently and not show that she had been listening in to his conversation. Then finally when the conversation had come to an end she could not resist the quip.

'Oh yes, I like to end my p-p-p-parties with a bang. I make my own fireworks, you see. I'm something of an expert.'

'Aren't fireworks made with potassium nitrate?'

'That gives them the whoosh and the colour. All standard shop-bought fireworks use it. I like to add a little ammonium nitrate. I find it gives them an extra vroom,' he said, punching the air with his fist for additional emphasis.

'Anyway, let's get on with the interview. You are . . .' He looked down at a notepad on his desk.

'Sarah Jenkins and you want me to consider you for the job of CEO's Right Hand?'

'That's right.'

'Excellent. Read this . . .' He held up a large board that had been lying face down on his desk. 'You want me to read that?'

'That's right. Aloud!'

'Peter Piper once Picked a Peck of Pickled Peppers. Now he's the CEO of Peter Piper's Petroleum Pipeline.'

'Excellent. Now wow me.'

'I beg your pardon?'

'Ask me something that shows you've done some research. I don't mean some contrived Ivy League-style question. Ask me a question that makes me think, "Wow, she's done her homework".'

'Why did you choose that name for your company given your particular speech characteristic?'

'If you mean "stutter", say "stutter". I hate euphemisms. Anyway, what makes you think I have a stutter? Who told you I had a stutter?'

'You don't have a stutter, well, not a conventional one anyway. They usually affect all plosives, all fricatives or all sibilants. You seem to have difficulty with some plosives but not all. You obviously don't have a problem with *bs*, but you obviously do with *ps*.

'Everywhere in your company, except in your company's name, you manage to avoid an initial P. Take this job for example, most places would call it Personal Assistant, you call it CEO's Right Hand. I've read through your company documents, and I notice that you have a Human Resources department, not a Personnel. You don't have a Pension Plan, you have a Retirement Investment Fund. You don't have Projects, you have Ongoing Concerns. In your staff canteen, you have an extensive range of sandwiches on offer, but no pastrami, pâté, roast pork, paprika, peppers, or pickled cucumbers. The list is endless. Nowhere is there in your company a function, department, or division that begins with the sixteenth letter of the alphabet.

'When I was researching your company I thought that maybe you were just a little eccentric and had something against this letter, but having met you I now realise that you have a problem pronouncing *p*s. You appear to be very careful to avoid troublesome *p*s, and yet you call your company Peter Piper Petroleum Pipelines. Why choose a name you can't pronounce?'

'Very astute observations – excellent. The reason's straightforward: I think it sounds good (unless I try to say it of course). Throughout my life associates, colleagues, and classmates have found my stutter amusing. It doesn't help that I can't even say my own name. One of the main objectives of the job you sent your resume for is to shield me from the outside world. I am the most successful chemical engineer of my generation and don't want to be mocked.

'Now that I have enough money, I want to hire someone who I can rely upon to avert this. The CEO's Right Hand will answer all my calls, chair meetings, and act on a day-to-day basis as if they were me. Occasionally, I will have to deliver a talk, and so my Right Hand will ensure my notes are free of those troublesome letters. The job is yours, if you want it. $80K starting salary, six monthly reviews, car, health care, and share offerings.'

Main Course

'P-P-P-Peter P-P-P-Piper p-p-p-picked a peck of pickled p-p-p-peppers. P-P-P-Peter P-P-P-Piper . . .'

'I don't know why you torture yourself so much,' Sarah said as she watched her husband standing in front of the full-length mirror struggling with both his bow tie and his pronunciation. 'Just use the *b*-for-*p* substitution that your therapist suggested. With any luck, after tonight, your problem will be gone forever.'

'You know very well why I must torture myself. I'll be standing in front of my contemboraries and won't even be able to enunciate my own name,' he said turning round. 'What do you think?'

Sarah looked up from the computer screen. 'You look great,' she said. 'I've made a few minor amendments if you'd like to take a look.'

Sarah went into her dressing room to finish preparing for the evening. Peter sat down in front of her laptop computer, but instead of reading the speech his wife had prepared for him, he started Mozilla Firefox and entered the URL for the Evoke Lounge web site.

'You're supposed to be reading the script,' his wife's disembodied voice called out from the other room, 'not messing around. If you want to listen to music, why don't you use the hi-fi? What is that crap anyway?'

'It's a bit before your time, love. It's "Helter Skelter" by the Beatles.'

Peter knew he would not need to check her work; she had been doing an excellent job ever since he hired her six years before. He read through the text anyway to remind himself of its contents and also to remind himself of the alterations that he had made that his wife did not know about.

'You look stunning,' he said as his wife came back into the room ten minutes later.

'Thank you. Shall we go?'

*   *   *

Peter was silent during the journey to Ithaca. His young wife glanced over at him in the back of the dimly lit limousine. This was a big night for him for many reasons, not least because he was confronting his tormentors in the most public way imaginable.

Ever since she first met Peter Sarah had been desperate to help him to overcome his unfortunate speech characteristic. At first she had thought that the extremes he went to publicly avoid words with an initial 'P' were just a part of his eccentric personality, but as she had got to know him, first as his personal assistant (although he would always insist on the title CEO's Right Hand) and then as his wife, she had realised that the problem had a much deeper psychological effect on him. He was such a brilliant man who had allowed himself to become trapped by a mild speech impediment.

After five years of persuasion, he had finally agreed to seek professional help. Rather than consult a speech specialist, Sarah had suggested a psychotherapist. This had proved to be an excellent decision. Through a number of sessions, they had 'discovered' the root of the problem.

Fate had dealt Peter Piper a cruel blow by providing him with parents who had an alliterative taste in child-naming and a predisposition to stumble over initial plosives. He had been brought up in Honey Creek, a mining town in Iowa where boys left school to follow their fathers down to the pits, and girls left school to produce the next generation. His parents were different: His mother taught English at the High School, and his father was the football coach. His father was something of a local hero; the only boys ever to leave Honey Creek did so with football scholarships thanks to Mr Piper Snr.

When Mrs Piper produced a son the whole town assumed that in time he would take over his father's position as football coach. But unlike his father he was short of stature and lacking any aptitude for, or interest in, football. Worse still, he was shy and prone to stuttering when nervous.

Children can be heartless when they sense weaknesses, and the young Peter Piper had more than his fair share. Having a mild nature and a sensitive disposition he had sought refuge within himself. He lost himself totally in his schoolwork, opting out of all forms of physical sport. He found that he had a natural aptitude for science, chemistry in particular.

By sixteen he had exhausted the school library and the local library and completed the entire high school curriculum. He applied to study chemistry at Cornell University.

He did not come across well in the interview, but his submitted written work was well received. What persuaded the faculty to offer him a place despite his young age was his intimate knowledge of each element in the periodic table. He also had an insight into the bonding mechanisms and complementary properties of radioactive carbon isotopes that far out-weighed the usual grasp that high-school graduates had and even challenged that of most college graduates who had majored in chemistry. The icing on the cake was the hobby that he had listed on his application: big bangs. The head of Chemistry was a fellow pyromaniac who enjoyed a good explosion every bit as much as the next man.

Unfortunately, Peter felt as much out of place in upstate New York as he had in Iowa. The rough and ready mining folk were replaced by prep school educated sons and daughters of old money families. He was disappointed to note that most had obtained their places at the college by virtue of their talents on the football pitch rather than in the laboratory. And they were as unforgiving of his speech imperfections as his erstwhile high school mates. Coming from circles priding themselves on perfect bodies, clothes, homes, cars, and teeth, the adolescent Peter Piper was the perfect foil for their cruel jibes. It did not help that in the same year that he embarked upon his degree, Jerry Lewis had a massive box office success with *The Nutty Professor*. A nickname for Peter was inevitable.

And so the cycle continued. Peter hid behind his test tubes and chose avoidance over confrontation. He completed his degree and PhD in less than four years. He was offered a chair to research carbon dating techniques, but this entailed an element of teaching, and he could not face the prospect of constant lampoonery. He chose instead to go into industry, the oil industry to be precise, where he quickly became an expert in underground explosives and mining.

He made Chief Engineer at Epsilon Fuels by the time he was twenty-five. The higher he rose in the company, the less time he spent getting his hands dirty, the more time he spent in meetings. He decided to create a company for laying pipelines for the oil industry, a brilliant move that had made him a very wealthy man. He had managed to become increasingly successful and increasingly remote from the outside world.

Having unravelled Peter's background over a number of sessions, the therapist had concluded, 'To avoid being teased about your stammer, you have withdrawn as much as possible from public life.'

'Thank you Doctor, very insightful!' he had retorted impatiently. 'Do you have any suggestions, or have I just been wasting your time and my money?'

'Your withdrawal has served to reinforce your affliction rather than to cure it. Don't hide yourself away behind your aides. Face your demons. Go to them, and show them just how successful you've been despite them. Once you can stand before them and impress them with what you have achieved, you will be able build up your own self-confidence.'

The therapist had, of course, been talking metaphorically, but Peter had decided to take the advice literally. Twelve months ago Peter had bought several acres of land that bordered his old college fraternity house, the site of two years of near-daily humiliation. Since then a construction team had been building on the site, their work hidden behind vast hoardings. Each of the workers had been paid a hefty bonus to maintain secrecy. All the outside world knew about the project was that Peter Piper was preparing a large gift for his *alma mater* and that tonight he had assembled the dons, lecturers, and fraternity masters to a dinner at which he would formally present it.

So like Peter, Sarah thought. *Never one to do things by halves.*

Just Desserts

The dinner took place in an enormous marquee pitched at the top of the hill that overlooked the fraternity house and Peter's neighbouring building site. At the end of the meal a trumpet fanfare started, and Peter Piper rose to his feet amidst tumultuous applause. He abandoned his half-eaten peach melba and made his way round to a dais that had been built in front of the tables and addressed the audience.

'Tonight I will unveil the gift that I give back that I think suitably rebays you.'

Sarah smiled to herself as she alone noticed the consonant substitution that allowed her husband to complete his opening sentence without hesitation. She felt proud as he continued in that vein for a further fluent and stutter-free twenty minutes.

'And now, with the help of my state-of-the art remote control system . . .' At this point one of his aides wheeled on a trolley that contained four comically oversized mushroom switches. The audience laughed. With gusto Peter placed both hands on the first of them and used his full weight to depress it. There was a massive whooshing sound from the back. Everyone turned in their seats to see the rear wall of the marquee drawn back like a vast curtain. From every seat, the fraternity building and the scaffolding surrounding the new building was clearly visible.

Peter depressed the second switch. The scaffolding and hoardings fell outwards to reveal an immense domed structure. Peter depressed the third switch. Four vast sets of spotlights burst into life to illuminate the structure. From their vantage point the audience could make out an enormous football stadium complete with enclosed seating and commentary boxes that would rival any in the AFL or NFL. Peter was amused to note that the fraternity coach had tears rolling down his cheek as he got to his feet and instigated a standing ovation.

As his audience stood with their back to him, Peter depressed the final switch. Fireworks erupted on all sides of the new stadium. The sky was quickly alight with Catherine Wheels, Molten Lava, Sunflowers, Flying Pigs, Carousels, Roman Candles, and three dozen Whoppers. The ground shuddered under the power of rolling thunder, and then smoke billowed out, enveloping the entire stadium.

The grand finale was a four-way rocket launcher that set off from the centre of the football field. The rockets sailed vertically upwards and rose steadily and silently until they were mere orange pinpricks in the night sky. At the top of their flight they slowly turned and started to head back to earth. As they fell they appeared to gather speed. The audience gasped as they watched the four rockets that appeared to have been incorrectly aimed. The rockets landed with an undeniable vroom, each taking out one of the four corner pillars that supported the giant stadium. Sarah looked up at her husband in disbelief and was surprised to note a look of what was undoubtedly satisfaction. She looked back down the hill to the mayhem below. The entire stadium was gracefully collapsing like an enormous house of cards caught by a gust of wind. As she watched she realised that no piece of debris fell further than thirty feet from the slowly disappearing stadium. It took a little under ten minutes for the entire stadium to be levelled.

Sarah realised that the wayward fireworks had not been misaligned at all; they had been perfectly placed by an expert.

*   *   *

During the investigation that followed Peter Piper was questioned at length by the insurance assessor. At one point the assessor suggested that Peter might have deliberately caused the explosions, to which he replied, 'That pronouncement is perfectly preposterous!'

Sample Decamots 4

The two sample Decamots in this chapter were inspired by the following Decamot items: *large parcel, billabong, venomous snake, little black book, postman, black umbrella, Big Ben, castle, river boat, airplane ticket.*

Wheel of Fortune

Wheel of Fortune explores the dangers of living a lie and the importance of seizing opportunities when they present themselves. It has a central deception and an unexpected resolution.

Wheel of Fortune

Redundancy hit Roger Marshall hard. To his wife and neighbours, he epitomised Middle England. He was 'something in the City' yet found time to support his local community. He was a governor of the minor independent school attended by his twin daughters, treasurer of the local operatic society, volunteer postman at the local hospital most Sundays, and chairman of the Esher Round Table. Apart from the well-being of his family, his two greatest passions in life were rugby and classic cars. He was from a typical middle-class family. His father was a retired doctor, now living in Eastbourne with Roger's mother, a moderately successful ballet teacher and theatre buff. On the surface, his life was little short of perfection.

The trouble was that Roger harboured a secret that his redundancy would expose: He had never really amounted to much, but until two weeks ago, he had had no real worries either. On leaving school with insufficient grades for a decent university place, he had opted for that safe refuge of every grammar schoolboy since the Second World War: a career in banking. He joined Barclays in Threadneedle Street as a clerk on a path that could have led to middle management if he had had a modicum of ambition or talent; Roger lacked both. Throughout his twenty-year career he had remained a clerk; it suited his temperament, and he was very easily satisfied. He liked doing the same mundane tasks each day. At lunchtimes he liked to go for a walk for an hour. Some days he would cross over London Bridge and stroll along the river towards

Tower Bridge; on other days he would walk up to Westminster. He would always be back on time, even if it meant taking the tube to do so.

The combination of a heavily subsidised staff mortgage plus an unexpected inheritance from a maiden aunt had given him a considerable leg up the property ladder just before the major explosion in house prices in the early seventies. His large five-bedroom detached property on the edge of Esher Common suggested its owner must be someone with a successful City career.

The only spontaneous thing that Roger had ever done was to marry suddenly at the age of thirty-eight. Caroline was a stunning blonde with a cut-glass accent who was fifteen years his junior. They met on a river boat trip to Windsor Castle organised by the Runnymede Conservatives. Their romance was swift and almost as much of a surprise to each other, as it was to their friends. At the on-board disco in the evening, an infuriatingly catchy tune 'You're More Than a Number in My Little Black Book!' became 'their song' despite the fact that neither of them really liked soul music. Roger was into Gilbert and Sullivan whilst Caroline preferred the New Romantics.

When they had first met Roger had accidentally deceived Caroline about the nature of his work. He had said that he worked in the bank and was in charge of security. He often described his job like that to make it sound more interesting than admitting that he was merely a clerk. At the time he was working in the Property department and one of his regular tasks was to test the fire alarms of the properties in which the bank had an interest. Unfortunately, Caroline thought he meant Head of Securities. Such a job would explain where he lived, that he could afford several classic cars (including an immaculate MG A) and was considered by the women of the local Conservative Party to be one of the most eligible bachelors in Esher. It was not until four weeks later when he proposed to Caroline that he realised her misconception, by which point it was too late to put the record straight; she had already told her family and friends about the catch she had made. He reasoned that to tell them the truth would make him look a fraud; besides, he rather liked the reaction that people gave when they thought he had an important job in the City.

During the years that followed, he gave himself theoretical promotions. Fabricating his own career became the most imaginative thing that Roger had ever done in his life. By the time Charlotte and Victoria were born, Roger had made himself Regional Director. His colleagues in the Compliance department, where he was not even an assistant team leader, would not have recognised their inoffensive colleague's description of himself. To them, he was as dull as he was unimaginative.

Work and family were two different worlds. On one occasion, he had arrived home with a large parcel for Caroline's birthday, which he insisted she open immediately. She opened layer upon layer of paper and found boxes within boxes until she was left with a single envelope. On the outside of the envelope Roger had written: '*Pack your bags; we're waltzing off to the billabong. And don't forget your venomous snake repellent!*' Inside the envelope were two airplane tickets to Australia. 'Courtesy of my latest bonus!' Caroline laughed and blessed her good fortune.

Roger Marshall led a very successful double life for fifteen years. But then suddenly, Roger was made redundant. With a potential world recession looming on the horizon, the bank was downsizing. The policy was to keep the essential managers, the younger members of staff, and those with good IT skills. Sadly, Roger was barely computer literate and considered something of a dinosaur. At the age of fifty-two, he was at an awkward in-between age: too young for early retirement and too old for retraining, especially with his limited ability and experience. For years he had been supplementing his inadequate salary by dipping into his life's savings and his aunt's dwindling inheritance. Redundancy was not only an acute embarrassment, it was a financial disaster.

That was two weeks ago, and he had yet to tell his wife. For the past fortnight, he had continued to leave home every morning, black umbrella in hand, to catch the South West Trains 7.05 service to London Waterloo via Clapham Junction. He would then spend the day in various coffee bars scouring the appointments pages of every paper that he could lay his hands on. He was having little luck and was becoming more depressed by the day. His options were narrowing all the time. The longer he put off making a decision, the more desperate he felt. He even contemplated suicide.

Today, he was going to visit the London Eye on the south side of the Thames opposite the Houses of Parliament. A job as a pod guide had caught his eye in the *London Evening Standard,* and he thought he would do some hands-on research. Whilst the salary offered was less than he had been earning, he reasoned that if he did the job well, he might be able to supplement his income with tips, particularly if the ride was popular with Americans. Given that each trip took about thirty minutes and each pod carried about twenty-five passengers, he had worked out on a napkin whilst sitting in Prêt á Manger that even if only one in ten people tipped the guide, he could earn up to £50 a day in tips. He knew it was a pipe dream, but after two weeks of scouring the newspapers, he could see no better way to continue his pretence of a City career.

* * *

Roger got into the pod, removed his jacket, and placed it on the bench in the middle. He had brought his birdwatching binoculars along with him and had decided to spend about five to six minutes looking in each direction to get a feel for how much you can make out and start thinking about a script he might use to enlighten fellow passengers.

He thought that looking east would be a good starting point since this would overlook the many walks that he had made during his years working on Threadneedle Street. Roger raised his binoculars and decided to look for St Paul's Cathedral. He spotted Tower Forty-Two immediately then looked round to the left and there it was. He was distracted from his reminiscing by a voice at his side.

'Excuse me, son, can we ask you a question?'

Roger looked round startled, not so much by the unexpected interruption than by being referred to as 'son'. No one other than his parents had thought him young enough for this description for at least twenty years.

He realised the man was American as much from his clothes as from his accent; he was wearing stout walking shoes, knee-length checked shorts, Timberland shirt straining over a wide girth, and a broad- brimmed Stetson. His most noticeable features were his mane of white hair, long, well-trimmed goatee, and thick moustache twisted at the ends. He reminded Roger of Buffalo Bill in later life.

'Of course,' said Roger. 'How can I help?'

'Can you point out London Bridge?'

'Certainly. It's the third bridge in that group of three: there's Blackfriars, Southwark, and then London Bridge,' said Roger. 'Here, would you like to borrow these?'

'Gee thanks son,' said the American taking Roger's binoculars and looking along the Thames. After a few minutes he turned from the window. 'Hey, Sherry-Lou, come and take a look.'

Roger looked round and saw a rotund woman wearing a near identical outfit to the American gentlemen walking over from the other side of the pod. There was no mistaking that this was Sherry-Lou.

'This is Sherry-Lou, and I'm Bud.'

'Hi, I'm Roger.'

'Look along the river, honey, it's that third bridge. Do you see it?'

'Yeah, I got it.'

'It's quite different from the real one, ain't it, honey?'

'Sure is.'

'What do you mean, "the real one"?' asked Roger.

'The real London Bridge,' said the man. 'Here look.'

He reached into his inside pocket and brought out a photograph. It showed a magnificent Victorian bridge with four arches that crossed a river that could easily have been the Thames.

'That's the real London Bridge in Havasu, our hometown,' explained the American. 'It was falling down, you know, like in the nursery rhyme. Anyway, it needed replacing or repairing. You guys decided to replace it, and this guy called McCulloch bought it in the early sixties, shipped it over to Arizona, and rebuilt it, brick by brick.'

Roger vaguely remember his father telling him that story when he was a child and felt slightly embarrassed that it was a tourist telling him some English history.

'So why did he buy it?'

'For the money, why else,' said the American. 'He figured that he could turn it into a tourist attraction.'

'Did it work?'

'Sure did. Your London Bridge put Havasu on the map real good. We had a big ol' ranch in the middle of nowhere, which we turned, built a 150-room hotel, and turned our eight acres into London Village. We never have an empty room.'

'Which way's Buck House?' asked Sherry-Lou.

Roger cringed but pointed her in the right direction without comment. By now he realised that he was going to act as a guide for the couple for the rest of the ride. Still, it would prove to be a useful practice, and he decided to make the most of it. For the next twenty minutes the couple took it in turns with the binoculars while Roger identified the most obvious buildings first to the east side of the pod, then to the north and west.

'And there's Westminster, the seat of the British Parliament. You'll notice it's only a short walk from Downing Street, but not one that Mr Prescott ever takes.

'If you walk along the river on this side this evening, you'll get a beautiful view of the building across the water from a nice bar called the Piano and Pitcher, a great photo opportunity.'

'The Piano and Pitcher was that?' asked Bud. 'I didn't realise you guys had baseball here.'

Roger looked round at Bud and saw that he had been making notes in a small pocket book.

'Thought I'd plan out our itinerary for later. Your commentary's been great. Hope you don't mind.'

'Not at all,' Roger replied.

'Is that an Inspector Morse car driving across the bridge?' Sherry-Lou asked, handing Roger the binoculars. 'We get Morse on Channel 59, don't we, Bud? We love it. Nothing like our cop shows.'

'You're absolutely right. It's a Jaguar MK 2. I have one myself, and if I'm not mistaken, it's a '62. When it moves forward, I'll see if I can read its number plate. Yup, it's an A-reg . . . R O G 15 A . . .'

Roger's voice trailed away as he read off the number.

'Are you all right, son? You look a little pale.'

'That's my car.' 'That Jag?'

'Yes, it is. I bought it a few weeks ago. But it should be on my drive at home, not heading towards Big Ben. I think someone's stolen my car.'

By now the London Eye wheel had almost completed its circuit, and the other passengers in the pod were gathering together their belongings and were preparing to disembark.

'Let's go for a drink, and we can help you decide the best thing to do,' Bud suggested.

STANLEY JACKSON AND GAVIN JACKSON

'I wouldn't want to impose. I'm sure you've got plenty of other items on your itinerary.' 'Not at all. You've been so generous with your time, it's the least we can do.'

*   *   *

They found a coffee bar close to the London Eye and sat down to discuss Roger's options. 'Are you sure it was your number plate?'

'Absolutely.'

'And it's supposed to be at home on your driveway?'

'Yes. My wife drops me off at the station each morning in her car. Mine never moves during the week.'

'Why don't you call your wife to see if she knows it's missing? Maybe she's already reported it to the police.'

Roger wondered why he hadn't thought of that himself and removed his mobile from the inside pocket of his jacket.

'That's strange. Caroline says the car's still on the drive.'

'Hey, isn't that it?' said Sherry-Lou. Roger and Bud looked out the window and sure enough there it was, driving back across Westminster Bridge. The three of them rushed out of the coffee bar and ran to the road. Roger flagged down a passing cab.

'Follow that Jag,' he said when they had all clambered into the back.

'Gee this is exciting,' said Sherry-Lou.

They followed the car as it sped through Pimlico then along the south side of Hyde Park. It then headed north through Holland Park. Finally the car turned into a side street off Chiswick High Road. Roger asked the driver to stop.

'I think I'd better try to sort this out for myself. Enjoy the rest of your trip to London.' Roger got out of the cab and gave the driver a ten-pound note.

'Look us up if you're ever in London Village,' said Bud handing him a business card. Roger gave him one of his in return.

*　　*　　*

Roger walked round the corner, and there it was parked outside the office of a company called International Insurance Investigations. He walked slowly round the car. Everything about it was identical to his own: the colour, the upholstery, the trim, everything. Roger squatted next to the front axle placing his hand lightly on the bonnet. Lowering his head almost to ground level, he looked along the underside of the car. *Nice to see I'm not the only person to have problem with the sills*, he thought to himself.

A voice behind him made Roger stand up quickly. 'Can I help you, mate?'

'Sorry, sir, I was miles away. I've always loved the 1962 MK 2, 3.4 litre, manual plus overdrive, 132 brake horsepower. And in Carmen Red, it's the prettiest Jag ever made.'

'Yeah, sweet, ain't it. It's not for sale though, mate.'

'I don't want to buy it . . . again.'

'What do mean "again"?'

'Could I suggest we go inside and discuss this?' 'If you like.'

Roger followed the man into the building. His office was plush without being opulent and was equipped with an array of computers, printers, scanners, and a drinks dispenser. He closed the door behind and offered his hand.

'Roger Marshall, how do you do?'

'Carl Stuart. So, what do you think we need to discuss?'

'I have that exact same car, with that exact same number plate sitting on my drive in Esher. I paid £4,000, in cash, only six weeks ago.'

'What are you suggesting?'

'I'm suggesting that one of our cars is a fake.'

'I see. Let me tell you what my company does. We investigate write-off claims and ensure that those cars written off are disposed of appropriately. There is no way that a car we own is a fake.'

'Well, one of our cars is a fake.'

'Will you excuse me for a few minutes?'

Carl turned to his computer and punched a few keys. He then consulted a printout, went to his filing cabinet, removed a sheet of paper and proceeded to make a series of short heated telephone calls. His mood changed from studied indifference to agitated concern. Roger sat uncomfortably, fearing the worst.

'It would appear that your car is a fake, as you must have realised from the very low price you paid for it.'

Roger sank further into his seat. He had bought the car on an impulse, mainly because of its number plate. Six weeks ago the price had seemed low, but now that he had been out of work for two weeks,

£4,000 seemed quite a lot. Only that morning he had decided that at the weekend he would start doing it up with a view to selling it for something closer to its true value.

But that option was not possible any more. If he understood correctly, his Jaguar must have been written off before he bought it. Some unscrupulous entrepreneur had bought the car, done enough work on it to make it saleable, then searched for a legally registered version and had identical plates made up. It would only be a matter of time before the police detected the subterfuge. The car could never be driven on the road again; now it would only be good for spares. He would be lucky to get £1,500 for it. Just when he thought things could not get any worse, he would now be £2,500 or more out of pocket.

'I have some good news for you, though. I am instructed to make you an offer, Mr Marshall. It would appear that there was a . . . minor administrative error. A question of internal procedures not having been adhered to at this end. The car you bought should not have been made available for resale. We are willing to offer you what you paid for it.'

'Why would you want to pay me for a car that your company wrote off?' Roger was totally confused. He had no idea why anyone would offer so much for a load of spares.

'Let's just call it a good will gesture.'

'But all you need to do is to get the police to compare the chassis numbers on both cars with your paperwork. This would verify that mine has been recycled illegally, and then I would be forced to have it destroyed and you wouldn't have to pay a penny,' said Roger, trying to be helpful.

'You're a shrewd man, Mr Marshall,' said Carl. Both men sat regarding each other silently.

Roger was now totally bemused. Why did this man think he was shrewd? All he had done was state the obvious. He was sure the man was serious about giving him £4,000; but why?

Meanwhile, Carl was trying to weigh up his unexpected and unwelcome guest. Was he making an idle threat? Was he testing him? Was he bent? If so, how bent? If nothing else, he was certainly a calm customer. He needed to get rid of him, and quick.

'OK, let's cut the crap, Marshall,' he said eventually. 'We both know the score. Fifty thousand is as high as we'll go on this. Is it a deal?'

Roger could not believe his luck. On the train on his way home he decided that he would admit to Caroline that he had been made redundant and pretend that the £50,000 was a golden handshake. The money would buy him enough time to find a new job, and he would no longer have to endure the stress of lying to his wife. Caroline would obviously be shocked, but they were in a much better position than most who had been made redundant.

'Darling, I've got something to tell you,' Roger said when he got home. 'It's about my job.' Before he could say anything further he was interrupted by the telephone.

'It's for you, honey,' Caroline said handing Roger the handset.

'Hey, Roger, this is Bud, how're you doin'?' a familiar American voice asked. 'Did you get your car sorted out in the end?'

'Yes, I did,' said Roger.

'Mine turned out to be a ringer, but I got a little compensation.'

'That's good. Hey, listen, son, I've got a business proposition for you. Do you wanna hear it?'

'Sure.'

'We've been thinking of trying a new tourist angle. We get a lot of rich retired folk visiting Havasu in the winter. They drive their Winnebagos down from the north and stay for several months. They have time on their hands and tourist dollars to spend. They're a captive audience that needs entertaining.'

'I see,' said Roger, not actually *seeing* anything, but not wanting to seem dim.

'Well, our little adventure earlier got me thinking. "Designer Tours of London", a special service we'll offer to our wealthiest guests. It'll be a three- to four-day flying visit to your nation's capital tailored to their tastes. At your end, you arrange for someone to pick them up from the airport, take them to their hotel, and then consult with them to find out their likes and dislikes then arrange their personalised tour for them. They'll have the consultant with them whenever they need chauffeuring, making reservations, suggesting shows to go to, all that sort of thing. We'll supply the customers, and you'll supply the local knowledge. I've even thought of a slogan: "London: You've seen the theme park, now see the real thing." What do you think of the idea in principle?'

'Sounds good.'

'Let's get together later in the week before we fly home to talk through the details.'

'That'd be great.'

When he put the phone down, Roger's wife looked up. 'What did you want to tell me?' she asked.

'I've just been made a partner,' he said, smiling broadly and giving his wife a huge hug.

Killing Time

Killing Time features a policeman brought out of retirement. He is a crossword loving police inspector who could not be any more different from Inspector Morse, except of course for the crossword loving!

Killing Time

No one was surprised that Inspector Dudley was the first person to make it to the station following the news of the large parcel bomb; nor were they surprised that he had managed to pick up a takeaway meal on the way in; but the scene they surveyed as they arrived was peculiar even for 'Dudders'. He was sitting amongst a pile of discarded fortune cookie pieces and several copies of the *London Evening Standard,* carefully pasting a small strip of paper on to a large card. Meanwhile, several dozen small unopened metal containers wafting the distinctive smell of Chinese cuisine were neatly arranged on the desk behind him.

'Looks like you've got enough for a party, Gov,' Detective Burns observed as she approached his desk, eyeing the food greedily.

'Three parties of six to be precise,' replied Dudders without looking up from his paper-sticking task. 'Feel free to tuck in. I've nearly finished here.'

Not requiring a second invitation, his two junior detectives set about opening boxes and dipping into the various dishes they held. Knowing that they would get no further information about how their unexpected supper fitted in with the explosion at the Houses of Parliament until he was ready to give it, they quietly tucked in, allowing Dudders to finish.

'As you both know, tonight's blast is the most audacious attack on a parliament building since the death of MP Airey Neave in 1979,' said the Inspector five minutes later. 'But I am convinced this has nothing to do with the IRA (real, surreal, or otherwise) or any other typical terrorist organisation. We have had no coded messages, and the sophistication of the bomb is at a level never seen before. Security at the House is tighter than a tart's G-string – even the postman is a high-ranking MI5 officer – yet despite all our precautions, the private offices of the Foreign Secretary lie in rubble. Why?

'This is not a random, lone, or amateur attack. This was carefully thought out and well executed. I think this was a professional hit job. The only lead we have to go on is what the Minister didn't eat for dinner.'

'Without trying to sound rude, Gov,' Detective Harris said through a mouthful of spare ribs liberally coated in hoisin sauce. 'What are you going on about?'

'Let me explain. Tonight the Minister was called away from his late-night transatlantic telephone meeting in his office to sign for a

Chinese takeaway. Nothing particularly odd there. He often works late and orders food, and if his staff are not around, he'll sign for it. What was odd though was that the bomb went off before he could resume his conference call.'

'You mean he was saved by his chop suey?'

'Exactly.'

'And you think it was no coincidence.'

'That's right.'

'Why?'

'For three reasons: Firstly, no one could remember ordering the meal. Secondly, because of this message.' He held up one of the cards he had been working on when they arrived. 'It's from one of the fortune cookies delivered with the meal.'

'From one of the fortune cookies?'

'Yes, they've started adding them with your order. Normally you get two per person or ten when you order for a party of six.'

'What made you open the Minister's fortune cookies? We all know you've got a reputation for following eccentric hunches, but isn't seeking clues in fortune cookies a trifle "Charlie Chan"?' Burns scoffed scornfully.

'If you must know, I sat on the bag they came in, crushing the contents.' His junior officers sniggered at this revelation. 'Anyway, I was about to throw it away when I noticed the motto on this one: "Beware dangerous gifts that make party go with bang". It looks just like the rest, but the message didn't look like it belonged in a fortune cookie. So I looked at the others that came with his meal.'

He held up another board. This one contained three further strips of paper but whose messages were less innocuous:

* Grasp the orchid whilst in full bloom
* Nurture your friends like a gardener tends his flowers
* Haul the oysters before the day breaks

'The usual rubbish you'd expect really.'

'Meaning?'

'Meaning: Someone planted that message in that cookie for a reason. And I think that reason was to announce to anyone caring to look that someone is able to get close enough to the Foreign Secretary to kill him whenever they want. So I bought this lot to confirm that this message was a one-off.' He indicated their half-eaten meal. 'I have thirty mottos in total, and as you can see, they all contain equally inscrutable Asian baloney.'

'So a single Chinese message leads you to conclude that there is a hit man out there ready to harm the Foreign Secretary?'

'That, and this,' said Dudders, holding up a little black book.

'What's that?' asked Harris, finally abandoning his munching.

'This is the third reason for suspecting that the bomb and the message in the unordered Chinese meal are related,' said Dudders, tossing the book to Harris.

'It's the Foreign Secretary's diary, or at least an identical one. He found it in his briefcase where the real one should have been.'

'It's empty,' said Harris, quickly flicking through the pages.

'Try today's date.'

'Ah yes, there's an entry for today: "When the harmless taipan slithers back down to the billabong, have a crossword with the London newsman." What does that mean?'

'No idea. Well, not about the taipan anyway. I'm guessing the second bit's got something to do with the crossword in the *Evening Standard*, hence this lot,' he said, pointing to the newspapers. 'Take one each, the crosswords're on the back page.'

'What are we looking for?' asked Harris.

'Well, so far we've got an odd fortune cookie turning up in a Chinese meal and a harmless taipan, so my guess is we're looking for a crossword clue that might have something to do with the Orient. Something that might indicate what this person might want in exchange for the Foreign Secretary's safety.'

All three police officers were silent for about ten minutes until Harris exclaimed, 'I think I've got it, fifteen across: "A rum bell provides scant covering in a monsoon". You get monsoons in China, don't you?'

'Excellent. But what about the bell?' asked Dudders.

'How about Big Ben, the biggest bell in London?' offered Harris enthusiastically. 'Perhaps someone's going to attack . . .'

'No, no, no,' interrupted Dudders. 'We're looking for an umbrella. "A rum bell" is an anagram of umbrella. The crossword clue is "A rum bell provides scant covering in a monsoon". An umbrella in monsoon would be about as useful as a chocolate poker.'

'Aha – we need to check all people coming into the Houses of Parliament who are carrying an umbrella,' declared Harris.

'Oh, for God's sake, listen to the two of you! You're about to describe a scene from *The Thirty-Nine Steps*,' snapped Burns irritably. 'Use a bit of common sense: Why would someone send a warning in a crossword? These things are written way in advance. No one could know which one would be published. The story you're looking for is on the back page just above the crossword under the title: Snake Found in Politician's Hotel. It says, "Today, the Castle Hotel, much favoured by MPs for its proximity to the Houses of Parliament, and its accessibility by river boat taxi, had an unexpected guest: a highly venomous snake. This particular snake, a taipan originating from Australia, was, in fact, harmless, its fangs having been removed, a practice commonly used when such creatures are kept as pets. The hotel refused to divulge whose room the serpent was found in." I think we can probably guess whose room it was. That sounds like a warning to me.'

'Ah,' said Dudders sheepishly. 'Didn't notice that article. Good work, Burns. Of course, we're no closer to knowing who is responsible or whether there is still a threat. We'd better put the Foreign Secretary under close surveillance.'

*　　*　　*

Dudders was sitting inconspicuously on one of the sofas in the Departure Lounge at Heathrow Airport surreptitiously watching the Foreign Secretary's progress. He had explained his fears for the Minister's safety to the Chief Inspector, who had in turn explained that he could not justify the expense of a surveillance operation based on a set of hunches, even if they were from the *prescient* Inspector Dudley. As far as he was concerned, there was only one incident to investigate: terrorism, and that incident should be investigated by the experts – the Bomb Squad.

Dudley could neither blame his boss's caution nor could he blame his sarcasm; most of his previous bosses had been equally doubtful of his methods. But neither could he allow anything untoward to happen to a member of Her Majesty's Government whilst he was in the UK. So he, Harris, and Burns were doing a little unofficial and unpaid overtime. Just then his earpiece crackled into life.

'Male, late twenties, smartly dressed heading your way, Gov. Looks like one of his aides is carrying with him the Minister's airplane ticket,' whispered Burns.

Dudders looked up briefly from his newspaper and quickly took in the dapper civil servant with his pinstriped suit and bowler hat. *Not many of the old school left*, he thought to himself, *and fancy carrying an umbrella on a day like this.*

With this thought came a sudden realisation.

'MINISTER, LOOK OUT . . .,' he yelled at the top of his voice. The Foreign Secretary turned to see one of his civil servants running towards him being quickly pursued by an overweight man in his mid-fifties. The latter launched his massive frame at the former and grabbed him around the knees, bringing him to the ground with an impressive rugby-style tackle. The two men fell with a force that sent bowler hat and umbrella flying and knocked the civil servant senseless.

Burns and Harris, who had witnessed the entire sequence, arrived running.

'Harris, when this man wakes up, arrest him. Burns, retrieve that brolly and send it to Forensics.'

$*$ $*$ $*$

Dudders spent most of the next day persuading the Forensic Science Department to take his request seriously. To humour him (and to stop him nagging) the pathologist finally agreed to perform a cursory inspection of the umbrella. Much to his surprise, his initial tests found that its tip, curiously sharpened to a point, had traces of some form of poison, which a toxicologist later confirmed was venom from an Australian taipan. With what appeared great reluctance, they concurred that its presence had turned the accessory into a lethal weapon.

Meanwhile, Burns and Harris between them had found out that the civil servant was not, in fact, on the staff at the Houses of Parliament but that his fingerprints were to be found on a fragment of one of the dishes recovered from the ruined offices of the Foreign Secretary. Who the bogus civil servant was remained a mystery, but Interpol claimed he

STANLEY JACKSON AND GAVIN JACKSON

bore a strong resemblance to a known contract killer last photographed in South-East Asia eight years before.

Dudders had included all these findings in the report that the Chief Inspector was just about to finish reading.

'You know something,' the Chief Inspector said grudgingly, finally looking up and acknowledging Inspector Dudley's presence, 'You may have sufficient grounds for a court case.'

Sample Decamots 5

The two sample Decamots in this chapter were inspired by the following Decamot items: *photo, football club, school, shorts, builder, famous, council estate, hard-hat, Manila envelope,* and *sweetheart.*

Upon Reflection

In **Upon Reflection**, while carrying out renovations, a builder finds a photograph thought long lost, and in that photograph he finds something unexpected.

Upon Reflection

To most people, Barry Mason was a typical small-time builder and decorator, albeit one with an enviable local reputation for reliability. He drove a scruffy Ford transit van bearing the legend 'Barry Builds', wore faded denim shorts a size too small to accommodate his midriff, and sprinkled his sentences liberally with a wide range of Cockney expressions, despite the fact that he had never been near Bow church, let alone heard the sound of its famous bells. He was born and brought up on a council estate in Sheerwater, on the outskirts of Woking in Surrey. He had wanted to be a professional footballer but had failed to make the grade. As a result, he had rather wasted his grammar school place, spending more time on the playing field than in the classroom. Recently he had been making up for lost time with weekly visits to night school, where he was currently studying the history of photography.

Unlike many of his bolder brethren, Barry had not taken the opportunity to expand rapidly in the Thatcher boom years. He was happy to stay small and accept some subcontracted work from larger firms plus individual commissions for extensions and alterations to existing houses. He had also bought, renovated, lived in, and traded up a series of houses for himself. His relatively cautious approach proved to be very wise when the economic recession of the late eighties bankrupted many of his larger competitors. Come the new millennium, Barry had created a comfortable, if somewhat arduous lifestyle: a full order book and five full-time employees, including Ian, his teenage son, whom he was grooming to take over the business. But at least he had time to indulge his two passions: amateur photography and Chelsea Football Club.

Whilst Barry supervised and worked on each new assignment himself for the first two or three weeks, once the job was up and running, he let his team take over with day-to-day organisation of the more mundane work, satisfying himself with one or two visits per week to check on progress. This meant that he usually ran up to three jobs in tandem, a formula that had proved remarkably successful over the last twenty years.

The Central House project proved an exception to most of Barry's normal rules. Firstly, it was larger in scope than he would normally undertake on his own. Secondly, he was expected to be the foreman throughout the project. And thirdly, there was tight a deadline to meet; he normally avoided the added pressure of an ambitious timescale, often refusing to tender for a job if he felt the client's expectations were unreasonable. Barry took a pride in his work and did not like to cut corners. 'If a job's wurf doin', it's wurf doin' proper, innit?' was his usual response to any criticism of his time estimates. 'That's my guesstimate, take it or leave it.' Most people took it.

But Miss Spencer, owner of Central House, was not most people. She had her own opinions about every aspect of the project, and nothing that anyone said would dissuade her from the path she wanted the project to take. The project was huge, and time was tight. Not conditions that would normally attract Barry's attention. However, this particular project had something that made this job irresistible to Barry Mason: the chance to work on an original Talbot house. To most middle-class residents of West Surrey, George Talbot was a legendary figure. He had virtually invented the concept of executive housing at the turn of the twentieth century, erecting superb high-specification residences, to order, for the nouveau riche of the day: railway magnates and industrialists settling in the South. Wherever you find a sought-after private estate in the area, you are bound to find a Talbot house or two. It is not that George Talbot built houses in sought-after areas; it was more that areas where George Talbot built houses became sought-after. Each house originally stood in a minimum of one acre of ground, often more when wealthy clients bought several adjacent plots but only had one house constructed. Even in the year 2000, in some cases fully 100 years after their construction, an original Talbot house fetched a premium.

* * *

Barry had not been invited to Central House to discuss the project so much as summoned. The phone rang late one Saturday morning shortly before Barry was about to set off for Stamford Bridge to watch a testing home tie against Newcastle United.

'Barry Builds, 'ow may I 'elp you?'

'Miss Lydia Spencer here, Headmistress Central House School.'

Something about Miss Spencer's tone made Barry sit up straight and take his elbows off the table.

'I shan't keep you. I know you've got your match to get to. One of my mothers recommended you. She says you're a top-notch builder and Chelsea fan. Well, I won't hold the latter against you, but I would like your professional help. I'd like you over here on Sunday to discuss the details.'

'Er, OK. What time did you have in mind, luv?'

'At eleven o'clock of course, after church, and you can stay for lunch, we've got a lot to discuss. But you must be gone by 2 p.m. before the bridge club arrive. Oh and good luck for this afternoon.'

'Er fanks,' Barry said as the line went dead.

* * *

Barry turned up for his initial meeting with Miss Spencer promptly.

'Good morning, Mr Mason. Thanks for coming at such short notice.'
'That's all right, luv.'

'No, no, no! That won't do. Miss Spencer is fine, Lydia is fine, but please, Mr Mason, not "luv".'

'Ok Miss, I 'ear whatcha sayin'. Tell me what've you got in mind.'

'Let me take you for a walk around the house, and I'll tell you about the project.' Miss Spencer led Barry round the outside of the house and into the back garden. They stood at the bottom of well-tended grounds and looked up at the rear aspect of the house.

'Central House once stood surrounded by several acres of woodland at the end of Central Avenue. Over the years those trees have been eaten away by greedy developers, slowly encroaching on my privacy so that now I'm totally overlooked by those lesser dwellings.'

Barry looked in the direction that Miss Spencer was pointing and could just about make out the rooftops of several large, but new, executive homes appearing over the trees at the bottom of her long formal garden. *That must be Lilac Crescent*, he thought to himself. *Four- and five-bedroom houses, all detached, double garages, en-suites and family barfrooms, utility rooms and studies, and at least 'arf wiv swimming pools.*

'I've had many offers to murder my house, or "develop this site" as some of your bloodthirsty colleagues like to euphemise. They seem to like nothing more than to pull down magnificent homes like these and overcrowd the grounds with poky little apartments. As you can see, each of these I have resisted,' she said. 'Let's go in. I'll show you around and give you a quick history lesson.'

They went back into the house through the conservatory.

'I was left this house when my mother died in 1955,' she said. 'It was much too large for me, but I could not bear to sell it. So I turned it into a private school for three- to eleven-year-olds. Not only did it make good use of the building, it also kept me in hampers from Fortnum and Mason.'

They were now standing in the grand hallway. Barry gazed up at the wide winding wooden stairway leading off from the main entrance hall.

He was particularly impressed with the long, church-like windows that bridged two floors and brought such light and warmth into the heart of the house.

'For more than forty years this room has been the site of morning assemblies. You see that raised section?'

Barry nodded.

'At Christmas, that's our stage. It's seen every pantomime I've ever put on with my pupils. The parents sit and watch from here,' said Miss Spencer, opening double doors into a magnificent drawing room. 'Some of my old boys volunteer to help me to set up raised seating.'

I wonder if they volunteer or if they are press-ganged, Barry thought to himself.

Barry followed Miss Spencer upstairs until they reached the third storey.

'Originally, this floor provided accommodation for the servants. I remember coming up here to spend the odd afternoon with nanny when I was a little girl.' They were now in the largest room on the top floor that overlooked the front of the house. 'The low ceilings make it cosy up here, so I use it as a rest area for the smalls.'

'Smalls?'

'The three- and four-year-olds. It's too much for them to last the whole day at that age, so I treat them to warm milk and a biscuit, and they have a nap up here for an hour each day.'

Having completed the tour, Miss Spencer took Barry into the scullery that led off from a spacious kitchen. In its centre stood an ancient wrought iron Aga.

'Judgin' by the beige sides and the dark bran lids on the 'ot plates, I'd guess that's an original.'

'Well spotted, Mr Mason,' said Miss Spencer opening one of the doors on the front of the Aga. She withdrew a tray of mince pies.

'They're best when they're warm,' she said. 'Help yourself to a plate and to a pie, and then come through to the study.'

Miss Spencer's study had once been the dining room. It was a spacious reception room, featuring an Adams fireplace and oak panelled walls.

'I remember many a glorious family gathering here,' she told Barry. 'We used to gather round the piano and sing Christmas carols. They were wonderful times.'

'You 'ave one hell of an 'ouse, Miss,' Barry said. 'But you 'aven't told me what the job is yet.'

'Well, Mr Mason, I'm not getting any younger. I've been doing less and less of the day-to-day running of the school. In fact, I'm retiring at the end of term, which is this Friday. I have no children, nor any other relatives who can take over Central House, so the school is also retiring.

'As for the house itself, I've signed a deal with Community Care Ltd. They are going to take over Central House and turn it into a nursing home. In return, they guarantee me a place for the rest of my days. The thought of going into an institution to see out my days was anathema to me, Mr Mason. Can you understand that?'

'I can, but I still don't see where I fit in.'

'Part of the deal is that I get to design the conversion and oversee its creation,' said Miss Spencer. She placed a large blue folder on the desk. 'And here are the plans. Please take a look. I'd like you to be the foreman for the project.'

Barry spent the next quarter of an hour pouring over the plans. They were extensive, detailed, and very clear. The finished home would have a large day room, dining room, sun lounge, and two bedrooms on the ground floor. There were a further six bedrooms on the first floor and two shared bathrooms. The top floor was going to house an office and overnight accommodation for two nurses. She had included details of converting the workshop over the double garage into a laundry, ramps at the front and rear of the house, and a lift.

'You've got planning permission for all this, I take it?'

'Huh! If I took any notice of the local authority's absurd rules, I'd have been out of business years ago. Believe you me, Mr Mason, I have been in and out of fashion more times than I care to recall since I started this school. Besides, I taught most of the councillors right here in this house. I don't think they'll put up any opposition. So tell me, Mr Mason, are you interested in the job?'

'Before I answer that, tell me, am I right in finking this is a Talbot-built 'ouse originally?'

'It's not just a Talbot house, it's Talbot's own house. He built this house just before the Great War. He chose this location so that he could be close to all of his sites. It was in the heart of his building empire. That's why he called it Central House.'

'You know a lot about the great man.'

'I should, he was my grandfather.'

'So you're a Talbot!'

'That's right, and sadly the last. George was my mother's father. She was the youngest of his three children. Her two brothers died young in the Great War. As for me, I'm an only child and never married.'

'Well, to work for a Talbot would be a privilege and a pleasure, Miss Spencer. I can start a week next Monday. That OK for ya?'

'That will do nicely,' Miss Spencer said with a smile. 'And don't forget your hard-hat!'

'Once the team are up and running I'll pop by twice a week to make sure everyfing's all right and everyone's 'appy.'

'No, no, no. That won't do.'

'Beg pardon, luv . . . er Miss Spe . . .'

'No. I need you here full time as the foreman.'

'But . . .'

'No buts. I'm paying for the best, so I want the best here at all times.'

We'll see, Barry thought to himself.

*   *   *

Barry had now been working on the project for over six months and had one room to go. Any thoughts he had had to delegate some of the foreman's tasks had long since been forgotten. He took the odd afternoon off to check up on some of the other ongoing projects, but not without seeking Miss Spencer's permission in advance. Each morning he arrived at Central House at 8 a.m. to discuss the day's plans with Miss Spencer over coffee and croissant; each evening he gave her a brief update before going home.

During this time, he came to fully appreciate the Talbott trademarks, his eye for detail, the quality of the basic bricks used, the exquisite workmanship.

On one occasion, as he was about to remove the panel above the fireplace in the study; it slid sideways to reveal a Manila envelope, yellowed with age, tucked behind it. Inside the envelope, was a sepia photograph. The picture was of a young army officer in his dress uniform leaning against a full-length mirror. Judging by the style of the uniform, Barry guessed the photograph had been taken during the First World War; perhaps it was the last picture taken before the subject saw active service. There was something strange about the photograph that did not appear to be quite right, however, but he could not figure out what.

'Good Lord, where did you find that?' asked Miss Spencer coming into the room with his mid-morning refreshment.

'Oh! I'm sorry to be so rude,' Barry replied still studying the picture in his right hand whilst absent-mindedly holding out his left hand for the proffered tea. 'That's OK. I just haven't seen it for years. Where was it?'

'It was hidden behind a secret panel over the fireplace. I saw it contained an old photograph and couldn't resist taking a look. I love photography. In fact, we are experimenting with sepia in my night class at the moment.' Seeing the slightly surprised look on her face he added, 'There's more to me than meets the eye, Duchess. At school, I always wanted to be a soccer star, so spent all me time training and neglecting me studies. I never got good enough at football and failed all my exams. Ever since then I've been taking night classes to try to catch up.

'Anyway, I love photographs, particularly old ones. I think they tell you so much more than words.'

'Well that one certainly has quite a tale to tell. It's of my uncle,' replied Miss Spencer, taking the photograph gently and peering at it closely. 'It was amongst his few possessions that returned from the front when he, alas, did not. All the family got back was that picture and a pair of old shoes.

'My grandfather had the picture framed and hung it in pride of place in this very room, over the fireplace. In fact, not more than a matter of inches away from where you just found it. He had other pictures of both my uncles, but for him, this was the one that meant most to him. And there it hung for thirty years until one day he ordered one of the servants to remove and destroy it.'

'Why did he do that?' Barry enquired.

'Well, he found out something about his favourite son that upset him greatly and could no longer bear to set eyes on him every day as he sat at his desk. My grandma intercepted the picture before the servant could carry out her master's wishes and hid it away. She never told anyone

STANLEY JACKSON AND GAVIN JACKSON

where she'd hidden it; ironic that she should have chosen that spot. For the last few years of my grandfather's life, my uncle was still so close by.'

'I hope you don't mind me saying so, but there's something about it that doesn't look quite right.' 'Oh?' replied Miss Spencer, raising an eyebrow and smiling mysteriously.

'I've been looking at it closely for a while, and there's something odd about the mirror. I can't work out which is the person and which the reflection, they both seem equally real.'

'You're only the second person to notice that unprompted,' said Miss Spencer. 'Let me explain a little about that picture. It was common for soldiers to carry with them pictures of their loved ones. Perhaps a holiday snap sharing a loving embrace or a fond farewell in a departure lounge. This was my uncle's picture.'

'Of himself?'

'Not exactly. Look a little closer. There's more to it than meets the eye.'

Barry took the picture back and peered at it closely. Suddenly he noticed that the young officer on the right was fractionally taller than his reflection and maybe a little thinner.

'My God! It's not a reflection! It's two men, not one. The composition is brilliant. Even down to the buttons and insignia reversed on the young officer on the left. Where did they manage to get an army uniform made in reverse?'

'They had my mother to thank for that. She was doing her bit for King and country in Munitions. She brought home several real uniforms and painstakingly made the mirror-imaged version. She even reversed the fly buttons on the trousers.'

'Who's the other officer? And why the elaborate illusion?'

'Well, he wasn't an officer. In fact, he never made it into the forces. He was turned down on medical grounds: persistent migraines. Ironically, he spent most of the war as a farmhand driving tractors, not the best job to do if you are prone to headaches! You see, the other young man was my uncle's "special friend". They took that photo so that he could take a picture of his sweetheart with him into battle without anyone realising what it was. You have to understand that they lived in less enlightened times than today, Mr Mason.

'And nobody, other than my grandmother and my mother of course, did realise what it was for fully thirty years. It was my father, who spotted it. I remember the day clearly. The whole family were here for Christmas dinner when he suddenly rushed over to the picture, took it off the wall, and hurried over to the window where he held it in the light and studied it intently for a few minutes before declaring, just like you did: "My God! It's not a reflection; it's two men, not one." He then went on to say that the picture had bothered him ever since he'd started courting my mother, but he could never work out what it was about it that looked so strange. Now that he knew, he could stop worrying.

'But that was the beginning of the problem with the picture, not the end. Not realising what my grandfather's reaction would be, my mother came clean about her role in the subterfuge, something she always regretted.'

'What happened to your uncle's friend?'

'He died a few days after news of my uncle reached the family. A barn suddenly burnt down. No one knows what happened. An empty bottle of paraffin was found in the barn. The police suspected foul play, but they never got very far with the investigation.'

*   *   *

Barry Builds completed the conversion of Central House on time and under budget. Miss Spencer took up residence in her newly furbished ground-floor private apartment, having moved her belongings from the third floor. She lived for five more years before slipping peacefully away one Sunday morning. In those years she helped train thirty young

STANLEY JACKSON AND GAVIN JACKSON

nurses in the demanding business of caring for the elderly, although not one of them realised they were being so schooled.

Barry noticed her obituary in the local newspaper. Two hundred people, the majority of whom were former pupils of Central House Preparatory School, attended a memorial service at the local church. The residue of her estate she left to the Terrence Higgins Trust.

Three days later, Barry Mason received a letter from solicitors acting for Miss Spencer's estate. Inside was an envelope containing a sepia photograph and a short handwritten note that simply said, 'Thanks for all your hard work. Grandpops would have been pleased with the job you did.'

The Photo Shoot

In **The Photo Shoot** there is another unexpected photograph, this time found by a Premiership footballer. Aside from the significance of the photograph, the two stories sharing these Decamot items could not be more different.

The Photo Shoot

Dino Jones was the new and rising soccer star who had recently signed with Chelsea Football Club from Blackburn Rovers for £5 million. A first team scout had noticed his tremendous ability as a striker and snapped him up as soon as the season had come to an end.

Dino had moved with his wife from a council estate in Blackburn to a newly built private estate on the outskirts of Cobham near to the Chelsea training ground and, if you got the timing right, a forty-five minute drive from Stamford Bridge. He was raking in the money now. To complement his generous salary, he was also benefiting from TV, radio, and promotional appearances. His next assignment was a photo shoot for Nike clothing.

Sandy, his wife of four years, liked to follow him everywhere. So naturally, on the day of the photo shoot she accompanied him. Sandy and Dino had married the day after they both left the same school, both aged at sixteen. She had been attracted by his great physique, film star good looks, thick dark hair, and olive skin that he had inherited from his Sicilian grandmother. When they started dating, she instantly became the envy of the rest of the girls in her year. Those same good looks were beloved of advertisers' cameras and hoards of women wherever he went. She trusted her childhood sweetheart explicitly, but you could never be too careful: Men are so weak.

The studio was bright, and strewn across the floor was white sand and fake palm trees. Dino emerged from the dressing room wearing only his football shorts, Nike boots, and cap. His muscular stomach glistened. As he struck various poses, he looked like a modern-day Adonis strutting around on the white beach of a Mediterranean island.

'That's a wrap,' shouted the photographer after an hour-long session. 'I'll get my assistant to give you the initial proofs if you don't mind waiting here for half an hour or so,' he said, turning to Dino and packing his equipment up at the same time. 'And if you don't mind me saying so, you've got lovely skin. Do you moisturise?'

Thirty minutes later the photographer's assistant appeared with a Manila envelope. She was short, pale-skinned, and dressed all in black. *She could almost be attractive if she only had a little more colour about her*, thought Sandy. The assistant handed Dino the envelope with a huge grin and winked as he took it.

'Thanks,' he said and turned to go. Sandy followed Dino, but not before she gave the assistant a hands-off-he's-mine stare.

Sandy was eager to look at the photos and tried snatching them from his hand as they walked to the car. 'Be patient,' he snapped. 'Wait until we get home.' Sandy sat sullenly in the passenger seat and remained silent until they arrived home. She was outwardly petulant, but secretly admired his manly tone.

As Dino flicked through the photos one by one, Sandy looked over his shoulder.

STANLEY JACKSON AND GAVIN JACKSON

'I wonder how that one slipped in,' said Sandy as Dino came to the final picture.

The picture was similar to the others: naked torso, firm stomach, and dashing good looks. But rather than football boots, he was wearing Doc Marten's; rather than football shorts, he was wearing cut-off jeans with the zip fastener half undone; rather than a Nike cap, he was wearing a yellow builder's hard- hat; and most notably, the olive-skinned body was not Dino's.

'I wonder who that is,' Sandy said inquisitively.

'Yeah, me too,' said Dino hesitantly. He made as if to throw the picture in the bin.

'Wait,' said Sandy. 'There's something written on the back.'

Dino turned the photo over. Towards the bottom in small neat italic handwriting were four words: *Sample for your consideration*

'There you go,' said Dino. 'That's obviously the photographer's comment. The assistant must of got his mixed up with mine. I think they're crap. They look like a bunch of cheap holiday snaps. I'll get him to send me the second reel. Maybe they'll be better.'

Dino went up to the bedroom to change. He threw his photos into the bin by the side of Sandy's dressing table. The rogue one of the man in the yellow builder's hard hat he folded carefully and placed in an old shoe at the back of the cupboard.

The next day the photographer's assistant showed up at the training ground with the second reel of photographs for Dino's approval. He left the pitch to take them from her amongst jeers and whistles from his fellow teammates. Again a Manila envelope. Again a grin and a wink.

Dino waited until he was alone before reviewing the second set of pictures. This set was undoubtedly better, but Dino was flicking through them quickly, not paying much attention to them until he reached the last one. As before, it was not of him, and as before, it was of a man with a naked torso, Doc Marten's and builder's yellow hard-hat; but this time, no cut-off jeans. He was standing as if preparing for one of Dino's famous free-kicks with his hands preserving his modesty.

Dino turned over the picture with shaking hands. Written in the same neat italic handwriting were the words: *Next time all will be revealed*

Dino screwed it up and shoved it in his back pocket.

After training he rushed home before his wife returned from her mother's. He hurried upstairs, retrieved the previous day's picture from its hiding place in the closet, and hurried into the garden. He took a small can of paraffin from the shed and set light to the photos on the barbecue.

Next day he received a Manila envelope through the post. He waited until Sandy had gone shopping before daring to open it. This time the envelope contained a single photo. It was of two males in a naked embrace. One was clearly the builder (complete with hard-hat) from the other two pictures; the other was clearly Dino Jones. He slowly turned the picture over, fearing the worst. In small neat italic handwriting were the words '*250k for the negatives or they go to* The Sun'. He tore the picture into tiny pieces, threw the pieces into the fireplace, and set light to them. He sat watching the pieces burn with his head in his hands; he felt a migraine coming on. He was finished. He had a reputation as being a red-blooded heart-throb, a positive babe-magnet. This had gained the respect of his fellow footballers every bit as much as his playing ability; it also brought in extra cash from advertisers. *Would they still be knocking at his door if they knew about his other preferences? Would the crowd and Stamford Bridge still chant 'Deeeno' enthusiastically?* The scandal would destroy his marriage and humiliate his family. What could he do?

The answer came to him in a flash. He scribbled a note to his wife and left for the airport. Two hours later he was in the Departure lounge waiting for a flight to Palermo.

*　　*　　*

Sandy arrived home later that night to find Dino's note: *Gone to visit Grandma, she's very sick. Back soon.*

　　STANLEY JACKSON AND GAVIN JACKSON

Sandy started to panic. She phoned her mother. She phoned *his* mother. She phoned the coach. He had told no one else about this emergency trip. Eventually, she tracked down the number of his grandmother: She sounded perfectly well and was as surprised about her grandson's imminent arrival as everyone else. Sandy's initial panic turned to anger. If he's gone AWOL, a girl was bound to be involved.

Three days later, Dino reappeared just as suddenly as he had disappeared. He waltzed into the kitchen on Sunday morning as if nothing untoward had happened, carrying the newspapers under his arm. Sandy questioned him about his absence at length, but he declined to comment, preferring instead to read out bits of stories that caught his attention. She gave up trying to get a straight answer. She knew about his reputation and drew her own conclusions about his recent whereabouts. She blamed herself, of course, and vowed to try harder to satisfy his voracious appetite.

She picked up the other newspaper and started idly leafing through it, not really paying much attention. Suddenly a headline and a picture caught her eye: *Man Shot in Front of Own Home, Police Suspect Professional Hit*

'Take a look at this, Dino,' she said. 'I'm sure I've seen this guy someone before. Do you recognise him?'

Dino gave the picture no more than a cursory glance. 'Never seen him before.' He passed the paper back having scarcely looked at the handsome man (no longer wearing a hard-hat) smiling up from the page. Sandy finished reading the article before starting to prepare lunch.

Next day Dino went to the training ground in the morning and returned home at the usual time in the evening. Sandy prepared dinner and did the washing-up. Life was back to normal. As for the Manila envelopes, no more arrived at the Jones's house.

CHAPTER 3

Turning a Decamot into a TV Screenplay

This chapter is devoted to explaining how to turn a Decamot into a TV screenplay. It uses as a worked example the story **Wheel of Fortune** and the associated TV screenplay that appears later in this book.

What is a Screenplay?

A screenplay is the telling of a story in a set of scenes that you might see in a TV programme or a film. Each scene within a screenplay uses a set template that comprises the following basic elements:

- **Title**: this provides an outline of where and when the scene takes place.
- **Introduction**: this is a paragraph or two of short declarative sentences that describes who's in the scene, where they are, and what they're doing.
- **Characters**: the people saying the lines in the scene.
- **Directions**: this optional element explains how a character delivers a specific line.
- **Dialogue**: these are the lines that the characters say to each other and form the bulk of most scenes.

Example Screenplay Scene

The visual design of a screenplay is very basic; this provides minimal distraction from the text and maximum clarity for the reader. By having distinct placement of the various elements, each element can be rapidly identified. When you read a screenplay, you can see immediately which are the spoken lines, who's saying each line, and which parts of the text describe the action.

The following is a simple sample scene written using the various screenplay elements and illustrates the simplicity of its design:

INT—SOUTH BANK—COFFEE BAR NEAR WESTMINSTER BRIDGE—MIDDAY

ROGER, BUD, and SHERRY-LOU are in a COFFEE BAR close to Westminster Bridge. The coffee bar is very full. They are perched on high stools at a narrow table near the window. They are discussing Roger's options.

> BUD
> Are you sure it was your number plate?

> ROGER
> Absolutely.

> BUD
> And the Jag's supposed to be at home on your driveway?

> ROGER
> Exactly. My wife drops me off at the station each morning in her car. I only drive the Jag at weekends. Caroline never does. She's not that keen on it to be honest.

```
            BUD
Call your wife. See if she knows it's
missing. Maybe she's already reported
it to the police.

            ROGER
        (hesitating)
That's going to be a bit awkward. . .
you see, I shouldn't really be here.
```

Basic Stages to Creating a Screenplay

When creating screenplays from our short stories, we've identified the following five stages:

Stage 1 - Creating discrete scenes for each portion of dialogue in the original short story.
Stage 2 - Deciding what new scenes are required to complete the story.
Stage 3 - Fleshing out the new scenes.
Stage 4 - Writing the new scenes.
Stage 5 - Identifying and fixing the flaws.

Stage 1 - Creating Discrete Scenes for Each Portion of Dialogue in the Original Short Story

Creating discrete scenes involves

- Maximising the dialogue
- Minimising the narrative
- Incorporating as much of the remaining essential narrative into the newly created scenes as possible by turning it into dialogue form.

In most short stories, you'll probably have large blocks of narrative interspersed with passages of dialogue. If so, at the end of this stage you will end up with several discrete isolated scenes and a lot of narrative left over.

In the case of the **Wheel of Fortune**, at the end of Stage 1 we had the following five scenes:

1. Roger speaking to an American couple in a passenger pod on the London Eye.
2. Roger talking to the same American couple in a nearby coffee shop, having spotted his own car driving over Westminster Bridge when their passenger pod was at the top of wheel.
3. Roger confronting the driver of the car that appears to be identical to his own.
4. Roger having a phone conversation with the American man that he met on the London Eye.
5. Roger announcing to his wife that he has had the offer of a partnership.

We also had two lengthy pages of narrative from the start of the Decamot. This narrative provides some important details about the story and so had to be converted into dialogue form during Stage 3.

Stage 2 – Deciding What New Scenes Are Required to Complete the Story

Having created a small number of discrete, isolated scenes and having some narrative detail left over that needs a good home, you need to identify what scenes are required to produce a satisfying programme or film. As a starting point, it's a good idea to write a chronological list of the main parts of the story that need to be covered. This is our chronological list for the **Wheel of Fortune**:

1. Roger, our hero, is off to work, smartly dressed and with a briefcase.
2. Roger, his wife, and their daughters leave together in Roger's wife's car. Another car (an old Jaguar) is also sitting on the drive.
3. His wife drops him off at the station.
4. Roger exits the train at Charing Cross Station, buys a newspaper, crosses over the bridge towards South Bank, and heads into a Costa coffee bar.
5. We next see Roger waiting in the queue for the London Eye. He's at the front of a long line of people, and is the last of thirty people to get into a passenger pod before the doors close.

6. Roger enters the passenger pod, makes himself comfortable by the east-facing window.

7. When the passenger pod is nearing its highest point, Roger is approached by an old American couple. He helps them to identify various London landmarks. When the passenger pod is about eight minutes from coming to rest, the American woman spots an Inspector Morse-style Jaguar, which resembles the one that we saw sitting on Roger's drive.

8. Roger and the couple exit the passenger pod and go together to a cafe to discuss the mysterious appearance in central London of Roger's car.

9. Roger opens up to the couple about having been made redundant from his job in the City.

10. As they are talking, Sherry-Lou spots the car that resembles Roger's as it passes in front of the coffee bar, heading back to towards Westminster Bridge.

11. All three rush out of the coffee bar, jump into a taxicab, and take chase after the Jag.

12. Roger points out the various landscapes as they speed pass them.

13. Roger parts company with the couple when the Jaguar stops in White City.

14. Roger examines the Jaguar outside the offices of International Insurance Investigations (III).

15. The manager of III confronts him and they go into the office to discuss the Jaguar.

16. They establish that Roger's car is a ringer, and as been sold to him 'in error'. The manager of III offers Roger compensation for the 'error'.

17. Roger meets his wife on their doorstep as the phone rings.

18. Bud calls to discuss a business proposal.

19. Roger tells his wife he's been offered a partnership.

Stage 3 - Fleshing Out the New Scenes

Each of the chronological points that you have listed in Stage 2 will become a scene for the first complete draft of the screenplay. Each of these scenes has a common purpose: to move the story forward.

Before starting to write any new scenes, you should summarise what you want to include in each scene in the screenplay. To do this, using 6 x 4 inch record cards (one for each scene, including those for which you've already written a first draft during Stage 1), write down the following:

- Heading
- Characters in the scene
- Rationale for the scene
- Where the scene starts (**in**)
- Where the scene stops (**out**)

By writing a brief summary of each scene on a single card, you can shuffle the order of the scenes around and insert extra scenes until you're satisfied that you've got roughly the right number of scenes for your first draft.

Based on the list in Stage 2, we identified and fleshed out the following nineteen scenes. The ones marked with an asterisk are those that we'd already written by the end of Stage 1; it's useful to include these on record cards; they may well need to change during this stage of the writing screenplay writing process.

1. EXT - AFFLUENT SUBURBAN STREET – ROGER MARSHALL'S DRIVE – EARLY MORNING

Characters:	THE MARSHALLS: ROGER, CAROLINE, 2 DAUGHTERS (11 AND 13), A NEIGHBOUR
Rationale:	To establish that Roger is a pillar of the community and to see his rather nice MK 2 Jaguar.
In:	View of the front of Roger's house.
Out:	Marshall family driving down the road in Caroline's RANGE ROVER.

2. INT – AFFLUENT SUBURBAN STREET – INSIDE CAROLINE'S CAR – EARLY MORNING

Characters: ROGER, CAROLINE, and DAUGHTERS

Rationale: To establish that the Marshalls are a well-to-do family, the children are well educated, and hint that they are a one-income family.

In: Marshall family chatting in Caroline's car. Out: Caroline arrives at the mainline station.

3.   EXT – SUBURBAN MAINLINE STATION – OUTSIDE CAROLINE'S CAR – EARLY MORNING

Characters: ROGER, CAROLINE, and DAUGHTERS
Rationale: To establish the expectation that Roger will be returning later that day, but walking home.
In: Roger leaning over to kiss his wife goodbye.
Out: Roger waves to Caroline and the girls and walks into the station.

4.   EXT – CHARING CROSS STATION AND THE BRIDGE OVER THE THAMES – EARLY MORNING

Characters: ROGER, FELLOW COMMUTERS, BUSKER
Rationale: To establish that Roger has arrived in Central London.
In: Roger exits the platform using his Oyster Card.
Out: Roger entering a coffee bar on the south side of the Thames.

5.   EXT – LONDON SOUTH BANK – QUEUE FOR THE LONDON EYE FERRIS WHEEL – MID-MORNING

Characters: QUEUE OF PEOPLE INCLUDING: ROGER, MOTHER WITH PUSH CHAIR, FOREIGN TOUR GROUP, ELDERLY COUPLE
Rationale: To establish that Roger is visiting the London Eye Ferris wheel and that he is unlike most of the people queuing on this weekday mid-morning; i.e. he's a smartly dressed businessman; everyone else is a tourist or a person of leisure.

| In: | Roger towards the front of the line waiting for the London Eye. |
| Out: | Roger entering the next available passenger pod. |

6. INT – LONDON SOUTH BANK – PASSENGER POD ON THE LONDON EYE – MID-MORNING *

Characters:	ROGER, ELDERLY COUPLE
Rationale:	To establish that Roger is more than just idly passing the time. He has prepared for this trip and has an objective in mind.
In:	Roger opening his briefcase and removing a book and a pair of binoculars.
Out:	Roger approached by the elderly American man.

7. INT – LONDON SOUTH BANK – PASSENGER POD ON THE LONDON EYE – MID-MORNING *

Characters:	ROGER, ELDERLY COUPLE: BUD and SHERRY-LOU
Rationale:	To establish that the elderly couple are wealthy American tourists on a sightseeing tour of the UK.
In:	Roger points out the various bridges that can be seen from the passenger pod. Out: Roger identifies the car Sherry-Lou spots as his.

8. INT – LONDON SOUTH BANK – PASSENGER POD ON THE LONDON EYE – MID-MORNING

Characters:	ROGER, BUD, SHERRY-LOU
Rationale:	To establish that Bud and Sherry-Lou are offering to help Roger out.
In:	Passenger pod returns to its starting position, and the passengers disembark.
Out:	Bud suggests they go for a coffee to discuss what Roger should do about the car.

9. INT – NEAR WESTMINSTER BRIDGE – COFFEE BAR – MIDDAY *

Characters:	ROGER, BUD, SHERRY-LOU
Rationale:	To establish that Roger has a secret.
In:	Roger confirms that the number plate of his car does match that of the Jag seen on the bridge.
Out:	Roger calls Caroline to confirm the car is still at home.

10. INT – NEAR WESTMINSTER BRIDGE – COFFEE BAR – MIDDAY

Characters:	ROGER, BUD, SHERRY-LOU
Rationale:	To establish that Roger's car is still on the loose.
In:	Sherry-Lou spots Roger's car for a second time as it crosses back over the Westminster Bridge.
Out:	All three dash out of the coffee bar.

11. EXT – NEAR WESTMINSTER BRIDGE – COFFEE BAR – MIDDAY

Characters:	ROGER, BUD, SHERRY-LOU, TAXI DRIVER
Rationale:	To establish that Roger, Bud, and Sherry-Lou are in pursuit of Roger's Jag.
In:	Roger flags down a taxi.
Out:	The taxi does a U-turn and heads north over Westminster Bridge towards the Houses of Parliament.

12. INT – PASSING WESTMINSTER, HEADING TOWARDS ST JAMES'S PARK – BLACK TAXI – MIDDAY

Characters:	ROGER, BUD, SHERRY-LOU, TAXI DRIVER
Rationale:	To establish that Roger has a near encyclopaedic knowledge of Central London and that Bud and Sherry-Lou love white-knuckle rides.
In:	Taxi passes statue of Nelson Mandela and heads towards St James's Park.

Out: Taxi gets stuck behind a bus.

13. EXT – WEST LONDON – BLACK TAXI – MIDDAY

Characters: ROGER, BUD, SHERRY-LOU, TAXI DRIVER
Rationale: To establish that Roger's car has come to a stop and that
                Roger is parting company with the American couple and
                exchanging contact details.
In: Sherry-Lou spots the Jag turning into a side street.
Out: Roger instructs the taxi driver to stop.

14. EXT – WHITE CITY – OUTSIDE OFFICE OF INTERNATIONAL INSURANCE INVESTIGATIONS (III) – MIDDAY

Characters: ROGER, ROGER'S CAR
Rationale: To establish that the car is very similar, but not identical,
                to Roger's.
In: Roger rounds the corner and spots the Jag parked.
Out: Roger crouches down to inspect under the Jag.

15. EXT – WHITE CITY – OUTSIDE OFFICE OF III – MIDDAY

Characters: ROGER, ROGER'S CAR, MAN IN A CAMEL HAIR
                OVERCOAT Rationale:
                To establish that there is something a little shady about III.
In: The man in the camel-hair overcoat approaches Roger.
Out: Both men head into the man's office.

16. INT – CHISWICK – IN THE OFFICE OF III – MIDDAY *

Characters: ROGER, MAN IN THE CAMEL HAIR OVERCOAT
Rationale: To establish that Roger's car is a fake. To hint that the man
                knew of its existence all along. To offer 'compensation' to
                Roger.
In: The two men introduce themselves.
Out: Roger accepts the compensation payment.

17. INT – ROGER'S HOUSE – BY FRONT DOOR – EVENING

Characters: ROGER, CAROLINE
Rationale: To establish that Roger has some news for Caroline. In: Roger arrives home.
Out: The phone rings.

18. INT – ROGER'S HOUSE – HOME OFFICE – EVENING *

Characters: ROGER, CAROLINE, and BUD (off-screen on the phone)
Rationale: To establish that Bud has a business proposition for Roger.
In: Caroline answers the phone.
Out: Roger accepts Bud's proposal.

19. INT – ROGER'S HOUSE – LIVING ROOM – EVENING *

Characters: ROGER, CAROLINE
Rationale: To reveal that Roger has a new future.
In: Roger ends the call with Bud.
Out: View of the front of Roger's house. And fade.

Stage 4 - Writing the New Scenes

Starting with an opening paragraph that describes who's in the scene and what you can see and hear, write a first draft of each of the scenes. At this stage it's worth creating a separate file for each scene. After you've written the first drafts, you might want to assess the order of the scenes and identify any other scenes that are required.

At the end of Stage 4 of **The Wheel of Fortune** we had the following scenes:

> 1, 2, and 3 as planned in Stage 3.
> 4 split into three scenes to help show where Roger arrived in London and where he was heading.
> 5 as planned in Stage 3.

6, 7, and 8 nearly as planned in Stage 3, but with the content and timing of each slightly different.

9 and 10 as planned in Stage 3.

11 split into two scenes to develop the anticipation of an impending chase.

12 became a set of thirteen short scenes that rapidly alternated between shots inside the taxi and external shots showing the progress of both the taxi and the Jaguar.

13 as planned except that the final location became a side road in Wood Lane instead of near Holland Park. Wood Lane seemed a more likely spot for a light industrial estate.

14 and 15 were combined into a single scene.

16 as planned in Stage 3.

17, 18, and 19 nearly as planned in Stage 3, but with the content and timing of each slightly different.

Along the way, some short scenes were added to help with the flow and a character was added to help further explain Roger's dilemma about admitting to his wife that his job in the City had come to an end.

Stage 5 - Identifying and Fixing Flaws

Flaws are parts of the screenplay that make the story as a whole less convincing. At the end of Stage 4, we felt the following areas needed to be considered carefully and amended to create a more plausible story:

Is Roger's dilemma believable?

Is Bud's and Sherry-Lou's involvement with Roger believable?

How likely is it that Roger would open up to the American couple?

What is the issue with the car?

Is it resolved convincingly?

Is Bud's offer to Roger credible?

Would Bud's offer resolve Roger's financial problems?

Sample Decamot TV Screenplays

The four sample screenplays in this section all started out as Decamot stories generated by ten Decamot items. They went through a period of revising and extending before going through the Decamot process described in **Chapter 3**. The original Decamot versions of **Helter Skelter, Wheel of Fortune,** and **Upon Reflection** appear earlier in the book.

HELTER SKELTER

By

Gavin Jackson

INT—ST HOLMBURY'S VILLAGE HALL—AFTERNOON

ST HOLMBURY'S VILLAGE COMMITTEE are meeting to discuss the annual village fair. COLONEL WORTHINGTON-SMYTHE is chairing the meeting. He is sitting at the head of a large trestle table. Seated around the table are 8 WOMEN and 11 MEN, all aged between about 40 and 75. Amongst them are: the VICAR, MARJORIE the Vicar's wife, MRS ORMSKIRK, EDWARD MASTERS, MARY JONES, and BARBARA DAVIS. There is also EMMA FORD, a 15-year-old-girl who represents the youth of the village. MARJORIE is taking the minutes.

Everyone has in front of them a notepad and pen, and a cup of tea. Across the middle of the table are strewn several empty plates, a plate containing a few sandwiches, and another containing a few slices of cake.

> EMMA FORD
> Why don't we get Peter Piper to open the fair?

> COLONEL WORTHINGTON-SMYTHE
> I'm sorry, my dear, but I've never heard of him, outside the nursery rhyme that is. Who or what is Peter Piper?

> EMMA FORD
> He's a DJ on Radio Active. Most people at school think he'll be the next Chris Evans. He's huge with students. And I think he may live near St Holmbury.

COLONEL WORTHINGTON-SMYTHE
Oh, I see.

The Colonel offers the last plate of the
sandwiches around the table.

COLONEL WORTHINGTON-SMYTHE cont'd
I must defer to your greater knowledge
of these matters, young Emma. All
those in favour of Emma approaching
Mr Piper, please raise your hand.

All 20 people sitting round the table raise
their hands.

COLONEL WORTHINGTON-SMYTHE
Motion carried . . . and if we can rely
on Mrs Ormskirk, as ever, to supply
the ornamental flourishes . . . ?

The COLONEL looks over to a plump little woman
of about 50.

MRS ORMSKIRK
(not looking particularly
enthusiastic)
Of course, Colonel.

COLONEL WORTHINGTON-SMYTHE
In that case, we are now on to any
other business. Is there any?

Emma raises her hand.

EMMA FORD
Err, I have one.

          COLONEL WORTHINGTON-SMYTHE
              (sounding slightly surprised)
     Really? OK, go ahead, Emma.

          EMMA FORD
     Why don't we ask Mr Henderson to put
     up his helter skelter for the fair?

No one says anything. Several people around the
table exchange glances.

          EMMA FORD cont'd
     My parents told me how great it was
     in the old days.

Emma looks around the table. Some of the
committee members avoid eye contact; some even
look down at their empty plates.

          EMMA FORD cont'd
              (sounding less confident now)
     My American cousin, Jed, is coming
     over to visit soon . . . he mentioned
     sliding down the helter skelter as a
     kid . . . and I just thought it'd be
     kinda nice to . . .

There is an uncomfortable silence for a few
moments. The Colonel leans forward in his chair.

          COLONEL WORTHINGTON-SMYTHE
              (talking quietly)
     Frankly, Emma, nothing would give
     us greater pleasure than to have
     Mr Henderson participate again. But
     since the tragedy of 40 years ago,
     he has shut himself away and is very
     rarely to be seen out and about. My
     wife has tried many times to shake

him out of his crippling despair, but
nothing seems to work.

EMMA FORD
Perhaps rebuilding the helter skelter
would take his mind off his problems.

EDWARD MASTERS
Emma does have a point. Working on
Henderson's Helter Skelter could be
therapeutic.

MARY JONES
That's very true. And pride of place
in our village fair always used to be
the fifty-foot multicoloured marvel
that was Henderson's Helter Skelter.

EDWARD MASTERS
Put St Holmbury's Village Fair on the
map. Made us a nationally renowned
event. We even used to stock a
postcard of it in the village shop.
Hugely popular with tourists.

BARBARA DAVIS
But what about the tragedy? We can
hardly overlook that now, can we?

EMMA FORD
What happened? I know it had something
to do with Mrs Henderson and their
son, but I don't know what.

COLONEL WORTHINGTON-SMYTHE
It was in the evening of Saturday,
27 April 1968, the eve of the annual
fair. Sally Henderson and her five-
year-old son Mark were crossing the

road from the shop to the village green. They were going along to watch the final preparations of the helter skelter – Mark was looking forward to his first ever slide down it the next day.

Suddenly a little white BMW came hurtling round the corner. He hit Mrs Henderson and young Mark, they both died on the way to hospital. The driver, whose own six-month-old son was a passenger in a carrycot in the back of the car, was later convicted of manslaughter, served six months imprisonment, and was banned from driving for two years.

Max Henderson saw everything from the top of the helter skelter. Devastated the poor man. The entire village turned out for the funeral of Mrs Henderson and young Mark three days later. Their graves have been tended by a grief-stricken Max Henderson ever since.

That was the last time that any of us has seen the helter skelter. As far as I know, it remains packed away in Mr Henderson's garage.

Grief's a personal thing, and we should respect his privacy.

                    EDWARD MASTERS
            (looking directly at the Colonel)
Oh come, Percy! Grief's one thing, but his has been going on for years.

STANLEY JACKSON AND GAVIN JACKSON

The Colonel looks affronted at the usage of his first name and goes to say something but is cut off:

                    MARY JONES
          Perhaps we'd be better neighbours to
          Max if we stopped pussyfooting around
          and helped him to confront his loss,
          and perhaps he'd able to move on. I
          think we'd be doing him a favour.

Several people around the table start nodding.

                    EMMA FORD
          So can I do it? Can I go talk to Mr
          Henderson?

                    COLONEL WORTHINGTON-SMYTHE
               (less enthusiastically than before)
          All those in favour of Emma trying to
          persuade Mr Henderson to bring the
          helter skelter out of retirement,
          please raise your hand.

13 people sitting round the table raise their hands. The Colonel is not one of them.

                    COLONEL WORTHINGTON-SMYTHE cont'd
          Well, it's close, but . . . the motion
          is carried.

INT—THE FORD'S KITCHEN—EVENING

EMMA FORD, MR FORD, and MRS FORD are sitting round their kitchen table discussing Emma's meeting with the committee.

MRS FORD
So how'd it go?

EMMA
All right I s'pose. I was the youngest
person there of course — everyone
else was ancient.

MRS FORD
Did you agree to do anything for the
fair?

EMMA
I suggested we get Peter Piper to
open the fair. Lots of kids would
come to the fair just to see him. I
volunteered to ask him.

MR FORD
How are you going to do that?

EMMA
I thought I'd ask him live on air.
I also suggested we get the helter
skelter back in fair.

MR FORD
Old man Henderson's Helter Skelter?

EMMA
Yeah. I offered to persuade him to put
it up again.

MR FORD
That's more of an ask, isn't it?

EMMA
I know. I kinda wish I hadn't now.

MRS FORD
How're you going to persuade him?

EMMA
Dunno. I've got to think of an excuse
for talking to him first.

MR FORD
How about bob-a-job?

EMMA
Bob-a-what?

MRS FORD
Your dad's talking about what the cubs
used to do back when he was a boy:
They'd go round to their neighbours
and offer to do a job for a bob—that's
like a five pence now, but worth more
like a fiver in today's money. The
money would go to charity I think.
I don't think they do that kind of
thing anymore, love.

EMMA
I'm a bit old for cubs, and I'm not a
boy!

MRS FORD
How about D of E? You're doing that at
school, aren't you?

EMMA
That's hiking and camping, how's that
going to help?

                    MRS FORD
But don't you also need to do community
service of some sort to get a D of E
award?

                    EMMA
Oh yeah, doing good deeds for old
fogeys! Mr Henderson could be my old
fogey.

EXT—MR HENDERSON'S DRIVEWAY

Emma is standing outside MR HENDERSON's house.
It's pouring with rain and she's only just keeping
under cover by standing in the porch. She rings
the doorbell and waits. A few minutes later the
door opens.

                    EMMA
Mr Henderson?

                    MR HENDERSON
Whatever you're selling, I'm not
interested.

                    EMMA
I'm not selling anything, I'm here
for . . .

                    MR HENDERSON
            (interrupting Emma)
Whatever it is, I'm not interested.

Mr Henderson goes to close the door.

                    EMMA
            (blurting out very quickly)
Bob-a-job?

MR HENDERSON
You're a bit old for that, aren't you?

EMMA
Yes, and I'm not a boy. I just wanted
to stop you closing the door.

MR HENDERSON
OK, what do you want?

EMMA
Community service.

MR HENDERSON
Community service? You're a young
criminal, are you?

EMMA
It's nothing like that, it's part of my
D of E, doing good deeds for old . . .
I mean, for senior citizens.

MR HENDERSON
D of E? Duke of Edinburgh award?

EMMA
Yeah, my school's really big on it
'forms a part of a holistic education'
or something like that.

MR HENDERSON
Well, that's all very well, but there's
nothing I need doing.

EMMA
There must be something I could do
for you. Mow your lawn, wash your
car . . .

                    MR HENDERSON
          In this weather?

Mr Henderson goes again to shut the door, but
then stops.

                    MR HENDERSON
          Actually, there is one thing you can
          help me with.

                    EMMA
          Yes?

                    MR HENDERSON
          I've got some silverware in the attic
          I've been meaning to get rid of a
          while - perhaps you can help me shine
          it up and then take it down to the
          antique shop in the village for me.

                    EMMA
                (brightening)
          Love to.

                    MR HENDERSON
          I guess you'd better come inside.

EXT—MR HENDERSON'S HALLWAY

EMMA is standing in MR HENDERSON's hallway.
Mr Henderson is not present. Emma is looking
round. It's a very large space, bigger than most
people's living rooms. There is a hat stand near
the door, a large oak table under the window, a
cupboard, and several bookshelves.

In one corner there is a piano. Emma approaches
it. The lid over the keyboard is closed. There

is a small booklet of sheet music on the stand. Emma takes a look at the page to which the booklet is opened and smiles.

Emma looks over her shoulder. There is no sign of Mr Henderson.

> EMMA
> Mr Henderson?

There's no response. Emma hesitates. She seems drawn to the piano. At last she sits down on the piano stool and opens the lid of the piano to reveal the keyboard. She starts playing the right-hand part of the piece very quietly.

We hear Beethoven's FÜR ELISE. Emma plays a little tentatively at first, but increasing in confidence, and getting louder as she progresses through the piece.

Emma stops then goes back to the beginning, this time playing both the left- and right-hand parts together. As she reaches the bottom of the page, she turns the page over and continues. She suddenly stops and turns round.

Mr Henderson is standing in the doorway holding a large cardboard box filled with assorted silverware. He has a tear rolling down his cheek. Emma leaps to her feet.

> EMMA
> I'm really sorry, I shouldn't't've done that. I just couldn't . . . I'm so sorry.

                    MR HENDERSON
Don't be.

                    EMMA
Thing is, I just saw the piece open
on the piano and . . . well, it's
something I've learnt recently . . .
and it . . .

                    MR HENDERSON
And it needs finishing.

                    EMMA
What?

                    MR HENDERSON
It needs finishing. You've got about
20 bars to go. Why don't take it from
the low A with the left hand, just
before the 4-bar flourish with the
right hand, and take it to the end.

Emma sits back down on the piano stool. She
hesitates for a few minutes, then starts playing
again. Mr Henderson is still standing in the
doorway holding the box. Finally, Emma finishes
the piece. She lays her hands in her lap and
looks downwards. She's too embarrassed to turn
to face Mr Henderson.

                    MR HENDERSON
That was very good, but it could sound
better.

                    EMMA
I know; I'm not very good. I've not
been playing very long.

MR HENDERSON
Not you. The piano could sound better.
The E-flat is too flat, and the notes
around middle-C are all a little
strained. The top-end keys sound
a little clicky. And I can see you
working the sustain pedal, but it's
not releasing fully enough, so the
notes are running on for a little
too long. But these things are easily
fixable.

Mr Henderson's whole demeanour has lightened. He
puts the box down on the oak table and walks over
to the cupboard next to the front door. He opens
the cupboard door and carefully removes a large
toolbox. He places it next to the cardboard box
on the table and opens it out.

Inside is a huge array of pliers and small
screwdrivers. There are also rolls of piano wire
of different thicknesses, offcuts of felt, some
small lengths of wood, several round wooden
pegs, a large tube of superglue, a small oil
can, and several tuning forks.

EMMA
Are you a piano tuner?

MR HENDERSON
Used to be. Or should I say, piano
tuning's one of the things I used to
do. In fact that's how I met Sally, my
late wife.

EMMA
Really?

                    MR HENDERSON
She was 18 at the time, and still
living at home. This home in fact –
she inherited it a few years later
when her father died.

She was playing when I got here; her
father let me in. I waited just here
and listened until she got to the end
of the piece before getting started
with the tuning.

Mr Henderson selects two pairs of pliers. He
walks around to the back of the piano and removes
the panel protecting the strings.

                    EMMA
What was she playing?

                    MR HENDERSON
It was another Beethoven piece:
Moonlight Sonata; very calming, very
dreamy.

                    EMMA
I know that one. Mum's got it on CD.

                    MR HENDERSON
You can't beat hearing it in person.
Now, play a scale with 2 flats in it
for me. Just the right hand.

Emma does so.

                    MR HENDERSON
Could you hear that? B-flat was fine,
but the E-flat not quite so.

                    EMMA
          I think so.

Mr Henderson uses the pliers to make some adjusts
to one of the strings.

                    MR HENDERSON\
          And again please.

Emma plays the same notes again. Mr Henderson
makes another small adjustment, then tightens
two other strings.

                    MR HENDERSON
          One more time please.

Emma plays the notes again.

                    MR HENDERSON
          Much better. Now let's see what we can
          do with that pedal. Play the first 8
          bars, pressing the sustain pedal as
          you're playing the left-hand triplets,
          and releasing as the right hand takes
          over each time.

Emma plays the first 8 bars while Mr Henderson
bends low and looks along the line of strings.
He then walks round to the front of the piano
and crouches down into the footwell.

                    MR HENDERSON
          First 8 bars again please.

Emma plays the first 8 bars again.

                    MR HENDERSON
          Got it.

Mr Henderson hurries over to the toolbox, selects a screwdriver and picks up the small oil can, and hurries back. He crouches into the footwell again, removes one of the levers, and squeezes a few drops of oil on to it. He then replaces the lever.

> MR HENDERSON
> One last time with the 8 bars.

Emma plays the first 8 bars for a third time.

> MR HENDERSON
> Much better. Can you hear the difference?

> EMMA
> I think so. The sustained notes stop much more quickly now when I lift the pedal.

> MR HENDERSON
> Exactly. Now let's hear the whole thing, but without the repeats.

Emma plays the whole piece through without stopping. Her playing is much more confident now, and she makes no errors. When she gets to the bottom of each sheet, she deftly turns the page with her right hand and smoothly continues.

The whole time Emma is playing, Mr Henderson watches from the doorway as he had before, but this time he is smiling broadly. When Emma gets to the end, he claps.

> MR HENDERSON
> Much better.

INT—MR HENDERSON'S KITCHEN—AFTERNOON

EMMA and MR HENDERSON are sitting at the kitchen table. Both are polishing silver plates. In the middle of the table are a stack of plates that have been polished to a high sheen. On the side is the cardboard box that MR Henderson had been holding earlier; it is now empty.

>   EMMA
> So what did you do apart from piano turning?

>   MR HENDERSON
> General woodworking: cabinet-making and boat-building.

>   EMMA
> Boat-building? But we're miles from the coast.

>   MR HENDERSON
> True. But we do have 36 miles of canals in the Cotswolds, 60 odd miles of the Thames not far off. Lichfield's not far away, and there's miles of canal that way too. I've had plenty of work over the years.

>   EMMA
>   (hesitating as she speaks)
> Is that er . . . is that how you came to build the helter skelter? Being the master woodworker in the village?

>   MR HENDERSON
> You know about the helter skelter?

                    EMMA
          Yeah. My parents mentioned it, and
          I've seen a postcard it was on.

                    MR HENDERSON
          I don't remember whose idea it was,
          but yes, that's why I was asked to
          build it. We put it up each year for
          10 years, until . . .

Mr Henderson falls silent. He stares down at the
plate he's been polishing and sighs, but doesn't
continue.

                    EMMA
               (very quietly)
          Until the car crash?

                    MR HENDERSON
          Yes. Yes, the car crash.

                    EMMA
               (almost under her breath)
          It must have been terrible.

                    MR HENDERSON
          It was. I was depressed for the longest
          time. The next year, I couldn't face
          rebuilding the helter skelter. Nor the
          next year, nor the next. In the end
          the village committee stopped asking
          me, and I shut myself away more and
          more.

Emma walks over to the dresser. There are several
photographs in frames, including one of a YOUNG
WOMAN and a SMALL BOY. The woman is surprisingly
similar to Emma: She has the same long, thick,
near-black hair, pale skin, and green eyes. Also

STANLEY JACKSON AND GAVIN JACKSON

like Emma, she looks quite slim without being skinny. She could almost be Emma's older sister.

>   EMMA FORD
> Is this them?

>   MR HENDERSON
> Yes. That was taken on Mark's third birthday.

>   EMMA FORD
> He's a real cutie.

>   MR HENDERSON
> Yes, he was.

>   EMMA FORD
> Yes, of course, was. Sorry.

>   MR HENDERSON
> Don't be. To be honest, I'm sick of people treading on eggshells around me. It was sweet at first, and I'm sure they all meant well, but it's got to the point where I don't feel I can walk around the village any more. It's nice to be able to talk about them with someone.

Emma and Mr Henderson are silent for a few minutes. Emma returns to the table and finishes polishing the final silver plate.

>   EMMA
> Do you still have the helter skelter?

>   MR HENDERSON
> Yes, I could never quite bring myself to get rid of it. It's taking up half

of my garage. It's probably not up to
much anymore. Do you want to see it?

             EMMA
I'd love to.

INT—MR HENDERSON'S GARAGE

EMMA and MR HENDERSON are in the garage, one
of which is taken up with several large humps
covered with dust sheets. Mr Henderson removes
the dust sheets one by one.

             MR HENDERSON
This is it: Henderson's Helter Skelter.
Those long straight panels make up
the bulk of the ride. That pile of
struts make up the framework. Those
curved pieces make up the slide. And
that last pile makes up the turret.

             EMMA
Wow, all the pieces look in pretty
good nick.

             MR HENDERSON
This garage is completely weatherproof,
so there's been no water damage or
anything like that.

             EMMA
Do you think it could be put up again?

             MR HENDERSON
I should think so. There might be the
odd strut that needs replacing, and
the panels need a good repainting,
but I think it could.

STANLEY JACKSON AND GAVIN JACKSON

                    EMMA
Would you be prepared to build it one
last time? For the fair this year?

                    MR HENDERSON
No, I don't think so.

                    EMMA
What! Why not?

                    MR HENDERSON
Who'd be interested in a helter skelter
these days?

                    EMMA
Loads of people would.

                    MR HENDERSON
It was old-fashioned when I first made
it. That was nearly 50 years ago. Kids
like theme parks nowadays; my helter
skelter is somewhat tame.

                    EMMA
But it's famous.

Mr Henderson scratches his head and looks
over the various piles tutting all the while.
Eventually he says:

                    MR HENDERSON
No! It'll be a lot of effort, and I
really don't think it's worth it.

        EMMA
Why did you keep it all these years if
you had no intention of ever putting
it back up?

        MR HENDERSON
It's like everything else round here,
Sally . . . er sorry, Emma. It's just
one more thing that I've been meaning
to get rid of, but just could not
quite get round to.

        EMMA
How about giving it one last go? Then
you can get rid of it for good.

Mr Henderson sighs. He says nothing for a while.
He walks over to the pile of panels. He picks up
a panel and leans it against the side wall of
the garage. He takes a few steps backwards to
look at it. The paint is flaking, but the words
'Henderson's Helter Skelter' are still visible.

        MR HENDERSON
Oh, what the hell – why not! Although
I think I'll need some help to put it
up. I'm not as young as I used to be.

        EMMA
Oh, thanks, Mr Henderson.

Emma throws her arms around Mr Henderson's neck
and kisses him gently on the cheek.

INT—RADIO ACTIVE'S STUDIO B

PETER PIPER is sitting at the control desk. He is holding several sheets of paper and is reading from the top one. He is wearing headphones and is talking into a microphone. JO NICKS is in the mixing studio watching him through the soundproof glass and listening in through her own headphones.

> PETER PIPER
> That was 'The Long and Winding Road' by the Beatles. And now we have our Friday request. Who do we have lined up Jo?

> JO NICKS
> On line one, we have an Emma Ford from St Holmbury. That's your neck of the woods, isn't it?

> PETER PIPER
> That's right. I'm just a few miles down the road. Hi, Emma, what's your request?

> EMMA (O.S.)
> I've got a request, but it's not musical.

> PETER PIPER
> This is Friday's song request slot, Emma. No exceptions, sorry.

> JO NICKS
> I think you could at least listen to Emma's request, Peter.

PETER PIPER
Oh, go on then. What did you have in mind, Emma?

EMMA (O.S.)
Will you come open the St Holmbury's Fair?

PETER PIPER
I'm afraid that really is something that I can't . . .

EMMA (O.S.)
        (cutting across PETER and gabbling
        slightly)
We're reopening the helter skelter.

JO NICKS
You mean the one and only Henderson's Helter Skelter?

EMMA (O.S.)
That's right.

JO NICKS
I remember hearing about that. It's been out of action for years, hasn't it?

EMMA (O.S.)
That's right, but Mr Henderson himself has agreed to put it up again.

JO NICKS
Wow. Didn't realise he was still alive. This is truly historic. Peter, you don't really want to miss out on this one, do you?

                    PETER PIPER
Well, it's er . . . well, not really
the sort of thing that I'd, er normally
do. But I . . . er. Henderson's Helter
Skelter eh?!

                    (beat)
You know what, I think I might make
an exception on this occasion.

                    EMMA (O.S.)
Thanks, Peter, you're sick.

                    PETER PIPER
Er thanks, I think. Emma, stay on
the line and let Jo take your details
while I play some more music . . .
and in the circumstances, this seems
quite appropriate: Robbie Williams,
'Let Me Entertain You!'

EXT—VILLAGE GREEN—EARLY EVENING

Posters festoon the neighbourhood. They are on
every tree, on every lamp post, and in most of
the shop windows; several are pinned on to the
doors of the village church, and there's even
one attached to the door of the police station.
On each poster in large block capitals are the
words:

            ST HOLMBURY'S ANNUAL FAIR

            TO BE OPENED BY RADIO ACTIVE'S
            PETER PIPER

FEATURING HENDERSON'S HELTER
SKELTER

EMMA and JED are sitting in the middle of the
village green admiring the famous helter skelter.

                EMMA
        Did you enjoy your week in Oxford?

                JED
        Sure did. Brought it all back - don't
        think the city's changed in 40 odd
        years.

                EMMA
        Where did you go?

                JED
        All the usual touristy places: the
        colleges, bookshops, took a punt along
        the river, and did a real cool Alice
        in Wonderland tour.

                EMMA
        Sounds like fun.

                JED
        Sure was. And now here's that old helter
        skelter, exactly as I remember it.

                EMMA
        Mr Henderson's done a great job,
        hasn't he?

                JED
        Sure has. Where's he got to now?

                    EMMA
Think he went off to the pub for a
well-earned rest.

                    JED
Cool. So shall we have quick go on the
slide while no one's around?

                    EMMA
Absolutely not. The first person to go
down it has to be Peter Piper.

                    JED
Why?

                    EMMA
Village tradition: Whoever opens the
fair has the first ride on the slide.
That's how they always used to do it.

                    JED
Shame. Look, I picked up this vintage,
pre-digital camera on my travels. It
would have been the latest thing when
I was last here in England.

Jed removes a camera from his rucksack and shows
it to Emma. It's an old SLR 35mm camera about 4
times the size of a digital camera and made of
sturdy black plastic. On its upper side it has
a huge flash.

                    JED cont'd
It's a Nikon F, made in 1960. You
even have to load it with film and
get someone to develop it for you,
something you've never had to worry
about!

                    EMMA
Hmm, very nice, but what's it got to
do with the helter skelter?

                    JED
Well, look at this bit here.

Jed points to a small lever on top of the camera's
casing.

                    JED cont'd
That's the timer control. It's the
only gimmick that the camera's got.
You get a delay of about 15 seconds,
so you have to set up the shot, set
the camera, run round to the other
side, and then . . . BOOM, you can
take a shot of yourself.

                    EMMA
Still not seeing where you're going
with this.

                    JED
I just thought it would be a bit of
fun to give it a whirl in the old-
fashioned way. I thought I could set
up the camera at the bottom of the
helter skelter near the landing area.
We could run up the inside and get
caught on camera as we land. Then
get the film developed, have several
weeks' anticipation without knowing
how well it will turn out, you know,
the whole sixties thing.

                    EMMA
Sounds like fun - I'm up for it. But
why can't this wait 'til tomorrow?

                    JED
Well, in the heat of the moment would
we really get a chance to set up the
camera? People will be too keen to
clamber up the famous helter skelter
to wait for us messing around. Do it
now, and we can take as long as we
like setting up the shot. Maybe you
can be waiting at the top of the slide
already, so only one of us has to run
up to the top.

                    EMMA
You do have a point I s'pose.

                    JED
So shall we go for it then? No one
will know.

                    EMMA
Yeah, go on then!

Emma climbs to the top of the helter skelter
while Jed sets up the camera on a box and
activates the timer by pushing the silver lever.
He then rushes up the winding inside staircase.
At the top, they both squeeze on to the same mat
and come swirling down the slide, barely able
to contain their excitement. As they land the
camera flashes. Several seconds later the camera
flashes a second time.

                    JED
Brilliant. Not sure why it flashed
again, but I'm fairly sure we were spot
on with the first flash. Thank you so
much. I'll send you a copy of the photo
when I get back to the States.

EXT—VILLAGE GREEN—MORNING

The village is swarming with people eagerly awaiting the opening of the annual fair. A crew from the local TV station has set up cameras and are filming the event.

About 5000 people have squeezed on to the village square. On the centre of the green is the giant helter skelter towering over the crowd. The woodwork is shiny and looks well polished, the paintwork on the lettering on the side of the helter skelter has been newly done, and the entire structure is covered in red, white, and blue bunting. There is a ribbon tied across the riders' entrance to the helter skelter.

In the centre of the crowd are the VICAR and his wife MAJORIE. Next to them is the local MAYOR dressed in his ceremonial gown topped off with the chains of office. On the other side of the VICAR dressed in a very smart suit is PETER PIPER, and next to him, a smartly dressed MAX HENDERSON.

The final person in the small group is dressed as an old- fashioned town crier. In one hand he is holding a hand bell and in the other an oversized pair of scissors. The TOWN CRIER starts to ring the bell, and the crowd fall silent.

> TOWN CRIER
> Oh yeah! Oh Yeah! People of St Holmbury - welcome to our annual fair. Please show your appreciation for Mr Peter Piper.

The crowd cheers. The town crier hands the oversized scissors to PETER PIPER. PETER cuts the ribbon. PETER turns to wave at the crowd who cheer even louder. He then disappears inside the helter skelter. After a few moments, he emerges at the top of the slide, holding a large coconut hair mat.

After riding the helter skelter without mishap, Peter Piper takes the microphone to declare the Annual St Holmbury's Fair open.

> PETER PIPER
> You can probably guess that Peter Piper is only my professional name. My real family name would have been known for the very worst of reasons to any of you who were living in the village 40 years Ago. It was my father's car that caused a fatal accident near this very village green. I was a passenger in that car. He had been drinking, and we took the bend much too fast.
>
> Of course, I was far too young to know anything about it at the time but, as a young reporter, I read the cuttings and knew what devastation it had caused Max Henderson and his family. I have never been able to drive through this lovely village without feeling the shame of what my father had done. Emma Ford somehow found all this out and introduced me to Max.
>
> Today, thanks to the marvellous generosity of spirit shown to me by Max Henderson, I have been able to atone. Sir, I will be eternally

grateful to you, and I believe that
today we have both achieved closure.

The two men embrace in front of 5000 cheering
people, tears filling both their eyes.

INT—EMMA'S LOUNGE—AFTERNOON SEVERAL WEEKS LATER

EMMA is sitting on the sofa. There is a pile of
letters on the coffee table in front of her.

On the top of the pile is an airmail package with
a US postage stamp. Emma opens the letter and
empties the contents on to the table in front
of her. There is a letter and a small envelope.
She unfolds and reads the letter.

She then opens the envelope and removes two
photographs. She looks at the first one. It
shows Emma and Jed tumbling on to the landing
mat together at the bottom of Henderson's Helter
Skelter, grinning like Cheshire cats.

She then picks up and looks at the second
photograph. She gasps and drops it on to the
coffee table face up. It contains two people:
a YOUNG WOMAN and a SMALL BOY. We've seen them
before in a picture on Mr Henderson's mantelpiece:
They are Mrs Sally Henderson and her five-year-
old son Mark. Both are sliding down Henderson's
Helter Skelter and both are waving and smiling
at the camera.

FADE OUT

CLOSING CREDITS

WHEEL of FORTUNE

By

Gavin Jackson

EXT—AFFLUENT SUBURBAN STREET—ROGER MARSHALL'S DRIVE—MORNING

We are outside a large detached house on an affluent street in a generic suburb of Tonbridge Wells. There are two cars on the drive: a maroon Mark II Jaguar with the number plate ROG 15A and a navy blue RANGE ROVER.

ROGER MARSHALL, a fit-looking 52-year-old, is at the back of the Range Rover amid schoolbags and related paraphernalia which he is loading into the back of the Range Rover. He is smartly dressed, wearing a gunmetal grey suit, crisp white shirt, and broad-striped tie.

Roger's wife CAROLINE is sitting in the driver's seat and his two daughters, CHLOE and PHILIPPA, are sitting in the back. The girls are smartly dressed in matching blazers, blue blouses, and cotton, tartan skirts.

Roger is about to load a lacrosse stick into the car when TONY, a neighbour, approaches.

> TONY
> First day for Chloe, eh?

> ROGER
> (turning towards the voice)
> Morning, Tony. Yup. Both at St V's now.

> TONY
> That'll hit the old wallet a bit.

                    ROGER
No kidding!

                    TONY
Still on for the Round Table meeting
on Thursday?

                    ROGER
          (turning back to complete the car
          loading)
Not a problem. 8 o'clock, right?

                    TONY
Right. Hey, nice try you scored on
Sunday for the OJs.

                    ROGER
Thanks, mate. Glad to see I've still
got it.

                    CAROLINE
          (calling from inside the car)
Come on, love, the girls don't want
to be late.

Caroline starts the engine.

                    ROGER
          (closing the back of the Ranger
          Rover)
Gotta go, Tony. See you Thursday.

Roger picks up his LEATHER BRIEFCASE, gets into
the passenger seat, and closes the door. The
car leaves the drive and heads off down the
road.

**INT—AFFLUENT SUBURBAN STREET—INSIDE CAROLINE'S
CAR—MORNING**

The traffic is reasonably light. The girls are
CHATTING in the back. The RADIO is playing
quietly.

>   CHLOE
>   Will I be any good?

>   PHILIPPA
>   'Course you will. It's a lot like
>   hockey really, 'cept you can scoop up
>   the ball and run with it.

>   CHLOE
>   Why's it called lacrosse?

>   PHILIPPA
>   Dunno.

>   CHLOE
>   Dad. Why's it called lacrosse?

>   ROGER
>   (turning slightly towards his
>   daughters)
>   It's a native American game, Iroquois
>   I think. Originally they played it with
>   some on horseback and between 100 to
>   1,000 braves on the field . . .

>   CHLOE
>   (interrupting)
>   You'd have to be brave with that many
>   on the field!

ROGER
True. Anyway, the French Canadians
watched the natives playing and
referred to it as 'le jeu de la
crosse', or in English, 'the game with
the stick'. We shortened 'le jeu de la
crosse' to lacrosse.

CHLOE
Wish we could have the horses too.
Way cool.

**EXT—TONBRIDGE WELLS STATION—OUTSIDE CAROLINE'S
CAR—MORNING**

Caroline's car turns into the car park of
Tonbridge Station Wells. Several other cars are
also stopping to drop off spouses. All around
smartly dressed MEN, WOMEN, and SCHOOLCHILDREN
are heading towards the ticket office.

CAROLINE
Darling, I've got to help Barbara with
the flowers this afternoon, then pick
up the girls. You OK to walk home this
evening?

ROGER
That's fine. Weather forecast looks
good for this afternoon, should stay
dry all day.

Roger leans over to kiss his wife goodbye.

ROGER
(turning to his daughters, smiling)
Good luck with your first day at St
Verucca's, Chloe.

PHILIPPA
(crossly)
Saint Veronica's, Dad.

ROGER
And get stuck in. Don't let anyone bully you off the ball. See you later, girls.

Roger gets out of the car and heads towards the station.

EXT—CENTRAL LONDON—CHARING CROSS STATION—MORNING

Roger is walking towards the ticket barrier along with many other commuters. He touches his Oyster Card on to the panel next to the barrier. The barrier snaps open. He walks through into the main foyer and turns sharply to the left.

Roger goes into the WH Smith concession, picks up a *Daily Telegraph*, and pays for it with a two-pound coin at the self-service counter. He retrieves his change, tucks the paper under his arm, and walks back into the foyer.

Roger then walks across the foyer and exits the station via the side entrance, heading towards the elevated walkway that leads to the Hungerford Bridge across the Thames. He is walking against the flow of commuters who are crossing to the north side of the river.

EXT—CENTRAL LONDON—ON HUNGERFORD BRIDGE—MORNING

Halfway across the footbridge that runs alongside
Hungerford Bridge a BUSKER is sitting on a small
plastic chair STRUMMING tunelessly on a ukulele
that has three strings tuned badly and one
string missing completely.

A large number of commuters are crossing over
the bridge. Mainly they are heading from south
to north. All are walking purposely. Some are
talking on mobile phones. Most are oblivious
to everyone else around them. Virtually no one
notices a man on a chair hoping for loose change.

We then see a lone figure walking against the
steady flow of commuters. It's Roger. He is
walking across the bridge towards South Bank.
When he reaches the busker he bends down and
places the change he got from his paper into the
man's upturned hat.

> BUSKER
> Bless you, man.

> ROGER
> Morning, Jimmy. Here, I've got a
> present for you.

Roger crouches down next to the busker. He
reaches into the top pocket of his shirt and
brings out a small bundle that looks like a
length of cheese wire that's been folded over
several times.

> ROGER
> To replace your missing string.

> (reaching for the ukulele)
> May I?

Roger gently takes the ukulele from the man's hands. He threads the new string on to the fret board and tightens it using the pegs on the neck of the instrument. He then plucks and tightens each of the strings in turn. When he's satisfied, he passes the now-tuned ukulele back to the busker.

> ROGER
> We'll have you playing 'Stairway to Heaven' by the end of the year!

> BUSKER
> Thanks, man. You're a real gent.

The busker resumes his now more tuneful strumming. Roger continues on his way across the bridge.

EXT—SOUTH BANK—NEAR THE THAMES—MORNING

We see Roger entering a COFFEE BAR just along from the old County Hall.

EXT—LONDON SOUTH BANK—QUEUE FOR THE LONDON EYE—MIDDAY

We see a long, snaking queue of people who are waiting to go on The London Eye. There are groups of tourists and groups of schoolchildren. There are visitors from overseas and young parents with toddlers and pushchairs.

Every so often the queue shuffles forward.

An ELDERLY COUPLE, both wearing stout walking shoes, knee-length checked shorts, Timberland shirts straining over wide girths, and broad-brimmed Stetsons, are CHATTING loudly. The woman is holding a bucket-sized cold drink container. The man's most noticeable feature is a mane of white hair and a luxuriant beard, not unlike Colonel Sanders's.

In front of the elderly couple we see the only smartly dressed businessman waiting for The London Eye. It's Roger.

INT—LONDON SOUTH BANK—PASSENGER POD ON THE LONDON EYE—MIDDAY

Finally, Roger is at the front of the queue for The London Eye. He gets into the passenger pod, removes his jacket, and places it on one of the benches in the middle.

He opens his briefcase and removes a pair of binoculars and a slim book that we see has the title *London 360*. He chooses the east window and raises his binoculars to his eyes. He opens the book and makes a few notes.

As the pod slowly rises, St Paul's Cathedral appears. Roger turns slightly to his right. Tower 42 comes into view.

BUD, the elderly man we saw just behind Roger in the queue for The Eye, approaches him.

> BUD
> (with a Southern American accent)
> Excuse me, son, can I ask you a question?

Roger looks round quickly.

> ROGER
> (laughing)
> No one's called me son in over 30
> years! How can I help?

> BUD
> Can you point out London Bridge to me?

> ROGER
> (pointing through the window)
> Certainly. It's the third bridge
> in that group of three: there's
> Blackfriars, Southwark, and then
> London Bridge.

Roger offers the man his binoculars.

> ROGER
> Here, would you like to borrow these?

> BUD
> (taking the binoculars)
> Gee thanks son.

Bud stands looking along the Thames. After a few
moments he turns from the window and towards
the near identically dressed woman that we saw
him with outside. She's facing in the opposite
direction on the other side of the pod.

> BUD
> (loudly)
> Hey Sherry-Lou, come take a look.

The elderly woman turns, then hurries over.

                    BUD cont'd
                 (to Roger)
This is Sherry-Lou. And I'm Bud.

                    ROGER
Hi, I'm Roger.

                    BUD
                 (passing the woman Roger's
                 binoculars)
Look along the river, honey, it's that
third bridge. Do you see it?

                    SHERRY-LOU
Yeah, I got it.

                    BUD
It's quite different from the real
one, ain't it, honey?

                    SHERRY-LOU
Sure is.

                    ROGER
What do you mean, 'the real one'?

                    BUD
The real London Bridge. Here look.

He reaches into his inside pocket and brings out
a photograph. It shows a magnificent Victorian
bridge with four arches that cross a river that
could easily be the Thames, but clearly isn't.

                    BUD
That's the real London Bridge in Lake
Havasu, our hometown. It was falling
down. You know, like in the nursery
rhyme.

Anyhow, it needed replacing or repairing. You guys decided to replace it, and this guy called McCulloch bought it in the early Sixties. He shipped it over to Arizona and rebuilt it. Brick by brick.

      ROGER
That vaguely rings a bell. Remind me: Why did he buy it?

      BUD
For the money, son, why else! He figured he could turn it into a tourist attraction.

      ROGER
Did it work?

      BUD
Sure did. Fact, we wouldn't be here without it. Your London Bridge put Lake Havasu on the map real good. We had a big ol' ranch in the middle of nowhere in which we built a 150-room hotel and turned our 80 acres into London Village. We never have an empty room.

      ROGER
So business is good.

      BUD
Good? You betcha. This is the first vacation we've allowed ourselves in over 20 years. Although you could call it a bit of a working holiday.

                    ROGER
I see. I thought you might be retired.

                    BUD
Not a bit of it. We've made a fortune
so far, but we're not done yet, are
we Sherr?

He glances at his wife.

                    BUD cont'd
No, sir. We're always on the lookout for
new ideas and business opportunities.
Thought we'd come over to this side of
the pond for some inspiration. Can't
beat a bit of first-hand exposure. And
we love what we've seen so far.

We're looking to add some authenticity
to our London. We've got your bridge,
so we thought we'd see if we can buy
some of your culture too.

                    SHERRY-LOU
          (interrupting Bud and Roger's shop
          talk)
Hey, honey, which way's Buck House?

                    ROGER
Buckingham Palace you can see from
the other side of the pod. But not
just yet. At the moment it's blocked
by the Houses of Parliament.

Roger points towards Big Ben.

                    ROGER
Look, why don't I walk you both through
the sites on this side of the pod,

and then I'll point out Buckingham
Palace, Horse Guards' Parade, and The
Mall when the pod gets to the top.

                SHERRY-LOU
Gee, that'd be great, honey.

                BUD
Are you sure you don't mind, son?

                ROGER
Not at all. I'm here for the view just
as much as you are.

**INT—LONDON SOUTH BANK—PASSENGER POD ON THE
LONDON EYE—15 MINUTES LATER**

                ROGER
. . . and there's Westminster, the
seat of the British Parliament. You'll
notice it's only a short walk from
Downing Street, where successive PMs
live. Nowhere near as impressive as
your White House though.

If you walk along the river on this
side this evening, you'll get a
beautiful view of the building across
the water from a nice bar called the
Piano and Pitcher – a great photo
opportunity.

                BUD
                (chuckling)
The Piano and Pitcher, was that? I
didn't realise you guys had baseball
here.

Roger looks round at Bud and sees that Bud has been making notes in a small pocketbook.

> BUD
> Thought I'd plan out our itinerary for later. Your commentary's been great. Hope you don't mind.

> ROGER
> Not at all. And that's 'pitcher' as in water jug, not . . .

> BUD
> I know, son. I'm just playing with you.

> SHERRY-LOU
> (handing Roger the binoculars)
> Hey, honey, is that an Inspector Morse car driving across the bridge?

Roger starts scanning the cars moving across Westminster Bridge.

> SHERRY-LOU
> We get Morse on Channel 59, don't we Bud? We love it. Nothing like our cop shows.

> ROGER
> You're absolutely right. It's a maroon Jaguar MK 2. I have one myself. And if I'm not mistaken, it's a '63, just like mine. When it moves forward I'll see if I can read its number plate. Yup, it's an A reg—that makes it a '63: R O G 1 5 A . . .

Roger's voice trails away as he reads off the Jag's number plate.

>   BUD
>   Are you all right, son? You look a
>   little pale.

>   ROGER
>   That **is** my car.

>   BUD
>   That Jag?

>   ROGER
>   Yes, it is. I bought it about a month
>   ago. But it should be on my driveway
>   at home, not heading towards the old
>   County Hall. I think someone's stolen
>   my car.

INT—LONDON SOUTH BANK—PASSENGER POD ON THE LONDON EYE—5 MINUTES LATER

By now the wheel has almost completed its circuit, and the other passengers in the pod are gathering together their belongings and preparing to disembark.

>   BUD
>   Let's go for a drink, and we can help
>   you decide the best thing to do.

>   ROGER
>   I wouldn't want to impose. I'm sure
>   you've got plenty of other items on
>   your itinerary.

                    BUD
Not at all. You've been so generous
with your time. It's the least we can
do.

INT—SOUTH BANK—COFFEE BAR NEAR WESTMINSTER BRIDGE—MIDDAY

ROGER, BUD, SHERRY-LOU are in a COFFEE BAR
close to Westminster Bridge. The coffee bar is
very full, and they are perched on high stools
at a narrow table near the window. They are
discussing Roger's options.

                    BUD
Are you sure it was your number plate?

                    ROGER
Absolutely.

                    BUD
And the Jag's supposed to be at home
on your driveway?

                    ROGER
Exactly. My wife drops me off at the
station each morning in her car. I
only drive it at the weekend. Caroline
never does. She's not that keen on it
to be honest.

                    BUD
You should call your wife. See if
she knows it's missing. Maybe she's
already reported it to the police.

                    ROGER
                    (hesitating)

That could be a bit awkward . . . You
see, I shouldn't really be here.

        SHERRY-LOU
        (suddenly paying attention to the
        conversation)
No?

        BUD
Where should you be, son?

        ROGER
My wife thinks I'm at work.

        BUD
Everyone's entitled to a little time
off.

        ROGER
You don't understand. It's not quite
that simple.

        SHERRY-LOU
I sense a little scandal going on
here. A little lunchtime intrigue, eh?

        ROGER
I wish that's all it was. It's way
worse than that.

        SHERRY-LOU
Now you've got me really interested.

        ROGER
Well, thing is, I was made redundant.
Two weeks ago.

BUD
That's nothing to be ashamed of, son.
Happens to the best of us.

SHERRY-LOU
I'm sure you'll get yourself sorted
pretty quick.

ROGER
Yes and no. There's more. I've been,
I suppose you could say, living a
double life.

SHERRY-LOU
This gets better and better.

BUD
Shhhh, Sher! Let the man go on.

ROGER
Well, Caroline thinks I'm 'something
in the City'. A nebulous term for a
whizz with figures and an aptitude
for deals. A money maker, a mover and
shaker.

BUD
And you're not?

ROGER
Nope. Never was. I'm something in the
City, or at least I was, but not what
she thought I was. I had a career in
banking, but I was no wunderkind.

I joined Barclays Bank in Threadneedle
Street 20 years ago. I was on a career
path that could have led to middle

management if I'd put a little effort in, but I preferred to remain a clerk.

I love . . . loved . . . doing the same mundane tasks each day. I like to go for a walk for an hour each lunch. Some days I cross over London Bridge and stroll along the river towards Tower Bridge, on others I walk up to Westminster.

Some days I see the latest exhibitions at the Tate. During the summer I like to catch the events at the New Globe.

But making money hand-over-fist? That was never me.

> SHERRY-LOU
> What about that nice car of yours? How'd you afford that?

> ROGER
> I loved the car the minute I saw it, especially the price! But it's not everything it at first seems: superficially, it's Morse's car. But mine's a '63, not a '60. It's maroon instead of burgundy, and it's a 2.4 litre engine instead of 3.4.

> SHERRY-LOU
> And that all makes a difference?

> ROGER
> Makes the difference between a £40,000 plus car, and the 8 grand I paid for mine. And the car is just one of the

small white lies I've been living for years.

Roger is silent for a few moments. He stares out the window at the passing traffic. He seems to be trying to decide whether to go on.

> ROGER
> It's like this: A combination of a heavily subsidised staff mortgage and an unexpected inheritance from a maiden aunt gave me a considerable leg up the property ladder just before a major explosion in house prices.
>
> My large five-bedroom detached property on the outskirts of Tunbridge Wells suggested I must be someone with a successful City career. This was the impression that Caroline got when I met her 15 years ago.

> SHERRY-LOU
> I take it impressions are important to your wife.

> ROGER
> Correct. She's from a good family, 15 years younger than me, and a real stunner. We met on a river boat trip to Windsor Castle organised by the Runnymede Conservatives. I couldn't believe my luck when she agreed to marry me.
>
> Problem was that when we first met, I accidentally deceived her about the nature of my work. I said that I worked in the bank and was in charge

of security. It made my job sound
more interesting. At the time I was
working in the Property department,
and one of my regular tasks was to
test the fire alarms of the properties
in which the bank had an interest.

So it was security that I was
responsible for. But, Caroline thought
I meant Head of Securities.

          BUD
Ah!

          ROGER
Ah indeed. Such a job would explain
where I lived, and that I could afford
several classic cars.

It was not until I proposed to
Caroline four weeks later that I
realised her misconception. By then
it was too late. She'd told her family
and friends about what a catch I was.
I thought telling the truth then
would make me look a fraud. I thought
Caroline would be put off and run a
mile.

Besides, I rather liked people's
reaction when they thought I had an
important job in the City.

          SHERRY-LOU
I see your problem, honey, but you
can't keep living a lie.

                    ROGER
I know that only too well.

The bank's redundancy policy is to
keep the essential managers, the
younger members of staff, and those
with good IT skills. I didn't qualify
on any criteria.

At the age of 52 I'm too young for
early retirement and too old for
retraining. For years I've been
supplementing my inadequate salary by
dipping into my life's savings and the
remains of my aunt's inheritance. But
that won't last long as the family's
sole income. I need a new job, and
soon.

For the last two weeks I've continued
to leave home every morning, come to
London at the same time as usual, and
then spend the day in various coffee
bars scouring the appointments pages
of every paper that I can find.

                    BUD
But no luck so far?

                    ROGER
No. There are too many young,
thrusting, and ambitious candidates
competing for all financial jobs. An
old fossil like me doesn't stand a
chance.

I've been dreading telling Caroline.
When I do, the whole truth will come
out.

                    BUD
And getting back to your car: You
only know about it because you were
on the Ferris wheel, and what's a top
executive doing on the London Eye in
the middle of the day when he should
be mixing it in the boardroom, or
forging the next deal?

                    ROGER
Aye, there's the rub!

Roger looks out the window and sighs.

                    ROGER cont'd
To phone, or not to phone? You're
right, Sherry-Lou, I've gotta bite the
bullet and get this done.

Roger reaches inside his jacket and removes his
mobile phone. He looks at his watch.

                    ROGER cont'd
She won't have left for Barbara's yet.

He dials his home number.

                    ROGER
              (to the phone)
Hi, darling it's me. I want to ask
about the Jag . . .

              (pausing as his wife responds, but
              we can't hear her words)
You did? Just now?

              (beat)
No, I don't mind at all.

> (beat)
> I was just going to say . . . oh, it's
> nothing. I'll see you later

Roger puts the phone back in his jacket pocket.

> ROGER
> That's strange. The car's still on the
> drive. Caroline had to move it a few
> minutes ago so that a delivery man
> could turn his truck around.

Sherry-Lou suddenly points out the window.

> SHERRY-LOU
> (tapping on the window and nudging
> her husband with her elbow)
> Hey, isn't that it?

Roger and Bud look out the window. We see a
maroon Jaguar with the number plate ROG 15A
driving back across Westminster Bridge.

> SHERRY-LOU cont'd
> Come on, let's get after it!

Roger and Bud turn round simultaneously and
see that Sherry- Lou is already heading for the
exit.

**EXT—SOUTH BANK—OUTSIDE COFFEE BAR NEAR THE
LONDON EYE—MIDDAY**

Sherry-Lou rushes out of the coffee bar quickly,
followed by Roger and Bud. All three stop at the
edge of the pavement facing towards Big Ben,
studying the traffic.

There are lots of people on the bridge. There are two ice cream vans both with crowds waiting patiently. There are loads of amateur photographers trying to get that memorable shot. There are several bicycle rickshaws touting for business.

The traffic is slow moving in both directions in the two centre lanes. The outer bus lanes are virtually empty. Then we see the Jag nearly at the end of the bridge. It is moving slowly but gradually getting further away.

Roger looks about ready to run after it. He's holding his briefcase and offers it to Bud. Before he can say anything, Sherry-Lou stops him by placing her hand on his arm.

>   SHERRY-LOU
> You'll never catch him on foot. Soon as you get close, the lights'll change and he'll be off. Even if you do get close, all he'll see is some loon chasing after him. He's not gonna stop and ask why. He's just gonna take off.

>   ROGER
> What do you suggest then?

At that moment, Sherry-Lou spots a BLACK LONDON TAXICAB moving slowly towards them. She starts waving frantically. The taxi moves swiftly into the bus lane and drives quickly towards them overtaking several cars on their inside and nearly taking out cyclist in the process. It pulls up right in front of them.

Sherry-Lou clambers into the back quickly, followed by Bud and Roger.

INT—NEAR WESTMINSTER BRIDGE—BLACK TAXICAB

Roger unfolds the seat behind driver and so is now facing Bud and Sherry-Lou, who are sitting on the back seat.

> SHERRY-LOU
> (laughing)
> Follow that car. I've always wanted to say something like that.

> BUD
> Gee, this is exciting.

> ROGER
> (turning to speak through the grill to the taxi driver)
> Did you spot that old maroon Jag that just went over bridge?

> TAXI DRIVER
> The Morse car? Yeah, I clocked that, she's a beaut!

> ROGER
> I need to speak to the driver, but I don't know where he's going. Could you follow her?

Before Roger can even finish his sentence, the taxi driver is already doing a U-turn, forcing the two lanes of traffic to allow him through. Several drivers sound their HORNS in annoyance.

> TAXI DRIVER
> No problem, mate. I love a challenge!

EXT—SOUTH BANK—ON WESTMINSTER BRIDGE

He moves the taxi into the bus lane and starts passing on the left-hand side, the now-stationary line of traffic that has now been stopped by red lights at the far side of the bridge. By the time lights go green, the taxi has caught up quite well, but is still about four cars back and is now stuck behind a bus letting on passengers.

Up ahead the Jag appears to be preparing to go round Parliament square, so the taxi has to move out into the right-hand lane.

INT—NEAR THE EAST SIDE OF WESTMINSTER ABBEY— BLACK TAXICAB

> ROGER
> (to Bud and Sherry-Lou, acting as an impromptu tour guide as the taxi pursues the maroon Jag)

The statue on the corner is of the late, great Nelson Mandela. One-time freedom fighter-turned-politician, and probably the best president South Africa will ever have.

And on your left, you'll see one of your greatest presidents: Abraham Lincoln.

The taxi turns left into Birdcage Walk.

> ROGER

We're now passing St James's Park. Nice place for a walk.

EXT—OUTSIDE BUCKINGHAM PALACE

The taxi is now nearing Constitution Hill.

INT—OUTSIDE BUCKINGHAM PALACE—BLACK TAXICAB

>   ROGER
>   (touching Sherry-Lou gently on the
>   knee)
> If you look over to your left now,
> you'll see we're about to go right
> past Buckingham Palace.

>   SHERRY-LOU
> Wow! I didn't realise we'd be able to
> get that close!

>   ROGER
> That road to the right is The Mall, it
> will take you to Trafalgar Square and
> our other Nelson.

INT—APPROACHING HYDE PARK CORNER—BLACK TAXICAB

>   TAXI DRIVER
> Looks like he's heading towards Hyde
> Park.

>   ROGER
>   (to Bud and Sherry-Lou)
> On the roundabout, you'll see
> memorials to our war heroes: there's
> one for the soldiers serving in the
> Royal Artillery and the Animals
> in War memorial for our furry and
> feathered friends who died serving in
> the British Military.

                    SHERRY-LOU
You Brits sure love your animals.

                    BUD
                (laughing)
We're more likely to shoot 'em than
salute 'em.

EXT—HYDE PARK CORNER

The taxi is exiting the Hyde Park Corner
roundabout heading north on the dual carriage
past the east side of the park.

INT—HYDE PARK CORNER—BLACK TAXICAB

                    ROGER
. . . and now into Park Lane. We're
heading along the left side of Mayfair
at the moment.

                    SHERRY-LOU
Park Lane and **Mayfair,** as in Monopoly?

                    ROGER
Correct.

                    SHERRY-LOU
Cool.

EXT—MARBLE ARCH ROUNDABOUT

We see the Jag turning left to take the Bayswater
Road that runs along the north side of Hyde Park.

                    ROGER
Up ahead are Marble Arch and Speakers
Corner, and once the site of the Tyburn
gallows used for public hangings.

                    BUD
And I thought it was tough in The
House - at least we don't execute the
speakers we disagree with.

INT—ON BAYSWATER ROAD—BLACK TAXICAB

                    ROGER
That's Lancaster Gate, former home of
the FA.

                    BUD
Controllers of your style of football,
right?

                    ROGER
Right.

INT—NEAR NOTTING HILL GATE—BLACK TAXICAB

The taxi is now passing the west gate of Hyde
Park.

                    ROGER
To your left, that's Kensington Palace,
which I'm sure you've heard of.

                    SHERRY-LOU
Oh yes. Princess Di's old home. Where
the little princes grew up.

                    ROGER
There's a fountain to her memory you
might like to find in the park later.

                    SHERRY-LOU
Sure would love to see that.

                    ROGER
To your right is Notting Hill—made
famous by Hugh Grant.

                    BUD
          (chuckling)
Who himself was made famous by Divine
Brown down on Sunset.

                    SHERRY-LOU
          (digging her husband in the ribs)
Shush, Bud.

                    ROGER
To the left we have Holland Park,
two of your countrywomen have lived
there: Ruby Wax and Madonna. In fact,
Ms Wax may still.

EXT—SW1A—APPROACHING SHEPHERD'S BUSH ROUNDABOUT

The Jag can be seen up ahead approaching the
Shepherds' Bush roundabout and signalling right
on to Wood Lane.

INT—ON THE SHEPHERD'S BUSH ROUNDABOUT—BLACK TAXICAB

                    ROGER
We're now heading towards White City.

                    TAXI DRIVER
Looks like he's turning into the old
Television Centre, mate.

                    ROGER
               (to the driver)
Can you stop just there? This is
probably as far as we want to go all
together.

               (to Bud and Sherry-Lou)
I think I'd better try to sort this
out for myself. Enjoy the rest of your
trip to London.

Roger gets out of the cab and gives the driver
a fifty-pound note through the window.

                    ROGER
               (to the taxi driver)
Can you drop them off outside the
Royal Albert Hall?

               (to Bud and Sherry-Lou)
You can enter Hyde Park from there.
Head towards the Serpentine, the big
lake in the middle, and you'll get to
Di's fountain. There's a cafe that way
too, good for an afternoon cuppa.

                    BUD
          (handing Roger a business card
          through the window)
Thanks for the guided tour, son. It's
been a blast. Look us up if you're ever
in Havasu and want to visit London
Village.

                    ROGER
I'll do that.

Roger gives him one of his cards in return.
Sherry-Lou waves to him through the back window
as the taxi moves off.

**EXT—SHEPHERD'S BUSH—SIDE ROAD OFF WOOD LANE—
EARLY AFTERNOON**

Roger walks round the corner and sees the car
parked outside the office of a company called
INTERNATIONAL INSURANCE INVESTIGATIONS.

He walks slowly round the car.

                    ROGER
          (muttering quietly to himself)
Everything's identical: same
colour, same upholstery, same trim.
Everything.

Roger runs his hand slowly over the bonnet of
the car.

                    ROGER
          (muttering)
No dent. And the crack in the bumper's
gone.

STANLEY JACKSON AND GAVIN JACKSON

Roger squats next to the front axle and places his hand lightly on the bonnet. Lowering his head almost to the ground level, he looks along the underside of the car.

> ROGER
> (muttering)
> Nice to see I'm not the only person to have problem with the sills.

A male VOICE behind him makes Roger stand up quickly.

> MAN
> Can I help you, mate?

> ROGER
> (turning round)
> I'm sorry. Couldn't resist a look. I've always loved the 1963 MK 2, 2.4 litre, manual plus overdrive, 132 brake horsepower. And in maroon . . .

> MAN
> Burgundy.

> ROGER
> Pardon?

> MAN
> The colour's burgundy like Morse's. Not maroon.

> ROGER
> Is it?

Roger spins round quickly to peer closely at the paint work.

                    ROGER
              (turning back to the man)
Burgundy. Maroon. Whatever. Prettiest
Jag ever made.

                    MAN
Yeah, sweet, ain't it. It's not for
sale though, mate.

                    ROGER
Oh, I don't want to buy it . . . again.

                    MAN
You a comedian? What do ya mean
'again'?

                    ROGER
Look, is this your office?

                    MAN
It is.

                    ROGER
Could we discuss this inside?

The man looks at his watch.

                    MAN
If you like. I've got a few minutes
before my next meeting.

Roger follows the man into the building.

INT—SHEPHERD'S BUSH—OFFICE OF INTERNATIONAL INSURANCE INVESTIGATIONS

The office is plush without being opulent. There is an array of FILING CABINETS, PRINTERS, SCANNERS and a DRINKS DISPENSER. Mounted on the wall over a large desk are three CLOCKS showing different times. The clocks are labelled New York, Tokyo, and Loftus Road. On the desk is a COMPUTER KEYBOARD, a MONITOR, and a TELEPHONE.

CARL, the man Roger met outside, closes the door behind Roger. Roger offers his hand for shaking.

>   ROGER
> Roger Marshall, how do you do?

>   CARL
> Carl Stuart. So what do you think we
> need to discuss?

Carl walks round to the far side of his desk and sits down. He indicates a chair on the other side. Roger sits down.

>   CARL
> So, Mr Marshall, what do you think we
> need to discuss?

>   ROGER
> I have the exact same car.

>   CARL
> I'm not interested in joining the
> Jaguar owners' club if that's what
> you're after. You a rep or something?

                    ROGER
No, I mean I have the **exact** same car.
With the same number plate. Sitting
on my driveway in Tonbridge Wells. I
paid £8000, in cash, only six weeks
ago.

                    CARL
What are you suggesting?

                    ROGER
I'm suggesting that one of our cars
is a fake.

                    CARL
I see.

Carl is silent for a few moments. He looks Roger
in the eye but says nothing. Finally he leans
forward on his chair, his elbows on the desk.

                    CARL
Let me tell you what my company does,
Mr Marshall. We investigate write-
off claims and ensure that those
cars written off are disposed of
appropriately. Let me assure you,
there is no way that a car we own is
a fake.

                    ROGER
Well, one of our cars is a fake.

                    CARL
Will you excuse me for a few minutes?

Carl turns to his computer and punches a few
keys. A printer in the corner springs to life.
He walks over to it and consults the printout.

Carl then walks over to one of the filing cabinets and removes a file. He returns to his desk. He picks up the phone and dials a number.

> CARL
> Tom? Carl here. Slight problem with one of the motors. The burgundy Jag.

Carl listens to a reply that we can't hear.

> CARL
> Yes, the Morse special. Looks like there might have been a double-up.

Carl makes a few notes on the printout.

> CARL
> Very embarrassing, I know.

Carl listens again for longer this time.

> CARL
> No, I can't right now. The owner's with me.
> (beat)
> Yeah, that could work.

Carl puts the phone down.

> CARL
> (sounding a little less sure of himself than before)
> It would appear that your car is a fake. A fact that you must have been aware of from the very low price you paid for it.

                    ROGER
I wouldn't say that low.

                    CARL
Come, come, Mr Marshall. I think we
both know the score.

                    ROGER
I bought it in good faith. It's far
from perfect, but I thought it would
make a good weekend project. Paperwork
all appeared in order.

                    CARL
Of course you did, of course you did.

Look, I have some good news for you.
I am instructed to make you an offer,
Mr Marshall. It would appear that
there was a . . .

                    (beat)
minor administrative error. A question
of internal procedures not having
been adhered to at this end. The car
you bought should not have been made
available for resale. We are willing
to offer you what you paid for it.

                    ROGER
What? Why would you want to pay me for
a car that your company wrote off? If
what you say is true, its only worth
is as a donor car for spares.

                    CARL
Let's just call it a goodwill gesture.

                    ROGER
Goodwill gesture? All you need to
do is to get the police to compare
the chassis numbers on both cars and
cross-check it with your paperwork.
This would verify that mine has been
recycled illegally, and then I would
be forced to have it destroyed. You
wouldn't have to pay a penny.

Carl sits back in his chair.

                    CARL
You're a shrewd man, Mr Marshall.

                    ROGER
I am?

                    CARL
We both know you are.

Both men sit regarding each other silently.
Finally, Carl glances at his watch.

                    CARL
OK, let's cut the crap, Marshall. I'm
a busy man. 10 grand's as high as
we'll go on this. I'll even send one
of the boys round with a flatbed to
pick it up for you at the weekend. Is
it a deal?

                    ROGER
          (sounding somewhat surprised)
I can live with that.

Roger stands up, and the two mean seal the deal
with a handshake.

INT—CHARING CROSS STATION—SECOND CLASS CARRIAGE—LATE AFTERNOON

Roger is in a carriage waiting for the train to depart. The train is slowly filling up with COMMUTERS. As yet, no one is sitting near Roger.

Roger has his BRIEFCASE open on his lap. From it, he removes today's *London Evening Standard*. He opens it and turns to the classified advertisements towards the back.

Something in the newspaper catches his eye. He folds the paper back over on itself and removes a highlighter pen from briefcase. He draws a circle around an advert and reaches for his mobile phone. He looks more closely at the advert and dials a number.

> ROGER
> (talking into his phone)
> Hi, my name's Roger Marshall. I'm calling about your ad in the *Standard*. . . . Yes, that's right: Necropolis Tours.

Roger listens to his phone for a few moments as other passengers board the train and walk past him to find a seat.

> ROGER
> Yes, I know London very well. Like the back of my hand you might say. I've been working in Central London for nearly 20 years. . . . Yes that's right, 20 years . . .

Roger loosens his tie a little.

> ROGER cont'd
> Er 52 . . . 23k . . . I see.
> No, no, I'm still interested . . . Yes,
> I can be in London on Friday.

Roger ends the call and sighs. He returns the phone to his briefcase. He then refolds the newspaper and places it in the briefcase alongside the binoculars that we saw him with earlier. He closes the briefcase and places it on the seat next to him. He folds his arms and watches out of the window, and the remaining passengers on the platform hurry on the train.

> PLATFORM ANNOUNCER (O.S.)
> This is a Thameslink train to Hastings calling at Waterloo East, Orpington, Sevenoaks . . .

INT—CHARING CROSS STATION—SECOND-CLASS CARRIAGE—FIFTEEN MINUTES LATER

The train has left Charing Cross station and passed through Waterloo East. Through the window we see the Kent countryside rushing by.

Roger is staring out the window.

> ROGER (V.O.)
> (rehearsing in his head his later
> conversation with his wife)
> Caroline, I've got some good news and some bad news. Too flippant.

> Caroline, I've got some news to tell you about my job. Too serious. She'll know something's up immediately.

                    TICKET COLLECTOR
          Tickets please!

Roger absentmindedly reaches into his inside
pocket and hands the ticket collector his
driver's license.

                    TICKET COLLECTOR
                    (peering closely at the driver's
                    license)
          Thank you, Mr Marshall. Nice picture,
          but it was your ticket I was more
          interested in.

                    ROGER
                    (now a little flustered)
          Sorry about that.

Roger reaches back into his inside pocket. This
time he hands over his Osyter Card.

                    TICKET COLLECTOR
          That's better, sir. Thank you.

The ticket collector continues his walk down
the train.

                    TICKET COLLECTOR (O.S.)
          Tickets please!

The train is slowing. Roger looks out the window.
We see the train has arrived at Tonbridge.
Several passengers are getting out. Roger
remains seated. The train moves off again.

                    ROGER (V.O.)
          Where was I? What to say to Caroline.

Caroline, Caroline, Caroline.

                    ROGER (V.O.)
Start with the car perhaps. Caroline,
I thought I'd get rid of the car. Oh,
and by the way, I'm not the man you
thought I am. I've been living a lie
for the last 15 years.

Too much of a shock. But I've got to
be honest. Tell it to her straight.

                    ROGER (V.O.)
               (smiling to himself)
I'm getting rid of the car. I've got
rid of my job. You'd better play your
cards right, because you could be
next.

                    JANE
You're very quiet this evening, Roger?

Roger visible jumps. He looks round quickly. He
notices that he's been joined in the carriage by
someone he knows.

                    ROGER
Oh, hi, Jane. Didn't notice you there.

                    JANE
Charming.

                    ROGER
Sorry. Didn't mean to be rude. Miles
away.

                    JANE
You're not kidding! What's the joke?

                    ROGER
Joke?

                    JANE
Well, something made you grin like a
Cheshire cat. You could of course be
losing the plot. I'm giving you the
benefit of the doubt here!

                    ROGER
It's nothing. I've just got a lot on
my mind.

                    JANE
Anything I can help you with?

                    ROGER
Oh no, no. Just something I've got to
get straight in my head.

                    JANE
Often helps to talk, you know. It
might not seem so big if you talk
about it.

                    ROGER
          (hesitating)
Oh, what the hell, why not.

                    JANE
Don't let me bully you into it.

                    ROGER
No, no. You'll do.

                    JANE
Gee thanks. I'm rapidly considering
changing my mind.

                    ROGER
You're a woman, right?

                    JANE
Your powers of observation do you
credit, Mr Holmes!

                    ROGER
What I meant was . . .

                    JANE
I know what you meant. You want a
woman's perspective on your problem.

                    ROGER
Well, yes.

                    JANE
Right. Fire away.

                    ROGER
OK. Suppose you're a woman . . .

                    JANE
Yup. Got that down pat!

                    ROGER
. . . and your husband/boyfriend has
got some news . . .

                    JANE
And it's not exactly good news?

                    ROGER
No. Well, I mean it's kind of . . .
No, it's not really very good news. I
mean, it will all turn out all right
in the end, but . . .

                    JANE
But, right now, it's not too good?

                    ROGER
          Correct.

                    JANE
          Well, I'd want to know it all. No
          matter how bad.

                    ROGER
                    (sounding doubtful)
          Really? Everything?

                    JANE
          Everything. But I'd want a little
          sugar-coating too.

                    ROGER
          What?

                    JANE
          Don't just blurt it out. Soften her up
          a little first.

                    ROGER
                    (quietly, almost to himself)
          Hmm, soften her up a little. Flowers
          perhaps?

                    JANE
          Do you normally buy her flowers?

          Roger thinks a little before answering.

                    ROGER
          Valentine's Day, or er . . .

                    JANE
          Not flowers then.

          ROGER
Not flowers?

          JANE
If you don't often bring home flowers,
and then you bring home flowers
when it's not Valentine's Day or her
birthday, she'll think you're having
an affair.

You're not having an affair, are you?

          ROGER
No, no. Of course not.

          JANE
Well, think of something else, and
think fast!

          ROGER
Fast, why?

          JANE
'Cos we're coming into to Tunbridge
Wells right now.

INT—ROGER MARSHALL'S HOUSE—KITCHEN—EVENING

Roger has just arrived home. Caroline is cooking.

          ROGER
You know, I think I ought to get rid
of the Jag.

          CAROLINE
Oh, thank God.

                    ROGER
               (slightly taken aback)
          Sorry?

                    CAROLINE
          I didn't want to say anything because
          I know you love it, but . . . well,
          it is a bit of an eyesore, isn't it?

                    ROGER
          Eyesore?

                    CAROLINE
          Yeah. And the exhaust does stink
          rather. I'm not surprised that people
          stare at us when we stop at lights.

                    ROGER
               (sounding affronted)
          I think that's admiration.

                    CAROLINE
          Do you think you'll get your money
          back on it?

                    ROGER
          I've already sold it. For two grand
          more than I paid for it.

                    CAROLINE
               (stopping what's she's doing briefly)
          Really? Wow, one born every minute I
          guess. Pass me that courgette, will
          you?

Caroline continues the preparation of the
ratatouille.

                    ROGER
          Darling, I've got something to tell
          you. It's about my job.

Before he can say anything further he is
interrupted by the telephone ringing. Caroline
answers it.

                    CAROLINE
          It's for you, darling.

Caroline passes Roger the cordless phone.

                    BUD
               (voice off camera)
          Hey, Roger, this is Bud, how're you
          doin'?

Roger takes the phone into his home office and
sits down at his desk.

                    ROGER
          Hi, Bud. I've only just got back in.

                    BUD
          Did you get your car sorted out in
          the end?

                    ROGER
          Yes, I did. Mine turned out to be a
          ringer.

                    BUD
          Ringer?

                    ROGER

          Yeah, a ringer, . . . a er, a fake.
          But I got a little compensation. The

guy's even going to come round at the weekend to pick it up and dispose of it for me.

                    BUD
That's great. Hey listen, son, I've got a business proposition for you. Do you wanna hear it?

                    ROGER
Sure.

                    BUD
We've been thinking of trying a new tourist angle: We get a lot of rich retired folk visiting Havasu in the winter. They drive their Winnebagos down from the North and stay with us for several months. They have time on their hands and tourist dollars to spend. They're a captive audience that needs entertaining.

                    ROGER
          (sounding uncertain)
I see.

                    BUD
Well, our little adventure earlier got me thinking: 'Designer Tours of London' - a special service we'll offer to our wealthiest guests. It'll be a three- to four-day flying visit to your nation's capital tailored to their tastes.

At your end, you arrange for someone to pick them up from the airport and take them to their hotel and then

consult with them to find out their
likes and dislikes, then arrange
their personalised tour for them.

They'll have the consultant with them
whenever they need chauffeuring,
making reservations, suggesting shows
to go to, all that sort of thing.

> ROGER
> It sounds good. Really good. I'd go on
> a trip like that.

> BUD
> You won't have time, son! You'll be too
> busy being the Executive Consultant.
> We'll supply the customers, and you'll
> supply the local knowledge. I've even
> thought of a slogan: London. You've
> seen the Theme Park, now experience
> the real thing. What do you think of
> the idea in principle?

> ROGER
> (sounding really excited now)
> Well, yes. Yes I'd love to.

> BUD
> Let's get together later in the week
> before we fly home to talk through
> the details.

> ROGER
> That'd be great.

Roger puts the phone down.

Caroline looks up as Roger walks back into the
kitchen. Roger leans on the kitchen counter

staring out the window, now seemingly distracted by his thoughts.

                    CAROLINE
          So?

                    ROGER
               (turning round quickly)
          What?

                    CAROLINE
          So what was the other news that you
          had? About your job.

                    ROGER
          Oh yes, that. I've just been offered a
          partnership.

Smiling broadly, Roger hugs his wife tightly.

                                   FADE OUT

UPON REFLECTION

By

Gavin Jackson

INT—WOKING—BARRY'S OFFICE—MORNING

BARRY MASON is in his office working. From the clock on the wall we can see it's late morning. He is casually dressed in jeans, a thick jumper, and Dr Martens boots. He is clean-shaven and has short, but not closely cropped, hair.

He is sitting at a desk with the architect's plans for a house extension laid out before him. He has written on various Post-it notes and stuck them on the plans, but the plans themselves are free of handwritten annotations.

There are two other desks in the room. Both are clear except for a computer screen, in-tray, telephone, and desk tidy.

There are several coat hooks near the door. One holds an overcoat and a blue-and-white scarf, the others are empty. It's obvious that no one else is around.

Barry is talking on the phone to a POTENTIAL CLIENT.

> BARRY
> Yes, Luv, that's the best I can do for you.

> POTENTIAL CLIENT (O.S.)
> It was a lot more than I was expecting.

> BARRY
> Quality costs, Luv, I'm afraid.

                    POTENTIAL CLIENT (O.S.)
Are there any savings that we can
make on materials?

                    BARRY
Well, there are shortcuts that some
builders might be willin' to make,
but that's not somefink that I do.

                    (beat)
Look, you've got your copy of the
plans there. Go away and fink about
it. Take 'em to another builder for a
quote if you want to.

                    POTENTIAL CLIENT(O.S.)
What about the cost of the plans
themselves?

                    BARRY
As I said when we met, our first step
is always to get our architect to
produce a first draft of the plans,
and if we don't end up goin' on to do
the job, there's no charge.

                    POTENTIAL CLIENT (O.S.)
That's very kind.

                    BARRY
Fink nothin' of it. We want you to be
'appy before we start. Take your time.

                    POTENTIAL CLIENT (O.S.)
I'll call you back by the end of the
week.

                    BARRY
OK Luv, ta.

Barry puts the receiver down. He gathers together the papers that he has been referring to while on the phone and puts them back in their folder. He walks around his desk and returns the file to the filing cabinet.

He then removes the scarf from the hook by the door and places it around his shoulders. As he puts his hand on the door, the PHONE RINGS.

Barry looks over towards his desk. He seems to be in two minds as to whether to answer it. He sighs. Hurries over to his desk, sits down, and picks up the phone.

> BARRY
> Barry Builds, 'ow may I 'elp you?

> MISS SPENCER (O.S.)
> (with an old-fashioned R.P. English
> accent)
> Miss Lydia Spencer here, Headmistress
> Central House School.

Barry looks at his watch.

> MISS SPENCER (O.S.)
> I shan't keep you. I know you've
> got your match to get to. One of my
> mothers recommended you. You did her
> music room recently.

> BARRY
> Ah, that'd Rosemary Spires.

> MISS SPENCER (O.S.)
> Indeed. Rosemary says you're a top-
> notch builder and Chelsea fan. Well,
> I won't hold the latter against you,

but I would like your professional help. I'd like you over here on Sunday to discuss the details.

                    BARRY
     Er, OK.

                    MISS SPENCER (O.S.)
     I'm on Central Avenue. You know it?

                    BARRY
     Yeah. Very nice road. Didn't know there was a school there. What time did you 'ave in mind, Luv?

                    MISS SPENCER (O.S.)
     Eleven o'clock, after church. You can stay for lunch, we've got a lot to discuss. But you must be gone by 2 p.m. before the Bridge Club arrive. Oh, and good luck for this afternoon.

                    BARRY
     Er, OK, fanks.

The line goes dead.

EXT—CENTRAL HOUSE—DRIVEWAY—AM

Barry has just parked his car, a LAND ROVER DISCOVERY in British Racing Green, outside a substantial suburban house. It's an old car, but immaculately kept. Barry is smartly dressed in fawn chinos and a brown sports jacket. He picks up a clipboard and pen that are on the passenger seat, gets out of the car, and locks the door.

The house has a wide frontage. There are steps up to an impressive oak front door and several windows on either side. From the height of the building, we can see that the house has three floors and possibly an attic as well.

On one side of the house, a huge rhododendron bush obscures the view down to the rear garden. On the other side of the house stands a detached double garage with a window over its doors, suggesting that there's a room of some sort above the garage.

Between the house and the garage there is a six-foot fence with a door in the middle that's currently closed.

EXT—CENTRAL HOUSE—FRONT DOORSTEP—AM

Barry walks up the drive to the front door and raps the knocker firmly. Within a minute the door opens to reveal MISS SPENCER.

She is 80 years old, but looks closer to 65. She is a tall woman with an upright posture. Her face is more creased than wrinkled and is framed with a mane of white hair loosely tied back in a pre-Raphaelite-style ponytail that goes halfway down her back. She's wearing a dark shawl over a white lace blouse, a brown calf-length wool skirt, and stout walking shoes.

>   MISS SPENCER
>   (a little more loudly than necessary)
>   Good morning, Mr Mason. Thanks for
>   coming at such short notice.

BARRY
That's all right, Luv.

MISS SPENCER
        (in a slightly scolding tone)
No, no, no. That won't do. Miss Spencer
is fine, Lydia is fine, but please Mr
Mason, not 'Luv'.

BARRY
Of course, Lu . . . er Ly . . . ydia,
er Miss Spencer. You can call me
Bazzer.

MISS SPENCER
Absolutely not! I might call you Barry
when you've earned it, but until then,
it will be Mr Mason.

BARRY
Right you are . . . Miss Spencer. By
the way, 'ow was the service?

MISS SPENCER
Service?

BARRY
Fought you wanted me over 'ere after
church?

MISS SPENCER
I do the flowers for the local Church
of England. The Vicar needs a little
help since his wife died. I drop them
off before his service, I don't attend
myself. Much too busy to waste time
with church services.

Miss Spencer looks at her watch.

>   MISS SPENCER cont'd
>   Now to business. We've got a lot to
>   get through. Let me take you on a tour
>   of the house, and I'll tell you about
>   the project.

Miss Spencer leads Barry round to the side of
the house, through the door in the fence, and
into the back garden.

EXT—CENTRAL HOUSE—BACK GARDEN—AM

Miss Spencer and Barry are standing in the
middle of well- tended grounds and looking up
at the rear aspect of a large suburban house.

>   MISS SPENCER
>   Central House once stood surrounded
>   by several acres of woodland at
>   the end of Central Avenue. Over the
>   years those trees have been eaten
>   away by greedy developers, slowly
>   encroaching on my privacy. Now I'm
>   totally overlooked by those lesser
>   dwellings behind us.

Barry turns round. He goes up on to his toes. We
can just about make out the rooftops of several
large, but new, executive homes appearing over
the trees at the bottom of her long formal
garden.

>   BARRY
>   That must be Lilac Crescent, on the
>   corner of Ridgeway and The Grove.

                    MISS SPENCER
That's right.

                    BARRY
Four- and five-bed 'ouses. Detached.
Double garages. En-suite and family
barfrooms. Utility rooms and studies.
And most wiv swimming pools.

                    MISS SPENCER
Quite. I've had many offers to
murder my house, or 'develop this
site' as some of your bloodthirsty
brethren like to euphemise. They seem
to like nothing more than to pull
down magnificent homes like these
and overcrowd the grounds with poky
little apartments. As you can see,
each of these offers I have resisted.
                    (beat)
Now come along.

Barry turns back round to find that Miss Spencer
is already halfway back to the house. He hurries
to catch up.

                    MISS SPENCER
             (without looking round)
We'll go in, I'll show you around,
give you a quick history lesson, and
if you're lucky, share with you a
little home economics.

Miss Spencer continues to walk back to the
house along the path running down the side of
the garden. She enters the house through the
conservatory with Barry in quick pursuit.

                    MISS SPENCER (O.S.)
                (calling loudly from inside the
                house)
        Shoes off and on the mat by the door
        please.

INT—CENTRAL HOUSE—GRAND HALLWAY—AM

Miss Spencer and Barry are now standing in the
GRAND HALLWAY of Central House. Miss Spencer is
now wearing slippers, and Barry is in his socks.

It is an impressive space from which we can see
several doors, all closed except the one leading
to the conservatory that Barry and Miss Spencer
have just walked through.

By the front door, there's a long line of about
20 coat hooks at waist height, all numbered.
Below the hooks and attached to the wall is a
long shallow bench. On the other side of the
hall between two doors is a quarter-sized grand
piano and stool. The lid on the piano is raised,
and there is some sheet music on the stand.

Barry gazes up at the wide, winding, wooden
stairway leading off from the main entrance hall
and is clearly impressed.

                    BARRY
        I like the long, church-like windows
        that bridge the two floors.

                    MISS SPENCER
        Yes, they are lovely. They have
        always let such light and warmth into
        the heart of the house. Such sweet
        memories.

Miss Spencer is quiet for a few moments.

> MISS SPENCER
> I was left this house when my mother
> died in 1955. It was much too large
> for just me, but I could not bear to
> sell it. So I turned it into a private
> school for 3- to 11-year-olds. Not only
> did it make good use of the building,
> it has also kept me in hampers from
> Fortnum and Mason for 50 years.
>
> This space has been the site of
> morning assemblies for half a century.
> You see that raised section?

Miss Spencer points to an area of the hall that's
about 18 inches higher than the rest of the
floor. Barry nods.

> MISS SPENCER
> At Christmas, that's our stage. It's
> seen every pantomime I've ever put on
> with my pupils. We also used it for
> Bollywood dancing during Diwali while
> Krishnan was with us.

Miss Spencer walks quickly to the other side
of the hall and opens a pair of double doors.
Beyond we see what appears to be a magnificent
drawing room.

> MISS
> And my parents sit and watch from
> here. Some of my old boys volunteer
> to help me set up the seating.

                    BARRY
              (quietly, almost under his breath)
          Volunteer or are press-ganged?

                    MISS SPENCER
          Oh, they volunteer, Mr Mason. I insist
          on it!

                    BARRY
          Of course, sorry Miss.

                    MISS SPENCER
              (now back to her previous brisk
              manner)
          Right. Onwards and upwards, Mr Mason.

Miss Spencer moves purposefully to the stairs.
Barry follows quickly.

INT—CENTRAL HOUSE—SECOND-FLOOR DORMITORY—AM

Miss Spencer and Barry are standing in a large
open-plan room at the top of the house.

                    MISS SPENCER
          This room has a rich and interesting
          history.

          Originally this floor was intended to
          provide accommodation for the servants.
          But then my uncle moved in up here
          when Gramps was training him up to
          take over the family business. I
          remember coming up here to spend the
          odd afternoon with nanny when I was
          a little girl. The low ceilings make
          it cosy up here, so I took down the

internal walls to create a single
dormitory. I use it as a rest
area for the smalls.

> BARRY
> Smalls?

> MISS SPENCER
> The three- and four-year-olds. It's
> too much for them to last the whole
> day at that age, so I treat them to
> warm milk and a biscuit, and they
> have a nap up here for an hour each
> day.

Barry moves over to one of the small windows
and peers out.

> BARRY
> Great view of the garden.

> MISS SPENCER
> Indeed. You'll notice there's a
> bathroom up here. That's been a
> godsend for cleaning up the odd child
> after a particularly vigorous play
> session in the garden. Can't send
> them back muddy now, can we!

> BARRY
> Boys will be boys I guess.

> MISS SPENCER
> And in my experience, as will the
> girls.

> BARRY
> Good point. Tina could get as mucked
> up as Liam when they were kids.

                    MISS SPENCER
          Your children?

                    BARRY
          Nah. Me sisters. They're all growed up
          now and work for me: Tina's my office
          manager, and I'm trainin' Liam up to
          be the onsite foreman.

                    MISS SPENCER
                    (turning her attention back to the
                    dormitory)
          Now get a feel for the size of this
          space, and remember that for later.
          I'll see you back in the kitchen in a
          few minutes.

Miss Spencer leaves the room. We hear her
FOOTSTEPS on the stairs going down.

Barry walks over to one of the windows on the
other side of the room and looks out. He runs
his hand over the window sill. He then walks
over to and opens several of the doors in the
dormitory. He makes a few notes on his clipboard.
He tries a few of the light switches and counts
the electric sockets. Finally he kneels down and
examines one of the radiators.

INT—CENTRAL HOUSE—SCULLERY—AM

Miss Spencer and Barry are in the scullery, a
small room that leads off of a spacious, clean,
but very dated kitchen. In the centre of the
scullery stands an ancient, well-worn, cast iron
AGA.

                    BARRY
Judgin' by the beige sides and the
dark bran lids on the 'ot plates, I'd
guess that's an original.

                    MISS SPENCER
Well spotted, Mr Mason. It was
installed in 1938.

Barry walks over to the wall opposite the Aga
and taps it firmly with his knuckle. We hear a
HOLLOW KNOCK.

                    BARRY
Fought so. This was once part of the
kitchen weren't it?

                    MISS SPENCER
          (slightly surprised)
Why yes, yes, it was.

                    BARRY
Smalls?

                    MISS SPENCER
Pardon?

                    BARRY
Bet you was worried about the smalls
comin' in and burnin' theirselves on the
Aga. And you could face gettin' rid of
it, so you added the partition and made
a little scullery.

                    MISS SPENCER
How could you possibly . . .

                    BARRY
Why else would you imprison such a
beauty in the smallest room in the
'ouse?

                    MISS SPENCER
Very good, Mr Mason. I knew you'd be
the right man for this job.

                    BARRY
You 'aven't actually told me what the
job is yet.

                    MISS SPENCER
All in good time, Mr Mason.

Miss Spencer opens one of the doors on the front
of the Aga. We hear a loud METALLIC SQUEAK. She
withdraws a tray of mince pies.

                    MISS SPENCER
They're best when they're warm.

                    BARRY
Don't mind if I do.

Barry reaches for the offered tray.

                    MISS SPENCER
    Plate!

                    BARRY
    Wot?

                    MISS SPENCER
'Pardon', never 'What'.

                    BARRY
Sorry. Pardon?

                    MISS SPENCER
              (nodding towards the cupboards on
              the wall)
         Plates are in the top cupboard on the
         right. You can take one down for me
         too.

Barry takes two plates out of the cupboard and
places a mince pie on each.

                    MISS SPENCER
         Now let's retire to the study.

INT—CENTRAL HOUSE—STUDY—AM

Miss Spencer and Barry are sitting on either
side of a large leather-topped, maple wood desk
in her study. It is a spacious reception room,
with an Adams fireplace, ornate mantelpiece, and
oak-panelled walls.

                    BARRY
         Now this is quite a study.

                    MISS SPENCER
         This used to be the dining room.
         I remember many a glorious family
         gathering here. We used to gather
         round the piano and sing Christmas
         carols. They were wonderful times.

                    BARRY
         You 'ave one hell of an 'ouse, Miss.

                    MISS SPENCER
         Thank you.

Miss Spencer sits back in her chair and sighs.

MISS SPENCER
Well, Mr Mason, I'm not getting any
younger. I've been doing less and
less of the day-to-day running of
the school. In fact, I'm retiring at
the end of the current term. I have
no children of my own, nor any other
relatives who can take over Central
House, so the school is retiring as
well.

As for the house itself, I've signed
a deal with Community Care Ltd. They
are going to take over Central House
and turn it into a nursing home. In
return they will guarantee me a place
for the rest of my days. The thought
of going into an institution to see
out my days was unconscionable, Mr
Mason. Can you understand that?

BARRY
I can. So where do I fit in?

MISS SPENCER
Part of the deal is that I design the
conversion and oversee its creation. I
want you to do the conversion.

BARRY
Wow. Now that's gonna be one 'ell of
a job. That's much bigger 'an what I
normally do.

MISS SPENCER
Oh, I know that, Mr Mason. But the
work that you have done is of top
quality. I've seen that for myself.

                    BARRY
'Ave you?

                    MISS SPENCER
Well, Rosemary Spires is the mother
of one my pupils, and the music room
that you that added for her is superb.
Then there's the attic library you
installed for the Russells.

                    BARRY
I was quite pleased wiv 'ow that one
turned out. Attics are notorious for
bein' cold in winter and stiflin' in
summer.

                    MISS SPENCER
Very clever usage of an isolated air-
conditioning unit to allow warmth
in the winter and cool in summer,
coupled with the tinted glass in the
skylights, triple glazing, and solid
wood shades. I remember young Master
Russell's first day at Central House.
And you've recently finished the
Smythe's garage conversion for their
twin sons.

                    BARRY
Yeah. Originally they'd wanted me to
fit removable sound-proofin' elements
on the boys' doors an' windas. But
I knew that'd never cover that God-
awful racket they make when their
band practises. But as no one 'ad
used that detached garage of theirs
for years, I fought that'd be a much
better option. And of course, it

meant they could 'ave the recordin'
equipment out all the time.

                MISS SPENCER
Well, that was brilliant. And you're
right: Jacques and Jean used to make
a God-awful racket when they were
students here, and they don't seem to
have improved now that their guitars
are electrified.

                BARRY
God knows why they'd want to record it.

                MISS SPENCER
Quite. You did the annexe with the
shared kitchen for the Arnolds . . .

                BARRY
When I saw Mrs Arnold's mother put
the kettle in the fridge, I knew she'd
feel 'appier bein' able to keep an
eye on 'er.

                MISS SPENCER
The conservatory/observatory for the
Moores . . .

                BARRY
Can you believe they were goin' to
chuck out that 'scope?

                MISS SPENCER
. . . and the garden offices in the
lake for the Jacksons. Very ingenious
to turn their frequent flooding into
a water feature, and the floating
walkway was inspired. Their son was
one of mine a decade ago.

Miss Spencer looks earnestly at Barry.

> MISS SPENCER
> So you see, Mr Mason, I've done my
> homework.

> BARRY
> Guess that comes with terry tory.

> MISS SPENCER
> All excellent, young man. And now I
> think it's time you pushed yourself a
> little more.

Miss Spencer opens a drawer on her side of the
desk. She removes a large blue folder and unfolds
four A2 sheets of paper with plans drawn up.

> MISS SPENCER
> Here are the plans. Bring your chair
> round this side, and I'll walk you
> through it.

As Barry walks round the table, Miss Spencer
spreads the plans out across the desk. They are
overlapping, but we can see that they entitled
GROUND FLOOR, FIRST FLOOR, SECOND FLOOR, and
GARAGE.

> MISS SPENCER cont'd
> On the ground floor, there'll be two
> bedrooms with en suite bathrooms, one
> of those will be mine. We'll convert
> the study back into a dining room
> and refurbish the kitchen. Across the
> back we'll have a day room and a sun
> lounge. We need ramps at the front
> and rear of the house, and a stair
> lift.

BARRY
Given the size of the great hall,
you could accommodate a proper lift.
That way you wouldn't spoil your
magnificent staircase.

MISS SPENCER
A very good suggestion. Now, there
will be a further six bedrooms on the
first floor and two shared bathrooms.
The top floor will house an office
and overnight accommodation for two
nurses.

And finally, we'll convert the
workshop over the double garage into
a laundry.

BARRY
Do you have a car, Miss Spencer?

MISS SPENCER
No. I don't drive.

BARRY
So you don't really need the garage
space. Might I suggest that you keep
the workshop intact and convert the
ground floor into the laundry. That
way you've a space for an 'andyman to
work in should you ever need one, and
the staff won't have to climb an extra
set of stairs when doin' the washin'.

MISS SPENCER
Now that sort of suggestion is exactly
why you are the right man for the
job. So tell me Mr Mason, are you
interested?

                    BARRY
You've got planning permission for
all this I take it.

                    MISS SPENCER
Huh! If I took any notice of the local
authority's absurd rules, I'd have been
out of business years ago. Believe you
me, Mr Mason, I have been in and out of
fashion more times than I care to recall
since I started this school.

                    BARRY
Er, I wouldn't really be very 'appy
even gettin' started on this project
wivout the plannin' perm. Miss
Spenc . . .

                    MISS SPENCER
              (sternly)
That was a joke, Mr Mason. I taught
most of the local councillors right
here in this very house. I had to
slipper some of them too. They didn't
put up any opposition whatsoever to
the planning application.

                    BARRY
Tell me, am I right in finking this
is a Talbott-built 'ouse originally?

                    MISS SPENCER
It's not just any Talbott house, it's
Talbott's own house. He built this
house just before the Great War.
He chose this location so that he
could be close to all his sites,
both the houses he built and the

materials he used. He built much of St George's Hill, owned some of the small businesses in Brooklands, and had a mill on the river at Addlestone. This house was in the heart of his building empire. That's why he called it Central House.

              BARRY
You know a lot about the great man.

              MISS SPENCER
I should. He was my grandfather.

              BARRY
So you're a Talbott!

              MISS SPENCER
That's right, and sadly the last. Richard was my mother's father. She was the youngest of his three children. Her two brothers died young in the Great War. Both officers: one a captain, the other a chaplain. As for me, I'm an only child and never married.

Barry and Miss Spencer sit silently for a few moments.

              BARRY
Well, to work on a Talbott would be a privilege and a pleasure, Miss Spencer. I've got a loft conversion booked in for next month, so we can make a start here after that, around mid-October. That OK for you?

MISS SPENCER
No, it most certainly is not. I need
to have the work completed during
November so that I can go away in
December, and be back here ready for
when the home opens. I'll need to make
sure that the nurses are ready to
receive our new residents in January.

BARRY
But I've agreed with the Andersons
that . . .

MISS SPENCER
I've already had a word with Elizabeth.
Under the circumstances, she's happy
to delay starting until the end of
the year. So I was hoping you could
start the week after next.

BARRY
Er, right you are then.

EXT—CENTRAL HOUSE—DRIVEWAY—AM

Barry is parking an old, but well-looked-after
transit van. He is dressed in an old, but clean
and well-cared-for boiler suit. Sitting next
to him is LIAM, his nephew, who is wearing an
identical but virtually brand new boiler suit.

They get out of the van and start walking up
the drive. Both are holding a sandwich box and
a thermos flask.

The front door of Central House opens before
they reach it. Miss Spencer emerges and walks
over to them.

                    MISS SPENCER
          Good morning, Mr Mason. Good to see
          you bright and early.

                    BARRY
          Mornin'. This is me nephew Liam. 'E'll
          be me second in command over the next
          few months.

Liam offers his hand for shaking.

          MISS SPENCER Good morning, Mr . . . ?

                    LIAM
          Brady Lu . . .

Barry nudges him with his elbow.

                    LIAM
          Er, Miss Spencer.

                    MISS SPENCER
          Right then, Ms Mason, Brady. Come
          along. I've got the kettle on. You'll
          be wanting to make a prompt start.
          There's a lot to get through.

INT—CENTRAL HOUSE—STUDY—AM

Barry, Liam, and Miss Spencer are in the study
sitting round the large desk. They have some of
the building plans spread out across the table.
On one quarter of the table there are three
mugs and a large plate with three part-eaten
croissants.

                    BARRY
We'll start off in 'ere, and we should
be able get the new dining room
completed by the end of the wee . . .

                  MISS SPENCER
               (butting in)
No, no, no. That will not work I'm
afraid, Mr Mason.

                    BARRY
It won't?

                  MISS SPENCER
Absolutely not. I can't lose this room
for at least four weeks.

                    BARRY
You can't?

                  MISS SPENCER

No. It's my rotation to host the Bridge
Club this week. Next week I've got the
Conservative Club and the WI. And at
the end of the month I've got the last
monthly Am Dram read through.

                    LIAM
The what?

                  MISS SPENCER
Amateur Dramatics Society. We have a
read through of the next play that we
intend to put into production at the
end of each month. This one will be
my finale as I'm retiring as society
president, but I obviously can't miss
my last one. I need to make sure they

select the correct person to take
over my role.

            LIAM
Guess we could start with the kitchen
then.

Barry looks at Miss Spencer. Miss Spencer shakes
her head.

            BARRY
I'm guessing not. If you've got those
meetings, you'll probably be needing
the kitchen to prepare refreshments.

            MISS SPENCER
Quite right, Mr Mason.

Liam sighs and raises his eyebrows.

            BARRY
This needn't be a problem. Will you
be needin' the drawing room, or any
of the back rooms?

            MISS SPENCER
No. You've got free reign there.

            BARRY
What I suggest then is that we start
off with gettin' your ground floor
suite underway. We can use that as a
reference for the other bedrooms.

            MISS SPENCER
That would be perfect.

                    BARRY
Now then, there's much more work 'ere
than Liam and I are goin' to be able
to get fru in four months. So what
I suggest is that we bring in some
extra 'ands in about two weeks. I've
got a couple of lads that I can bring
in to then do the rooms on the first
floor. They can use the first bed and
barfroom as a model. I've used 'em
before on lots of me jobs. They're
good workers.

                    MISS SPENCER
That is an excellent idea, Mr Mason.

INT—CENTRAL HOUSE—FIRST FLOOR—AM

Barry and Liam are addressing two teams of
contractors. He is briefing them on their first
day on the Central House project. They'll be
working on the two bathrooms and 6 bedrooms on
the first floor, using the completed rooms on
the ground floor as their model/yardstick.

                    BARRY
You'll be workin' in two teams of
free: the A-Team and the B-Team. Both
teams will 'ave free bedrooms and one
barfroom to complete. Liam and I 'ave
already done two beds wiv en-suites
on the ground floor. You can use those
as your reference. They've all got
to be up to that spec. It's a quality
finish we're after 'ere. No corner-
cuttin', but no wastage neiver.

                    (beat)
          Any questions?

                    CONTRACTOR 1
          If I'm in the A-Team, can I be Hannibal
          Smith?

                    BARRY
          Very funny. If you've go no real
          questions, before you get started,
          a bit ov 'ousekeepin', lads. When it
          comes to 'avin' your lunch, plates are
          in the kitchen.

BOB, one of the B-team, looks around at the dust
sheets and general building detritus.

                    BOB
          Plates? You're kidding, right?

                    BARRY
          Not at all. Miss Spencer's a stickler.
          She's our customer. That's her wishes.
          We 'ave to respect 'em. End of.

                    BOB
          You're the boss.

                    BARRY
          Now then, Liam's in charge up 'ere
          today. If you've any questions, direct
          'em to 'im. I'll be in the kitchen
          gettin' the prep done.

INT—CENTRAL HOUSE—KITCHEN—AM

Barry is disassembling the Aga. He removes all
the doors, the lids from the top, and the side

panels. When the Aga is down to the framework, he carefully covers it with a dust sheet. Barry picks up all the various parts of the Aga and takes them out of the back door.

He returns a few moments later with a large sledgehammer. He starts to knock down the wall between the scullery and the kitchen.

INT—CENTRAL HOUSE—KITCHEN—AM

Barry and Miss Spencer are in the fully refurbished kitchen. The wall dividing the scullery and the kitchen has now been removed, and so the room is about 50% bigger. New tiling, flooring, and cupboards make it impossible to tell that it had once been two rooms.

There are lots of new appliances in the kitchen. A dust sheet covers the space in which we previously saw the Aga.

Miss Spencer is making tea for herself and Barry. Barry places a bag from a local baker on the counter and takes two plates out of the cupboard. He puts a croissant on to each plate.

>   MISS SPENCER
> You've done a fine job in here.

>   BARRY
> Fanks. You ready to see the Aga?

>   MISS SPENCER
> Of course.

Barry bends down and takes hold of a corner of the dust sheet. In one swift movement of his arm, he removes the sheet to reveal what looks like a brand new Aga.

                    BARRY
          I stripped down all the various parts
          of the Aga, and part-derusted, part
          cleaned 'em up. I re-chromed the
          towel rail and the metal fittin's on
          the front and touched up and polished
          the nameplate. Plus I lubricated the
          doors.

Barry opens one of the doors on the front; it now makes no sound.

                    BARRY cont'd
          I powder-coated the insides of the
          doors wiv an 'eat-resistant, non-toxic
          paint to make future cleanin' easier.
          And 'cos it's a specialist job, I sent
          the lids off to be re-enamelled.

Barry closes the door again.

                    BARRY cont'd
          And finally I reattached the plumbin'
          on the back and re-routed the pipes
          so you can get 'ot water to the top
          floor that's on a system independent
          to the residents' rooms on the ground
          and first floors.

Miss Spencer walks over to the Aga.

                    MISS SPENCER
               (quietly, almost to herself)
          My, my, my.

She runs a hand over the top surface. She opens
one of the lids on the top. She crouches down in
front of the Aga. She caresses, then opens one
of the doors. She slides out the grill pan and
tray, it looks brand new.

                    MISS SPENCER cont'd
          My, my, my. You've done a great job,
          Barry. It really pops.

Barry looks up quickly with a surprised look on
his face.

                    MISS SPENCER cont'd
          'Pops'. That's what Rick on American
          Restoration says. Your fine work
          really pops out at you. It grabs your
          attention. It's a fine centrepiece of
          the new kitchen.

                    BARRY
          Fanks. I'm glad you like it.

                    MISS SPENCER
          So what have we got left to do?

                    BARRY
          Liam's workin' wiv the A-Team on the
          top floor today. I'll be startin' the
          prep for the study-to-dinin' room
          conversion.

                    MISS SPENCER
          Have you any thoughts on the
          panelling?

                    BARRY
          I was finkin' you'd probably want to
          get the walls in the dining room as

light as possible, so removin' the panels seems the best option. I've checked the wood and they all seem to be in good nick, so I fought we could treat 'em and reuse 'em in the laundry: add a bit of warmth and make a converted garage a little more 'omely.

                    MISS SPENCER
That sounds perfect, Barry.

INT—CENTRAL HOUSE—STUDY—AM

Barry is working alone in the study. He is carefully taking off the panels and stacking them one-by-one in one corner of the room. He has a step ladder with him that he takes over to the large Adams fireplace and starts removing the panels above the mantelpiece.

As he reaches up to remove a panel, it slides sideways to reveal a Manila envelope, yellowed with age, tucked behind it. Barry opens the envelope and removes from it a sepia photograph. The picture is of a young army officer in his dress uniform standing in front of a full-length mirror gazing at his own reflection. Judging by the style of the uniform, the photograph had been taken during the First World War.

Barry walks over to the window and stands so that the light from the window falls on to the photo. He studies it for a few moments.

Liam walks into the study.

                    LIAM
          Need a hand, Bazzer?

Barry looks up still holding the photograph.

                    BARRY
          Er, no fanks, mate, you're all right?

                    LIAM
          OK. Well, the paint's drying in the
          laundry, so I'll go see how they're
          doing upstairs.

                    BARRY
          Yeah, all right. Can you take this
          stack of panels out to the laundry
          the next time you go out there?

                    LIAM
          Yeah sure.

Barry takes the photograph over to the desk
and places it with the building plans that are
spread out over it. We see that the plans are by
now very well thumbed with numerous crossings
out and additions made.

Barry goes back to removing panels.

INT—CENTRAL HOUSE—STUDY—AM

Barry and Miss Spencer are in the newly
completed dining room discussing the completion
of the building project. The panels have all
been removed now, and the walls are painted
a light cream. The thick pile carpet has been
replaced with a new, dark brown, hard-wearing,
Berber tweed carpet. The picture window has been

replaced by French windows, and we can see that hardwood decking has been added to the outside of the house.

The only items of furniture that remain in the room are the large desk and the two chairs. Barry and Miss Spencer have the plans spread before them on the desk. There are more notations, additions, and crossings-out on plans than we saw last time, and the plans are looking quite worn.

>   BARRY
> Well, I fink we're just about done
> now, Miss Spencer.

>   MISS SPENCER
> Yes, Barry. You've done an excellent
> job. As I knew you would.

>   BARRY
> Just this desk to move up to the
> office on the second floor.

>   MISS SPENCER
> Is that going to be possible? It is
> rather large.

>   BARRY
> Not a problem. I was lookin' at it
> earlier. It comes apart. You can twist
> the legs off if you give 'em a bit
> of welly. And the centre of the desk
> comes off if you take out the drawers,
> slide your 'ands in, and push. 'Ere,
> I'll show you.

Barry slides back his chair and stands up. He removes one of the drawers and places it on the floor under the window. He then moves several of the plan sheets to one side. As he does so, he uncovers the photograph that we saw him find behind the hidden panel over the mantelpiece.

Miss Spencer spots the photograph.

>   MISS SPENCER
>   (picking up the photograph)
> Good Lord, where did you find that?

>   BARRY
> Oh yeah, I forgot all about the photograph. I found it in an envelope.

>   MISS SPENCER
> I haven't seen it for years. Where was it?

>   BARRY
> It was hidden behind a secret panel over the fireplace. I saw it contained an old photograph and couldn't resist taking a look. I love photography. In fact, we are experimenting with sepia in me night class at the moment.

>   MISS SPENCER
> You attend a night class?

>   BARRY
> There's more to me than meets the eye, Miss Spencer. At school, I always wanted to be a soccer star, so spent all me time trainin' and neglectin' me studies. I got into the Chelsea Academy, but broke me leg in me first season in the reserves. Never 'ealed properly. Buildin' was me back-up. And

I've been takin' night classes to try
to catch up me education.

A couple of years ago I took a night
class in photography. In fact, that's
where I met me partner, Chris.

                MISS SPENCER
You're not married then?

                BARRY
Er no, we've not been able to yet.
I went for the photos, and fell for
the teacher! I love photographs,
particularly old ones. I think they
tell you so much more than mere words.

                MISS SPENCER
Well, that one certainly has quite
a tale to tell. It's of my uncle,
Richard.

Miss Spencer takes the photograph gently and
peers at it closely.

                MISS SPENCER cont'd
That photograph was amongst the few
possessions of his that returned from
the front at the end of First World
War. He, alas, did not return. All the
family got back was that picture and
a battered harmonica.

My grandfather had the picture framed
and hung it in pride of place in this
very room. It was over the fireplace.
In fact, not more than a matter of
inches away from where you say you
found it. He had other pictures of

both my uncles, but for him, this was the one that meant most. And there it hung for 30 years until one day he ordered one of the servants to remove and destroy it.

                    BARRY
What! Why?

                    MISS SPENCER
Well, he found out something about his favourite son that upset him greatly and could no longer bear to set eyes on him every day as he sat eating his dinner. My grandma intercepted the picture before the servant could carry out my grandpa's wishes and hid it away. She never told anyone where she'd hidden it - ironic that she should have chosen that spot. For the last three years of my grandpa's life, my uncle was sitting just over his shoulder.

                    BARRY
I hope you don't mind me saying so, but there's something about it that don't look quite right.

                    MISS SPENCER
          (raising an eyebrow and smiling
          enigmatically)
Oh?

                    BARRY
When I first found it, I studied it quite closely for a while, and well, there's something odd about the mirror.

                    MISS SPENCER
          Odd in what way?

                    BARRY
          I can't work out which is the person
          and which the reflection, they both
          seem equally real.

Miss Spencer laughs.

                    MISS SPENCER
          Well observed, Barry. You're only
          the second person to notice that
          unprompted. Let me explain a little
          about that picture: It was common for
          soldiers to carry with them pictures
          of their loved ones. Perhaps a holiday
          snap, sharing a loving embrace, or a
          fond farewell in a departure lounge.
          This was my uncle's special picture.

                    BARRY
          Of himself?

                    MISS SPENCER
          Not exactly. Look a little closer.
          There's more to it than meets the eye.

Barry takes the picture back from Miss Spencer
and peers at it even more closely.

                    BARRY
          'Ang on a minute.

He takes a pen out of this his pocket and places
it flat on the photograph, and then rolls it from
one side of the picture to the other.

BARRY cont'd
The young officer on the left
is fractionally taller than his
reflection, and maybe a little thinner

He picks up the photograph and holds it very
close to his face and closes one eye.

BARRY cont'd
My God! It's not a reflection; it's
two men, not one. The composition is
brilliant. Even down to the buttons
and insignia reversed on the young
officer on the right. Where did they
manage to get an army uniform made in
reverse? And why on erf did they take
that picture?

MISS SPENCER
The young man on the right made the
uniform. Before the war, he was into
amateur dramatics in a big way. Not
just on the stage, but behind the
scenes too. He painted sets and built
props, but his speciality was making
costumes.

He studied my uncle's uniform carefully
and painstakingly reproduced it in
reverse. Look really closely, and
you'll see he even reversed the fly
buttons on the trousers.

BARRY
I still fink I'm missin' somethin'.
They went to a lot of trouble to take
a quite exceptional photo. Who was 'e?
And why the elaborate illusion?

> MISS SPENCER
> His name was Alfred Caine. He wasn't
> an officer in the Great War. In fact,
> he never saw active service. He was
> turned down on medical grounds:
> severe bronchial problems.

Dissolve to

INT—CENTRAL HOUSE 1914—ATTIC—AM

ALFRED CAINE, RICHARD TALBOTT, and ANNIE TALBOTT
are in Richard's room on the second floor of
Central House.

Richard is wearing his officer cadet's uniform.
Alfred is wearing what appears to be an exact
copy of the uniform, but we see that the
supporting strap attached to Alfred's Sam Browne
belt is worn over his left shoulder, and the
rank insignia is on his left sleeve.

The bed has been moved to one side. A large
free-standing, full-length mirror in a stand has
been placed between the two windows. Lying on
the bed is an empty picture frame that appears
to be the same size as the mirror. There is also
a small make-up bag and a large, professional-
looking sewing box with its double-handled lid
open and some of the contents spilling out.

There is a mahogany tripod with a huge Korona
camera mounted on it facing the mirror. Annie is
sitting on a chair behind the tripod.

We hear MISS SPENCER'S VOICE continuing the
story.

                    MISS SPENCER (V.O.)
Alfred wanted to go, desperately. He
didn't want to be separated from my
uncle. He would have done anything to
have gone with him. You see, Alfred
was my uncle's 'special friend'. My
mother took the photograph so that he
could take a picture of his sweetheart
with him into battle without anyone
realising what it was. You have to
understand that they lived in less
enlightened times than today, Barry.

                    ANNIE
Dickie, stand in front of mirror as
if you're admiring yourself!

Richard does so.

                    ANNIE
You're a natural!

Richard throws a rolled-up sock at his sister.
She ducks.

                    ANNIE
Now angle your right shoulder away
from the mirror. Remember, we need
to see you both in the shot, not just
Alfie and your back.

Richard moves to face towards the camera a
little more.

                    ANNIE
Now, Alfie, gently angle the bottom
of the mirror. We need to get Dickie's
feet into the reflection, otherwise
the illusion will never work.

                    (beat)
          A little more. A little more. Now
          stop. That'll do.

We see Richard reflected in the mirror in exactly
the pose that we've seen in the photograph that
Barry found, except that in the mirror, we see
Richard reflected not Alfred.

                    ANNIE
          Now, Alfie, you come round here and
          look through the lens while I measure
          where you should stand.

Annie and Alfie switch places.

                    ANNIE
          You've got to see how to stand to be
          Richard's reflection. You'll need to
          have your left shoulder slightly
          square. Richard's got his left hand on
          his belt with his thumb in his pocket,
          so that'll be your right hand. And
          you'll need your heels slightly closer
          together than your toes, Richard
          always was a little flat- footed.

Annie picks up a tape measure from the open
sewing box and bends down in front of her
brother. She measures the distance from each
of his feet to the mirror, and then measures
behind the mirror. Satisfied, she takes off her
own shoes and places them on the floor behind
the mirror.

                    ANNIE
          Alfie, my shoes are your marks. After
          we've moved the mirror, you'll need to

come round here and place your feet
exactly where my shoes are.

          RICHARD
I think my reflection wearing women's
shoes might be a bit of a giveaway,
don't you?

Annie tosses the rolled-up sock back at her
brother.

          ANNIE
Oh, very funny. Now Dickie, no more
moving. And Alfie, help me move the
mirror.

Afred hurries over to the mirror. Between them,
they carefully lift the mirror off its stand
and place it on the bed. They then take the
empty picture frame and hang it on the mirror's
stand. Now Alfred walks behind the stand. Annie
helps him to get his feet into the right place,
then takes her shoes away and throws them on to
the bed. She then walks back to the camera and
tripod.

          ANNIE
Dickie, remember: statues. Right now
Alfie, you need to move your left
foot back a bit. Other hand on your
belt . . . that's it. We're almost
there.

Annie stands up. She walks over to her brother,
holds his head in her hands, and studies his
face closely. She then picks up an eyeliner
pencil from the bed and walks over to Alfred.
She holds his head in her hands. She delicately
paints several small freckles on Alfred's cheek.

She then leans back to examine her work, then reaches over and smooths down his hair a little.

>   ANNIE
>   Perfect.

Annie walks back to the camera and tripod. She sits down and looks through the lens. The tableaux that we see is exactly as we've seen in the found photograph. There's a FLASH as she takes the picture.

INT—FIRST-CLASS TRAIN CARRIAGE, 1914—AM

Alfred, Richard, and Annie are travelling to Dover to see Richard off. There is no one else in their First-Class carriage.

Richard is dressed in his officer's uniform. Alfred and Annie are wearing their Sunday best. They look as though they could be on their way to church.

>   ANNIE
>   Aren't you at all scared?

>   RICHARD
>   Of course I am. I'd be crazy not to be.

>   ANNIE
>   How can you be so calm?

>   RICHARD
>   That's just a facade. Classic British
>   stiff upper lip, but inside, I'm all
>   butterflies.

                    ALFRED
I'd give anything to be going with
you. You know that, don't you? I'd even
go as your batman if they'd let me.

                    ANNIE
What's a batman?

                    RICHARD
It's like a servant for officers.

                    ANNIE
Well, I'm glad you're not going, Alfie—
at least I'll still have one of my
favourite boys at home.

                    RICHARD
And you'll have me back before you
know it. Some think it will all be
over by Christmas.

                    ANNIE
Really?

                    RICHARD
Yes, really. We've got the best cavalry
in the world. One charge from our
men, and the Bosch will be running
for the hills.

                    ANNIE
If it's going to be so easy, why do
the Germans want to fight us anyway?

                    ALFRED
Don't look at me. I got no idea what
it's all about. You'd have to ask the
politicians.

                    ANNIE
          Let's talk about nicer things. I know,
          I've got some presents for you both.

Annie reaches into her SATCHEL and brings out
the photograph that we've seen Annie compose
and Barry find decades later. She puts it on the
table for Richard and Alfred to see.

                    ANNIE
          It came out well, didn't it?

                    ALFRED
          That's amazing, you've done a great
          job there.

Richard picks up the picture and peers at it
closely.

                    RICHARD
          Stunning. Simply stunning.

                    ANNIE
          So you won't mind taking it with you?

                    RICHARD
          Not at all. No one would guess. If I
          didn't know, I don't think I'd guess.
          It's just a soldier contemplating his
          reflection for the last time before
          going off to war. That is some picture.

Richard puts the photograph back on the table.

                    ANNIE
          And now something for you both.

Annie reaches into her satchel for a second
time, and this time brings out two harmonicas.

ANNIE cont'd
I got you both one of these.

RICHARD
What do you expect us to do with them?

ANNIE
Well, play them, of course. Chose a time to play them, and each day it will be like you're doing something together, you'll feel a bond.

RICHARD
I like that. But I don't play the harmonica.

ALFRED
Neither do I.

ANNIE
There's nothing to it, just move it from side to side to go up and down through a simple scale. These two are in the key of E flat. That's a slightly melancholy feel, but you can still play something more upbeat with them if you want to. Let me show you.

Annie takes her brother's harmonica and plays 'Half a Pound of Twopenny Rice'. She then hands the harmonica back. Richard tries to copy his sister.

ALFRED
That's none too clever, old boy.

Now Alfred tries on his harmonica. He plays with gusto, but it sounds nothing like the tune that

Annie played. It's even worse than Richard's attempt.

>   ANNIE
>   (laughing)
>   You've got it the wrong way round,
>   silly.

Annie takes the harmonica out of Alfred's hands, turns it round, and hands it back.

>   RICHARD
>   And you think what I played sounded
>   stupid!

Alfred tries a second time. This time it's a lot better.

>   RICHARD cont'd
>   OK. So we've got the harmonicas. I can
>   hardly play children's nursery rhymes
>   in the battlefield.

All three are silent for a few moments.

>   ANNIE
>   How about this.

Annie plays several bars of 'The Last Post'.

>   RICHARD
>   What's that? I'm sure I recognise it.

>   ANNIE
>   You should: it's the bugle call that
>   the army play last thing at night. I
>   think it's called 'The Last Post'. As
>   you can see, it's quite easy to play.

                    ALFRED
        Easy for you perhaps, but not for us
        duffers, eh, Dickie?

                    RICHARD
        Oh, I don't know, I think I could give
        that a try.

Richard takes back his harmonica and tries to
copy the tune that his sister played. His first
two attempts are unrecognisable. The third
attempt is a definite improvement.

                    RICHARD
        A little more practice, and I think I
        could get there.

                    ANNIE
        So it's settled then. Each night while
        Dickie's away, you can both end each
        day playing The Last Post:

              (touching Alfred on the knee)
        You at home with me . . .

              (turning to her brother)
        . . . and you in Flanders.

Richard picks up the photograph from the table
and puts it in the inside pocket of his uniform
jacket. He then places the harmonica to his lips
again. But we hear instead the sound of the
train's WHISTLE.

                    ANNIE
        Looks like we've arrived.

Richard stands up and retrieves his kitbag from
the overhead shelf and swings it on to his

shoulder. When the train comes to a stop, he opens the door and Annie stands up. Richard stands to one side to let her alight first. Alfred remains seated. Annie leans her head back into the carriage.

          ANNIE
Come along, Alfie.

          ALFRED
I think that would probably look a little odd. You go, see off your big brother. I'll wait here and save the carriage for our return journey.

          RICHARD
Alfie's right. Family and girlfriends only at the final departure, I think.

       (to Alfred)
You take care of my little sister.

Just as Richard is about to leave the carriage, Alfred stands up and grasps Richard's hand below the level of the window. He squeezes it tightly for a second.

          ALFRED
       (softly)
Good luck, old man.

Annie and Richard both get out of the train. Annie closes the door behind her. Alfred sits back down on the bench in the now-empty carriage. He leans back and looks out of the window on the other side of the carriage away from the departing serviceman. A tear trickles down his cheek.

Dissolve to

INT—CENTRAL HOUSE—STUDY—AM

Barry and Miss Spencer are sitting in the newly completed dining room.

>   BARRY
> Blimey. That's quite a story, Miss Spencer.

>   MISS SPENCER
> No one, other than my grandmother or my mother, knew what the picture was for fully thirty years. It was my father who spotted it. I remember the day clearly:
>
> The whole family were here for Christmas dinner when he suddenly rushed over to the picture, took it off the wall, and hurried over to the window. He held it in the light and studied it intently for a few minutes before declaring, just like you did: 'My God! It's not a reflection! It's two men, not one.' He then went on to say that the picture had bothered him ever since he'd started courting my mother, but he could never work out what it was about it that looked so strange; now that he knew, he could stop worrying.
>
> Unfortunately, that was the beginning of the problem with the picture, not the end. Not realising what my grandfather's reaction would be, my mother came clean about her role in the subterfuge, something she always regretted.

She told him that my uncle and Alfred could not bear to be parted, and that she'd had a brainwave about how they could still feel a connection even when they were thousands of miles apart.

It didn't occur to her that her father hadn't known the nature of their friendship, nor that it would matter so many years later. So much had happened since.

                    BARRY
What happened to your uncle's friend?

                    MISS SPENCER
Alfred did his bit for King and country, and was every bit as brave as my uncle. And just as tragically, he died before the end of the war.

                                Dissolve to

INT—MUNITIONS FACTORY, 1917—PACKING ROOM—AM

There are rows of WOMEN working in a PRODUCTION LINE. They are all wearing dark boiler suits with their hair tied up and covered in headscarves. They are packing rifle shells into boxes.

We hear MISS SPENCER's VOICE continuing the story.

                    MISS SPENCER (V.O.)
He went to work in one of the munitions factory. Mother worked there too. Not surprisingly, there were not many

men there, two in fact: Alfred and
a retired major, a veteran of South
Africa, who was put in charge of the
factory.

We now see Alfred wearing a private's uniform.
He appears to be showing one of the women how
one of the machines work. He then starts to walk
along the length of tables stopping occasionally
to check one of the boxes.

> MISS SPENCER (V.O.)
> Because he was a man, and young,
> Alfred was given lots of duties,
> including training and fire officer.
> Anything deemed manly was assigned
> to him despite his health problems.

Alfred stops; he turns away from the line. He
is wracked by a chesty cough for a few seconds
during which time he places his hand on the wall
to steady himself. He then resumes his walking
along the line.

> MISS SPENCER (V.O.)
> Then late one afternoon as it was
> getting dark, there was a fire alarm.

We hear the sound of a SIREN.

> ALFRED
> (shouting loudly over the sound of
> the machinery)
> OK, Munitionettes, you know the drill.
> It's probably a false alarm, but we've
> got to be certain. Stop what you're
> doing and await my command.

All the women simultaneously stop what they are doing, back away from their tables, and stand to attention. Alfred hurries over to a wall where we see a helmet and a jacket hanging on hook and a large red emergency mushroom button.

Alfred strikes the button and the machinery falls silent. He quickly dons the helmet and jacket, both of which we now see have FIRE WARDEN printed on them. He picks up a clipboard.

> ALFRED
> OK, girls, single file starting at the door, follow Annie out in to the courtyard.

The girls start to file out. Alfred quickly checks that no one else is left inside and follows the last girl out.

EXT—MUNITIONS FACTORY, 1917—COURTYARD—AM

The Munitionettes are now lined up in the courtyard outside the factory. The women are standing to attention facing Alfred. They are grouped eight across and three deep.

Alfred is looking at the clipboard about to take roll call. Before he can start, his body is wracked again by a cough. One of the Munitionettes that we now recognise as Annie looks concerned.

> ANNIE
> Are you OK, Alfie?

Alfred looks up sharply, and frowns.

                    ANNIE
          Sorry. Are you OK, Private Caine?

                    ALFRED
          I'll be fine.

                    MUNITIONETTE 1
                    (shouting loudly)
          Fire! The factory's on fire!

Alfred turns quickly. We see smoke pouring out
of one of the windows.

                    ALFRED
                    (speaking rapidly, but calmly)
          OK, girls, let's not panic. We need to
          act quickly. Now then, there are 25
          names on the list, and only 24 of you
          in front of me. Who's missing?

                    MUNITIONETTE 2
          Oh my God, it's Lucy. She was packing
          parachutes on the upper floor. She
          couldn't have heard the alarm.

                    ALFRED
          Right then. Girls, you need to clear
          the courtyard. Wait for the Major on
          the other side of the road. I'll go
          get her.

Alfred hurries back towards the factory.

                    ANNIE
          Alfie, wait.

Alfred doesn't look back, but dashes into the
burning building. The other Munitionettes are
hurrying away from the factory. Annie is left

alone in the courtyard. Tears stream down her face.

INT—MUNITIONS FACTORY, 1917—STAIRS—AM

Alfred is rushing up the stairs. There is smoke everywhere. When he reaches the top of the stairs, we see there is a closed door in front of him. He crashes into it with his shoulder. The door flies open. We see inside and there is a Munitionette lying on the floor overcome by fumes.

Alfred hurries over to the stricken girl. She's still breathing, but unconscious. Alfred part drags, part carries the girl out of the room and to the top of the stairs, coughing the whole time. He manages to prop the girl up into a sitting position on the top step, and with an almighty effort, he heaves her over his shoulder.

EXT—MUNITIONS FACTORY, 1917—COURTYARD—AM

Annie is alone in the courtyard watching the door intently. It suddenly flies open and Alfred staggers through it. The girl is still over his shoulder. He is coughing violently.

Before Annie can react, there is a huge explosion from inside the factory. Alfred is knocked off his feet and the girl is thrown to the floor. Annie rushes over, and falls to her knees sobbing.

                              Dissolve to

INT—CENTRAL HOUSE—STUDY—AM

Barry and Miss Spencer sitting in the newly completed dining room.

>   BARRY
>   (in a whisper)
>   I take it he didn't make it.

>   MISS SPENCER
>   Sadly not. They rushed them both to
>   the village hospital. She survived.
>   My mother visited him every night,
>   but he died a few days later.

Miss Spencer leans forward in her chair and takes hold of Barry's hand.

>   MISS SPENCER
>   Thank you so much for finding this
>   Barry. I'll treasure it always.

INT—BARRY'S HOUSE—KITCHEN—AM

Barry is standing in his kitchen. He is wearing jeans, a thick jumper, and Dr Martens boots and has a blue-and-white scarf draped over his shoulders.

He has the various sections of the *Weekend Guardian* spread out across the work surface. He has opened and is studying the Sport section. He is drinking coffee from a large Chelsea FC mug.

We hear a doorbell RING. Barry hurries into the hall. He opens the front door. There is a POSTMAN on the doorstep holding a large cardboard box.

                    BARRY
          Morning.

The postman holds out an electronic receipt
device.

                    POSTMAN
          Got one to sign for.

                    BARRY
          Thanks, mate.

Barry takes the device. He makes an illegible
signature with the plastic pen and passes it
back. The postman hands him the box in return
and turns to go.

                    BARRY
               (to the postman's departing back)
          Thanks.

The postman raises his hand to shoulder height,
but doesn't look back. Barry closes the front
door.

INT—BARRY'S HOUSE—DINING ROOM—AM

Barry takes the large box through to the dining
room. He puts it on the table and starts to open
it. Inside we see that there is folded sheet of
notepaper, a sealed envelope marked Item 1, and
two parcels wrapped in brown paper marked Item
2 and Item 4.

Barry unfolds the notepaper. We see that it's
from a firm of Solicitors and is addressed to
Barry Stuart Mason. As Barry reads, we hear his
voice.

                    BARRY (V.O.)
      We regret to inform you of the death
      of our client, Miss Lydia Spencer of
      Central House Nursing Home.

Barry sits down quickly on one of the dining
chairs.

                    BARRY
      Oh no.

Barry continues to read.

                    BARRY (V.O.)
      In accordance with our client's last
      will and testament (a copy of which
      you are entitled to apply should
      you so wish) I am instructed to
      disclose the following: Miss Spencer
      has left to you certain items that
      are enclosed with this letter. They
      are to be addressed in the sequence
      indicated below as dictated to us by
      Miss Spencer.

      1) Envelope marked Item 1.

Barry removes the envelope marked Item 1 from
the box and places it on the table.

                    BARRY (V.O.)
      2) Parcel marked Item 2.

Barry removes the parcel marked Item 2 from the
box and places it on the table alongside the
envelope marked Item 1. It measures about eight
inches by four inches and is about one inch
think.

> BARRY (V.O.)
> 3) Envelope marked Item 3; you will
> find this inside the parcel marked
> Item 2. This is to be opened before
> you open
>
> Item 4. Miss Spencer was most
> insistent on this point.
>
> 4) Parcel marked Item 4.

Barry removes the parcel marked Item 4 from the
box and places it on the table alongside the
other items. It is much smaller than the parcel
marked Item 2. Barry looks back at the letter
from the solicitors.

> BARRY (V.O.)
> The residue of Miss Spencer's estate
> I have been instructed to sell by
> auction. The auction will be held on
> September 5. The proceeds of said
> auction will be donated to the Terence
> Higgins Trust.

Barry picks up the envelope marked Item 1 and
holds it for a while before opening it. As Barry
reads, this time we hear Miss Spencer's voice.

> MISS SPENCER (V.O.)
> My Dearest Barry, if you are reading
> this letter, I am no longer in the
> land of the living, and you have just
> received an unexpected delivery from
> the postman. I would like to thank you
> so much for making the transformation
> of Central House possible. It can now
> forever be a place for repose.

After the completion of our project I was able to embark upon a grand tour of my friends scattered throughout the Home Counties – a swan song if you will. On my return, I was able to welcome the new residents as they moved in. At the time of writing, only two vacancies remain. You'll be delighted to know that the nurses are coping admirably, after a little prompting from me of course.

Now please open the parcel marked Item 2.

Barry opens the larger of the two parcels. Inside we see a framed sepia photograph. It's the photograph that Barry found in Miss Spencer's study. He picks up the picture and looks at it closely. He then notices the envelope at the bottom of the box. He takes it out and places it on the table next to the photograph. It's marked Item 3.

CHRIS, a man a few years older, a little taller, and a little heavier than Barry, walks into the dining room. He's wearing a dressing gown, his hair is longer than Barry's and a little dishevelled, and he's not shaved for a few days. He leans over Barry from behind, drapes his arms over Barry's shoulders and across his chest. He kisses him gently on the cheek.

>   CHRIS
> Was that the postman?

>   BARRY
> Er yes. A parcel for me.

                    CHRIS
I've not forgotten your birthday
again, have I?

                    BARRY
Er no. You're in the clear this time.
It's from the solicitors of Miss
Spencer. Do remember 'er? The job I
did on Central 'ouse?

                    CHRIS
Oh yes. Massive place. You turned it
into the final staging post before
heaven for the affluent middle classes
of the Woking area.

                    BARRY
She died.

                    CHRIS
Oh, I'm so sorr . . . I didn't mean to
er . . . Hey, what's this?

Chris's attention has been caught by the framed
photograph of Miss Spencer's uncle and Alfie.
He picks up the picture and looks at it closely.

                    CHRIS
Wow. If I didn't know any better, I'd say
that was taken in the early 20th century.

                    BARRY
It was taken in 1914.

                    CHRIS

Really? Wow.

                    BARRY
          It's Miss Spencer's uncle. I found the
          photo when I was strippin' the panels
          off her wall. She knew I liked photos,
          so she's left it to me.

As Barry talks, Chris takes the picture over
to window to look at it in better light. He's
no longer paying attention to what Barry's
saying.

                    CHRIS
                 (to himself)
          A young officer contemplates his
          reflection before going off to war.

                    BARRY
          He took it with him when he went to Belgium.

                    CHRIS
          Whoever took this must have taken a
          long time on the composition.

                    BARRY
                 (raising an eyebrow and smiling
                 enigmatically)
          Oh yeah. Why do you say that?

Chris walks back over from the window and places
the picture on the table in front of Barry. He
leans over him and points at the photo.

                    CHRIS
          Well, first of all, look at the light
          sources: the two windows and the
          overhead bulb. Now look at the angle
          of the mirror and the shadows.

                    BARRY
OK.

                    CHRIS
Well, don't you see?

                    BARRY
See what?

                    CHRIS
Quite! You don't. You don't see the
photographer! You've got two windows,
and one carefully angled mirror. That's
three reflecting surfaces. You've got
no glare on the mirror, with a flash
from 1914. That in itself is amazing.
The reflection is almost as clear
as the real person, and crucially,
somehow, the photographer, has not
caught himself . . .

                    BARRY
          (almost inaudibly)
Or herself.

                    CHRIS cont'd
. . . in the reflection of the mirror,
or the windows. Next is the feet. Now
that is very clever.

                    BARRY
It is?

                    CHRIS
Oh yes. What do you notice about the
reflection?

                    BARRY
Well, I can see a pair of feet . . .

                    CHRIS
                (interrupting)
Exactly. You can see a pair of feet!
The mirror has been deliberately
angled to get the feet into the shot.
Without the feet, it's obvious which
is the reflection. With the feet . . .

                (beat)
. . . it's less obvious. The
photographer clearly wants the casual
viewer to take a second look.

Chris picks up the picture and holds it close to
his face again.

                    CHRIS
You know, it really is hard to tell
which is the reflection and which is
the real person. If it wasn't for the
slight height difference, the shot
would be perfect.

                    BARRY
Height difference?

Chris puts the picture back on the table.

                    CHRIS
Take a close look. The reflection
appears to be ever so slightly shorter
than the subject. It's probably because
of the angle of the mirror. Must be
the compromise the photographer had
to make to ensure that the camera and
flash wasn't caught in the shot. Most
people wouldn't notice it.

                    BARRY
          Certainly not somefink I'd've fought
          of!

Chris pats Barry on the shoulder.

                    CHRIS
          Well, you know photography's my
          passion. Can I hang it?

                    BARRY
          Do.

Chris takes the picture over to the mantelpiece.
We now notice that there are dozens of
professional-looking framed photographs covering
the wall above the fireplace. Some are of famous
people, some of famous architecture, some just
of random people taken at interesting angles or
with curious backdrops.

After a few moments, Chris removes from the wall
a perfectly composed photograph of the Taj Mahal
taken through an archway at sunset. He replaces
it with Miss Spencer's uncle Richard and his
'reflection' Alfred.

Meanwhile, Barry picks up the envelope marked
Item 3, and opens it.

                    BARRY
          Thank you so much for finding the
          picture.

Chris turns round. As Barry reads, we now hear
Miss Spencer's voice.

                    MISS SPENCER (V.O.)
          It meant so much to my uncle, my
          mother, and of course dear Alfie.

STANLEY JACKSON AND GAVIN JACKSON

As you can see, the frame has given
it a new lease of life. I've had it
hanging on my wall over the fireplace
in the beautiful rooms that you
created for me.

By now you'll know that I've left
the bulk of my estate to a charity
of which I'm sure you'd approve. But
there were a few items that I felt
must go to a more fitting home, the
photograph being one such.

The final two items you'll find in
the parcel marked Item 4. Please open
it now.

Barry does so. Inside we see two harmonicas. One
is badly dented and has spots of rust all over
it. The other looks brand new.

        MISS SPENCER (V.O.) cont'd
One of these was returned to my mother
in 1918, badly battered but intact. I
have kept it together with its partner
for the last 50 years. I want you
to take over their custodianship and
breathe new life into them.

Your dear friend, Lydia Barry looks up at Chris.

        BARRY
Here, one each.

Barry hands Chris the pristine harmonica.

        CHRIS
I don't play the harmonica.

BARRY
Neiver do I. But we can learn. I'm sure
we can find someone at Brooklands
College who does a night class in
music.

THE WISHING WELL

By

Gavin Jackson

INT—NEW YORK—JOSHUA'S APARTMENT—MORNING

JOSHUA CREASEY, a successful sports writer, is in his apartment in Winbourne Towers overlooking Central Park, New York.

Joshua is standing at the desk in his home office. He is leaning over the chair, arranging a notepad and a Monte Blanc pen. There is also a computer monitor and keyboard on the desk. The monitor is switched off.

He is dressed in a running outfit: Nike Performance Air MAX training shoes, black Gore Urban running shorts, and matching shirt. Mounted on his arm, he has an iPod, and we see he has the ear buds inserted. We can hear a tinny BASE beating, so we know he has the iPod switched on. Joshua looks at his wrist. He is wearing a Tom Tom GPS personal training watch. We see it's 10 a.m.

Apparently satisfied with the desk arrangement, Joshua walks over to the window and opens the blind. We see the view he has over Central Park: trees, pathways, a small lake, and, in the distance, the Manhattan skyline.

EXT—NEW YORK—CENTRAL PARK—AM

We see Joshua walking briskly into Central Park.

He stops at a park bench and places his left foot on its arm. He leans forward to touch his toe and to stretch his left hamstring. He repeats the procedure to stretch his right hamstring. He then stands up straight and catches hold of this

left toe behind his left knee to stretch his
left quad. He repeats the procedure to stretch
his right quad. He then stretches both calf
muscles.

Joshua stands up straight again, places one hand
on his hip and the other on his shoulder, and
does some rotational torso stretches. Finally,
standing with his back to the bench, he places
his knuckles on the ground in front of him
shoulder-width apart and hops his feet on to
the seat of the bench. He then starts to do very
deep, and slow, press-ups.

EXT—NEW YORK—CENTRAL PARK—AM

We now notice another exerciser approaching. His
outfit is very similar to Joshua's: Nike's, black
running shorts, and black running shirt. But
whereas Joshua is 5 foot 10, stocky, and white,
the newcomer is 7 foot 3, heavily muscled in the
shoulders and biceps but otherwise virtually
fat- free, and black. He is DEVLIN 'SLAM-DUNK'
SAUNDERSON, a professional basketball player.

> SLAM
> Another attempt to put off starting
> that novel of yours?

> JOSHUA
> Hey, Slam, how you doin'?

Joshua completes three more press-ups.

> JOSHUA cont'd
> (loudly)
> 98, 99, 100.

                    SLAM
          Yeah right, in yer dreams man. 20 if
          you're lucky, and that's 20 the easy
          way.

Slam bends over with his legs straight and places
his hands flat on the ground before him. He then
goes up on his toes and brings his legs in to his
chest. His toes leave the ground, and he slowly
lifts his legs, straight, into a handstand. He
holds his body perfectly vertically and perfectly
still.

Two passers-by, a YOUNG LAD and his FATHER stop
to watch.

Slam does 5 perfect inverted press-ups, then
slowly lowers his feet back to the ground, his
knees never bending.

                    JOSHUA
          No one likes a wise guy.

                    YOUNG LAD
          Wow! That was awesome, man.

Slam turns to face the boy and his father. They
clap. He does a mock bow.

                    SLAM
          Why, thank you, kind sirs.

                    YOUNG LAD
          Oh. My. God. It's Slam-dunk Saunderson.

                    SLAM
          In the flesh.

Slam walks over to the boy, leans down, and extends his hand for shaking. He towers over the boy. The boy timidly holds out his hand. Slam's enormous hand envelops the boy's. The boy tries to shake it, but Slam resists. The boy tries again. Slam resists again. Now the boy tries to shake Slam's hand with as much strength as he can manage. Slam does a three-quarter somersault, landing on his bottom with his

legs outstretched, still holding the boy's hand. He's now eye-to-eye with the boy.

> SLAM
> That's a mean handshake you've got there, lad.

The boy laughs.

> YOUNG LAD
> Will you do the slam-dunk for us?

> FATHER
> Leave the man alone son. He came here to exercise, not be bothered by the likes of you.

> SLAM
> That's no problem. Hey, Josh, give us a hand over here.

Joshua walks over to the three of them.

> SLAM
> Right, there's the basket.

Slam points to an ornate lamp post at the edge of the pathway. It's a very solid-looking, wrought

iron post with elaborate shapes on its length.
The light stands at about 10 foot off the ground.

                SLAM
        The light's the hoop. You, young man,
        you've got to stand right here and
        defend. And Josh, you come and stand
        over there. You'll feed me the ball
        when I run in.

                FATHER
                  (gabbling)
        Wait up! Wait up, wait up. Let me get
        my phone.

The boy's father fiddles in the inside pocket of
his jack. He takes out his phone and points it
towards Slam and the lamp post.

                FATHER cont'd
        Right. Got it in video mode. Ready
        when you are.

                SLAM
        Right, Josh, you ready? Feed me the
        ball.

                JOSHUA
        What ball?

                SLAM
        This one.

Slam starts to bounce an imaginary basketball.
He dribbles it round the boy's father, then
passes it to Joshua. Joshua makes no attempt to
catch it. The boy laughs.

STANLEY JACKSON AND GAVIN JACKSON

                    SLAM
          Can you fetch it, lad?

The boy runs to the bushes where the imaginary
ball would have landed.

                    SLAM
                (to Joshua)
          You know, you've really got to work on
          that imagination of yours if you're
          going to write a novel.

The young boy thrashes around for a few moments.

                    YOUNG LAD
          Got it.

The young boy mimes throwing the ball back to
Slam. His action resembles that of a shot-putter.
Slam leaps up and catches the ball at the top
of its supposed trajectory.

                    SLAM
          That's a netball pass, lad. Nothing
          wrong with netball, but you don't
          slam-dunk in netball. Here try again.

Slam mimes a basketball pass to the boy. The
young lad catches the imaginary ball and passes
it back to Slam.

                    SLAM
          Much better. Hope you're taking notes,
          Josh. Now then, let's go again.

Slam takes a short run-up. Then as Joshua mimes
a pass, he takes three loping strides as though
about to do a high jump. On the third stride, he
takes off vertically and 'catches' the imaginary

ball high over the boy's head. He turns in the air so is now moving backwards towards the lamp. He grabs high above his head with his left hand, catches hold of the lamp, and taps it with his right hand, as if scoring a basket. He holds on to the lamp for about five seconds with his knees bent up before dropping to the ground. He then drops to his knees in front of the boy, and they do a high five.

> YOUNG LAD
> Thanks man. The guys at school are never gonna to believe this.

> FATHER
> Come on, Son, we've got to get back home for lunch.

The young boy and his father leave. Joshua and Slam sit down on the bench that Joshua had been using for his stretches.

> SLAM
> So how long before we get your good self back on the sports pages?

> JOSHUA
> They allowed me a two-month sabbatical, and we're at the end of the first week.

> SLAM
> Well, the sooner you're back, the better. Your temporary alternate is really not up to the task.

                    JOSHUA
Can't pretend I'm not relieved to hear
that. Sounds like my job's safe!

                    SLAM
You still getting trouble started?

                    JOSHUA
Each time I sit down at my desk, my
mind goes blank.

                    SLAM
Well, that's your problem right there:
sit in front of a blank page or a blank
screen and you're bound to get a blank
mind. What you need is a little spark.
Take yourself away from your screen
and find your inspiration first.

                    JOSHUA
How do I do that?

                    SLAM
When I was doing my English major,
whenever I needed a little push, I'd
people watch. Worked every time.

                    JOSHUA
People watch?

                    SLAM
Yeah. You know, sit on bench, watch
people go by, and imagine what their
stories might be.

                    JOSHUA
But they're just people going about
their mundane lives. What could be
inspiring about that?

> SLAM
>
> Man, you have so much to learn about
> this city. Little dramas are playing
> themselves out all around you, all the
> time. You just have to open yourself
> up to seeing them.
>
> Look, you're all dressed up, me
> too: let's do a quick circuit, full
> obstacles. I'll even spot you a
> 60-second head start while I chin.
>
> Then get yourself changed, get
> yourself a notepad and pen, find
> yourself a nice place to sit, and
> let the stories come to you. Believe
> me, man, they're here, all around
> us. You just have to let yourself
> see them.

Slam walks over to the basketball lamp post,
leaps up, and catches hold of the cross member.
He starts doing chin-ups. He keeps his legs
pointing straight down throughout each rep.
He lowers himself each time as slowly as he
raises himself. Each rep is a smooth fluid
movement.

> SLAM
> (while continuing his exercise)
> Your 60-second start's dwindling,
> Josh. Fifty dollars says I catch you
> by the boathouse.

Joshua looks up at Slam, then leaps to his feet
and sprints down the path towards the lake.

EXT—NEW YORK—SHADY GLEN IN CENTRAL PARK—AM

Joshua is sitting on a bench in the middle of Central Park. It's a beautiful sunny afternoon and a beautiful location. Several paths cross in front of where Joshua is sitting. There is a gentle, grassy slope leading down to a small lake with a view of the downtown skyscrapers in the distance. There's a stream flowing into the lake with a decorative fountain part way down.

Joshua is now wearing khaki chinos; a dark green blazer over a white polo shirt; and brown, checked, Louis Vuitton loafers. We can see that he has the ear buds of his iPod inserted. He is holding a pen in one hand and is balancing a notepad on his knee. We see that there is nothing written on the notepad.

Joshua is watching his fellow visitors. They are dog- walking, jogging, rollerblading, strolling, book-reading, or, like him, just sitting and watching the world go by. There are children playing, children eating ice cream, and several couples in animated conversations.

Off to one side, there is a large group of Japanese tourists taking photographs of a clump of cherry trees. They seem particularly interested in the patterns of the blossom on the ground beneath the trees.

A man in his early thirties walks past. He stops when he recognises Joshua. The man says something to Joshua. The man has a *Sports Illustrated* under his arm. He holds it out to Joshua. Joshua removes his ear buds and takes the man's magazine. He leafs through it, stopping about three quarters of the way through. We see a photograph of Joshua in the magazine. Joshua signs his name below the photograph and hands the magazine back to the man. The man thanks him and continues on his way through the park.

Joshua carefully winds up the cable of his ear buds and puts them into his pocket. He then settles back on the bench, puts his hands behind his head with his fingers interlocked, and continues doing nothing.

EXT—NEW YORK—CENTRAL PARK—LATE MORNING

Joshua appears to be dropping off to sleep on the bench when his attention is caught by MILO, a shabbily dressed man in his mid-forties, apparently feeding pigeons.

> JOSHUA
> (to himself)
> As if there aren't enough of those feathered rodents fouling the park. Now we've got some hobo encouraging more.

But we now see that Milo is not feeding them at all; he has no food with him. He is crouched down low and ten pigeons are gathered around him, none closer than about six feet, all facing him. He appears to be addressing them, and they appear to be listening with rapt attention.

As Joshua watches, Milo reaches into his pocket and brings out what looks like a small metal pea-shooter. But he puts it to his lips sideways in the manner of a flute. He then starts playing.

We hear Rimsky-Korsakov's 'Flight of the Bumble Bee' played on a PICCOLO FLUTE.

As Milo plays, more pigeons join the ten already in front of him. They fly in from all the nearby trees. Soon ten become a hundred. Still pigeons come flying in to join the growing crowd. By the time he has finished playing, there must be over a thousand pigeons gathered in a circle round Milo.

Suddenly Milo stands up and raises his hands above his head in one swift movement. As one, the pigeons take off. They bunch together and appear to hover over the park for a few seconds. They start to soar and wheel resembling a murmuration of starlings. They then change direction and fly over the treetops as single organism.

Joshua stands and turns to watch as the massive flock of pigeons head northwards, temporarily darkening the afternoon sky.

> JOSHUA
> Wow, that's some trick.

Joshua turns back to where Milo had been standing. We see that Milo is walking straight towards him.

> MILO
> Can you spare any change, sir?

> JOSHUA
> Sure.

He reaches into his pocket and hands over two quarters.

                    MILO
          Why thank you, sir.

Milo touches the brim of his hat with his right
hand, turns, and walks back to where his tiny
audience had been just moments before. He then
tosses the two coins into the small decorative
fountain and starts to walk down the path away
from Joshua.

                    JOSHUA
              (shouting out to the old man)
          Hey! What did you do that for?

Joshua gets up and starts to follow Milo. He
calls out again, but Milo appears not to hear.
Milo is walking quite quickly, so Joshua has to
run to catch up with him.

Joshua taps Milo on the shoulder. Milo turns
round.

                    JOSHUA
          Hey, why did you toss my money into
          that fountain?

                    MILO
          I didn't.

                    JOSHUA
          You did, I just saw you.

                    MILO
          It was my money. You gave it to me.

                    JOSHUA
          OK, wise guy, why did you throw your
          money into that fountain? If I'd
          known you were just going to throw it

away, I wouldn't've given it to you.
I thought you wanted to buy a cup of
coffee with it.

                    MILO
With 50 cents? Are you kidding? Where
can you get a cup of coffee for less
than two bucks?

                    JOSHUA
Fair point. But why throw those coins
into the fountain at all?

                    MILO
That's no ordinary fountain. It's over
a wishing well.

                    JOSHUA
A wishing well?

                    MILO
That's what I said: You throw in some
change; you make a wish; the wish
comes true.

Joshua says nothing.

                    MILO
You look sceptical. I'm not surprised.
I was at first. But my father assured
me that it worked, and I've not been
disappointed in nearly 50 years. My
wish today was that the pigeons would
heed my advice and seek out a more
appropriate woodland home upstate
away from the pollution of the city.

JOSHUA
I thought you were feeding the
pigeons.

MILO
Why would I do that? That would just
encourage more to come. And that
would not be good for their health.

JOSHUA
Not good for their health!

MILO
Exactly.

JOSHUA
Is it just pigeons you're worried
about?

MILO
Oh no, I care for all birds. But I
find most others are a little . . .
flighty if you'll pardon the pun.

JOSHUA
Flighty?

MILO
Yes, flighty. Have you ever tried to
reason with a red cardinal?

JOSHUA
Er no, can't say I have.

MILO
Believe me, they're obstinate little
critters. Always think they're right.
Never willing to compromise.

STANLEY JACKSON AND GAVIN JACKSON

                    JOSHUA
               (a little hesitantly)
          This might sound a little odd, but
          do you want to tell me more about
          the pigeons, Central Park, and the
          wishing well over a coffee?

Milo's face breaks into a big smile.

                    MILO
          I'd love to.

INT—NEW YORK—DINER OVERLOOKING CENTRAL PARK—MIDDAY

Milo is telling Joshua about the part that the
wishing well and Central Park has played in the
lives of several generations of his family.

                    MILO
          The park and the wishing well have
          played a central role in the fortunes
          of my family for four generations.
          The park has been good to us, and,
          in return, we have been good to the
          park.

          We came originally from the little
          village of Xylokastro in the shadows
          of the Corinthian mountains in Greece.
          My great-grandfather settled in this
          city at the end of the 19th century.
          He came with nothing and had nothing
          until the creation of Central Park
          offered him a lifeline.

          He was one of the original labourers
          back in the 1870s. They were looking

for workers to help build the park, and he was a willing worker. When the park was finally opened in 1878, each worker was given an extra nickel in their pay packets as a bonus.

My great-grandfather, coming from the ancient mountains of Greece, was a deeply superstitious man. He had already spotted the well while working on the park and guessed at its powers. He had heard tales of such things in his childhood. If they exist in the ancient states of Greece, why not also in the states of the New World?

He threw his bonus nickel into the well (now marked by that small decorative fountain) and made a wish. He wished that the park would support all future generations of his family. And so it has. We've been sweepers, wardens, and gardeners.

At various times we have all made wishes at that same well, each of which has come true. My son works in a building just off the park. He makes regular trips to the park and makes regular wishes with the tips that he receives. His wishes are always related to his clients. He says it has never once failed him, and so the well actually helps him to fulfil his job.

**INT—NEW YORK—DINER OVERLOOKING CENTRAL PARK—
LATE AFTERNOON**

Milo finally stops talking. They have each had
half a dozen Americanos and several pastries
each over the course of the afternoon. The table
is filled with crockery.

> JOSHUA
> That's quite a story.

> MILO
> You don't believe me? That's fine.
> It's good to be sceptical. Why not
> give it a try? What harm can it
> do? As Niels Bohr is supposed to
> have once commented when hanging a
> horseshoe above the door to his lab:
> 'I understand it brings you good luck
> whether you believe in it or not.'

> JOSHUA
> But what about the pigeons?

> MILO
> What about them?

> JOSHUA
> Well, look over there. What are they
> still doing here?

Milo looks through the window. We see several
pigeons pecking at a discarded sandwich.

> MILO
> Having lunch I'd say.

> JOSHUA
> But why?

                    MILO
Because they're hungry?

                    JOSHUA
I thought you'd sent all the pigeons
way upstate where it was healthier
for them.

                    MILO
I did. But they're pigeons, not nuclear
physicists. I can only advise. It's up
to them how they act on that advice.
I'm not a miracle worker. At least
they're more sensible than passenger
pigeons.

                    JOSHUA
Passenger pigeons?

                    MILO
Beautiful, tall and slender dove-
like pigeons, with long mottled tail
feathers and a bright orange breasts
like an English robin. There used to
be millions of them in huge flocks,
up to a mile long, all the way up and
down the East Coast. They'd regularly
overfly New York in such great numbers
that they'd darken the sky.

                    JOSHUA
I think I might regret asking this,
but What happened to them?

                    MILO
Victims of small game hunters who
thought shooting ectopistes migratoria
by the thousands was legitimate sport.
They were eventually hunted out of

existence around 1900, largely down to their own arrogance, but Xerxes never forgave himself.

          JOSHUA
Xerxes?

          MILO
Xerxes Dimas. My great-grandfather. He always felt he could have done more to persuade them to flock in smaller numbers, and to move to Washington State, but they thought they could out- fly the hunters. One of his wishes at the well was that Central Park would forever be a green oasis in the heart of New York. A place that would forever provide a sanctuary for the furry and the feathered regardless of whatever other building developments should arise in the future.

          JOSHUA
You're saying that the continuing success of Central Park is due to that very first wish of your great- grandfather?

          MILO
Of course. It's still here, isn't it?

Joshua laughs.

          JOSHUA
Well, I certainly can't deny that!

Joshua looks at his watch.

              JOSHUA cont'd
     Look, I really should be going.

Joshua calls over the waitress and asks for the
tab. When he opens his wallet, he realises he's
not got enough money.

              JOSHUA
     Shit. This is embarrassing: I was in
     a rush earlier and forgot to go to the
     cash machine before coming back out
     to the park.

              MILO
         (picking up the tab)
     I'll get this.

              JOSHUA
     But I invited you.

              MILO
     Fuhgeddaboudit.

Milo reaches into his pocket and brings out a
roll of notes. He peels off two and places them
on the table. Milo gets up and heads towards
the exit of the cafe. Joshua hurries after him.

EXT—NEW YORK—OUTSIDE THE DINER—LATE AFTERNOON

Milo and Joshua are standing just outside the cafe.

              JOSHUA
     Why did you ask me for change if you
     had all that money?

                    MILO
     I needed the change for the wishing
     well. It only works if someone has
     been kind enough to give you the
     money. Here, give it a try on your
     way home.

Milo hands Joshua two quarters.

                    JOSHUA
     I'm not sure I could find that shady
     glen again.

                    MILO
     It's easy. Just take this path. Go as
     far as the fork near the oak tree, and
     follow the signposts for Inspiration
     Point. You can't miss it.

Joshua looks in the direction that Milo is
indicating.

                    MILO
     Just be careful what you wish for.

                    JOSHUA
     What do you mean?

Joshua turns back round, but Milo is already
someway off, heading towards 5th Avenue.

**EXT—NEW YORK—SHADY GLEN IN CENTRAL PARK—LATE
AFTERNOON**

Joshua cuts back through Central Park. He finds
the wishing well.

JOSHUA
I wish I could find inspiration in
everything around me.

He throws the two quarters that Milo gave him
into the fountain. He stands there for a few
minutes. Nothing happens.

INT—NEW YORK—JOSHUA'S APARTMENT—EVENING

Joshua gets back to his apartment at a little
after six thirty in the evening. He pours himself
a glass of red wine and sits down at the desk
in his study. He is careful to place his glass
on a coaster. He opens the drawer to the desk
and takes out a large notepad and places it in
front of him. Finally, he takes out his prized
Mont Blanc pen. He is ready to start.

In neat copperplate handwriting, Joshua writes.

    Fairy Tale of New York

He sits back and looks at the notepad.

JOSHUA
Perhaps something more dynamic.

Joshua draws a neat line under his first attempt.
He tries another:

    Barefoot in the Park

JOSHUA
Better. On the one hand, it gives
a sense of intimacy, innocence, and
freedom. And yet on the other hand,
it hints at poverty and hardship. The

complexity of Central Park in the heart of New York.

Joshua draws a neat line under his second attempt.

Joshua sits back and sips his wine for a few minutes. He looks at his watch, and then walks over to the window. He watches the city many floors below.

INT—NEW YORK—JOSHUA'S APARTMENT—OVERNIGHT

Overnight there is an almighty storm. We hear heavy rain lashing at the windows and the sound of thunder. First the thunder is quite distant, from Central Park. But then several claps get louder and closer. The storm climaxes with a lightning strike that hits Joshua's apartment block. The few lights that were still on (diodes of the hi-fi and TV on standby mode, electronic clock, telephone answering machine) go out, plunging the apartment into complete darkness.

Then Joshua's computer starts to boot up. Joshua sleeps soundly through the entire storm.

INT—NEW YORK—JOSHUA'S APARTMENT—MORNING

Next morning, Joshua comes out of the bathroom dressed for his morning run. As he is about to leave his apartment, he notices that the computer monitor is on in the study. He goes in, and we see that on the screen, the two titles that he wrote (and underlined) on the notepad are now on the screen. In both cases, the titles are in strike-through format:

~~Fairytale of New York~~

~~Barefoot in the Park~~

Joshua leans over his chair, picks up the mouse, and moves the cursor to the Start icon and selects Shut down. But the computer doesn't start the shut down routine. He switches off the monitor. It switches itself back on again.

Now a new title appears below the two struck-through titles:

The Wishing Well

Joshua tries to hit the delete key, but his hands seem drawn to the letter keys instead. Seemingly against his will, he starts to type:

> At the heart of the city lies Central Park; a slumbering titan, breathing life into the hopes and aspirations of its citizens. Wall Street may provide the city's financial security, but Central Park provides its soul. Without Central Park, New York would be a lifeless husk, just an ordinary city like any other.

Joshua stops typing and lifts his hands from the keyboard. He turns them over to look at his palms, and then the backs, as if they are not his own. He then plunges his hands back down on to the keyboard and continues to type. He is still leaning over the chair and looks very uncomfortable, but he doesn't seem able to stop pounding away at the computer.

STANLEY JACKSON AND GAVIN JACKSON

Suddenly Joshua's mobile phone MESSAGE ALERT sounds. Joshua stops typing. With seemingly superhuman effort, he wrenches his hands off the keyboard and picks up his phone:

HEY MAN, YOU RUNNING TODAY?

Joshua replies to the text messages.

SEE YOU AT THE LAKE IN 30

Joshua reaches under the desk and unplugs the computer's power cable. The monitor goes black. Joshua drapes the plug over the monitor.

With the spell apparently broken, Joshua walks over to the window and opens the blinds. Light floods into the apartment. It's a beautiful day, but Joshua gasps. He looks panicked. He frantically snatches up his notepad and starts scribbling notes manically.

Joshua takes several other notepads out, throws them on to the dining table. He goes back to the window. He looks out again, but in a different direction. He rushes to the table and starts scribbling on one of the new pads.

JOSHUA
(mumbling under his breath)
Why have I never noticed this before?

He then rushes back to the window. Then back to another notepad.

Finally he looks at his watch.

JOSHUA
Shit, shit, shit.

He tosses the pen across the apartment, snatches up his keys, and rushes out of the apartment, slamming the door behind him. We hear his footsteps going down the stairs. Then the footsteps stop. We hear footsteps coming back up again.

Joshua bursts back into the apartment, snatches up another blank notepad and stuffs it into his shorts, then rushes over to where he'd thrown the pen and scrabbles on the floor for a few moments. He stands up holding the pen, stuffs it into his pocket, and exits the apartment for a second time.

EXT—NEW YORK—SHADY GLEN IN CENTRAL PARK—AM

Joshua is sitting on a bench in the shady glen where he met Milo and then returned to make a wish in the well. We see that as people near him are having conversations, Joshua is occasionally making notes of their dialogue.

Several joggers are passing. One of them is Slam. He stops when he notices Joshua.

>   SLAM
> What happened to you, man? I did the
> lake 5 times before I gave up on your
> sorry ass.

>   JOSHUA
> Sorry about that. Got distracted. When
> I woke up yesterday morning . . .

>   SLAM
> Let me guess: You had the blues!

JOSHUA
No. I felt more alive than I'd ever
felt in my life. The park seemed very
different. All the familiar paths, and
trees, and grassy banks, and flower
beds, and kiosks were still there,
but they all seemed to be in sharper
focus. Colours seemed brighter and
sounds clearer.

SLAM
You changed your meds or something?

JOSHUA
Very funny. I seem able to find
inspiration everywhere now. I see
a greater depth of detail than I've
ever seen before. And the people
are no longer merely dog-walkers,
joggers, rollerbladers, strollers,
or book-readers. I can see them all
as potential characters, each with
their own back story just waiting to
be explored.

SLAM
Told you people watching would help.

JOSHUA
Even you. I don't see just a
professional basketball player.
I see a gifted kid from a tough
neighbourhood who started off as a
gymnast at high school who quickly
got selected for the basketball team
when he kept growing.

6ft at 13, 6ft 6 at 15, and topping
out at a 7ft 3.

A kid who in another area or in another body would have gone to college on intellectual merit, but who got a sports scholarship and had to fight with his coach to be allowed to actually attend lectures. A straight-A student who was one of the few alumni who went to college on a sports scholarship and majored in English rather than Sports Science.

          SLAM
You been reading my autobiography! It's all in there.

          JOSHUA
Yes, but I've known you for years. I've known your story for years. But now when I see you, it all floods back in an instant.

          SLAM
So what's the problem? You've now got instant recall and what seems like a limitless source of ideas. Sounds like progress.

          JOSHUA
I'm afraid it might stop.

          SLAM
So get it down!

Joshua waves several notepads in the air.

          JOSHUA
I'm getting down, but I don't know what to do with it.

                    SLAM
And you're coming to a professional
basketball player for literary advice.
Man, you are in trouble.

Slam starts to laugh heartily.

                    JOSHUA
We both know you're more than that.

                    SLAM
Aw shucks! But honestly, I really
don't think I can help. But I know a
man who probably can: Paul Austin.

                    JOSHUA
Who's he?

                    SLAM
Literary agent. He finds ghost-writers
for sports autobiographies. Did mine
for me.

                    JOSHUA
I thought you wrote yours.

                    SLAM
Just the title: He wanted to go with
'A Devlin from the Kitchen'. I told I
wasn't wanting to write a cookbook,
and I'm not from Hell's Kitchen. So we
agreed on 'From the Slammer to the
Slam-Dunker'.

                    JOSHUA
You've never been in the slammer.

                    SLAM
            (with mock indignation)
    I have. We played an exhibition match
    in St Quentin last summer. Scared the
    shit out of me.

EXT—NEW YORK—SHELDON PUBLISHING HOUSE—AM

Joshua carefully parks his white BMW M5 outside
SHELDON PUBLISHING HOUSE, four inches from the
kerbside, perfectly parallel. He looks up at
the tall building. He pauses for a few moments
before getting out of the car and closing the
door.

He is smartly dressed in light chinos and the
blazer that we saw him wearing in Central Park
when he met Milo. He is also wearing a crisp
white shirt and a Windsor-knotted tie. He heads
towards the building and walks through the
revolving door, and into the lobby.

INT—SHELDON PUBLISHING HOUSE—RECEPTION AREA—AM

Joshua takes the lift to the 42nd floor. There is a
long corridor opposite the lift. PAUL AUSTIN has
a corner office at the far end of the corridor.

Before Paul's office is the reception area. This
is the domain of TINA CORTÉZ, Paul Austin's
personal assistant. As Joshua comes round the
corner and into the reception area, we see that
Tina is sitting behind a vast desk piled high
with printed manuscripts, one of which she is
reading and marking up. Behind Tina are two
floor-to-ceiling glass walls through which we
can see into Paul's office.

STANLEY JACKSON AND GAVIN JACKSON

Paul's office is a huge L-shaped room with vast amounts of window and very little furniture. There is notably no desk, but there are two very long sofas offering impressive views over New York in two different directions. In front of each are several coffee tables.

> JOSHUA
> I'm Joshua Creasey. The sports writer.

> TINA
> Tina Cortéz. PA's PA. Go straight through.

Joshua looks through the glass wall and we can see Paul pacing up and down the length of the office speaking into a telephone headset. It's clear he's having an animated conversation.

> JOSHUA
> Really? He seems to be on a call.

> TINA
> Of course he is. That's what he does: walk and talk.

> JOSHUA
> I don't want to disturb him. I could just . . .

> TINA
> Nonsense. Off you go.

Joshua opens the door and hovers in the doorway to Paul's office.

INT—SHELDON PUBLISHING HOUSE—PAUL AUSTIN'S OFFICE—AM

We can now hear Paul's end of the telephone conversation.

>   PAUL
>   (talking animatedly into the
>   telephone headset)
> Shut the front door, Mr Fowler. Shut the front door.
>
>   (beat)
> Yeah? So sue me. Ya, cornstalker.

Paul turns back away from the window and sees Joshua standing in the doorway.

>   PAUL
> Come in. Come in.

>   JOSHUA
> Paul Austin? I'm . . .

>   PAUL
>   (cutting him off)
> Joshua Creasey. You need no introduction, my man. S-DS maybe the MVP, but you're the MVJ, the Most Valuable Sports Journo around. 'sides, Slam said you'd be over. What's on your mind? Wanting help to write your 'rags to riches'?

>   JOSHUA
> Er, no. I . . . . . .

PAUL
(interrupting)
Of course in your case it's a 'riches
to riches' story.

JOSHUA
Actually, I . . .

PAUL
I can find a ghost for you. Although
I'm surprised you think you think you
need one.

JOSHUA
I was thinking of a novel.

PAUL
Hope you're not thinking about a
sports novel.

JOSHUA
Anything but. I want to get away from—

PAUL
Or Scandi-Noire.

JOSHUA
Well, I'm not from Scandinavia, so not
much . . .

PAUL
I've got a Turk out in Queens who
can crank out a Scandi-Noire novel
whenever I need one.

JOSHUA
Thing is, I met this guy in Central
Park.

                    (beat)
This is going to sound fantastical,
but I'll tell you anyway: He corralled
a huge flock of pigeons and persuaded
them to fly upstate for the sake of
their health.

Anyway, he said he owed his 'power'
to a wishing well. I gave it a try and
since then, I've found inspiration
anywhere and everywhere I look. Loads
of ideas that I'm trying to channel
into a . . .

            PAUL
          (again interrupting)
You've met a mystery man in Central
Park who can talk to the birds. You
made a wish in a well and now you're
channelling your inner spirit.

            JOSHUA
If you put it like that, it sounds . . .

            PAUL
Like 'Magic Realism'. Like. ING. it.

            JOSHUA
I guess it . . .

            PAUL
Take that away. Treat us in two.
We'll work out whether it's floater
or a lurker — worth progressing or
regressing. You follow?

            (beat)
Later.

Before Joshua has a chance to reply, Paul is already walking back towards the window and speaking into his telephone headset to another client. Joshua backs out of Paul's office and closes the door.

INT—SHELDON PUBLISHING HOUSE—RECEPTION AREA—AM

> JOSHUA
> (sarcastically)
> Well, that went well!

> TINA
> Yes, I thought so.

> JOSHUA
> But I was in there no time at all. I barely had a chance to say anything.

Tina looks at her watch.

> TINA
> Two minutes and seventeen seconds. That's very good for a first meet. Means he likes you.

> JOSHUA
> He does?

> TINA
> And your column.

> JOSHUA
> Does he really read it?

                    TINA
          No.

               (beat)
          I do. Which is the next best thing.
          And he invited you back.

                    JOSHUA
          Yes. At least I think he did.

Tina looks at some notes on her desk.

                    TINA
          Treatment for a novel. Magic Realism.
          Return in about 2 weeks.

                    JOSHUA
          You were listening?

                    TINA
          Of course. I'm PA's PA.

INT—NEW YORK—COFFEE SHOP—PM

Joshua is looking very dishevelled. He is wearing
jogging trousers and a New York Red Bulls jersey.
He is in the coffee shop overlooking Central
Park that we saw him in with Milo.

He has two small reporter's notepads, one on
either side of the table he's sitting at. He has
a pen resting on each notepad. He has a third
larger notepad in between the two that he's
furiously writing on.

A couple nearby are having a conversation that
we can't hear. Joshua stops writing on the large
notepad. He leans over to his left, makes a few

notes with his left hand on the small reporter's notepad, and replaces the pen. He then sits up straight again and resumes his furious scribbling with his right hand. When he gets to the bottom of the page, he looks around the table and picks up a paper napkin. He smooths it out, places it on the large notepad, and starts to write on that.

RAINA, the waitress who served Joshua when he was last here with Milo, passes Joshua's table. She is holding a filter coffee jug. She stops and fills up Joshua's mug. Joshua looks up while continuing to write.

          JOSHUA
  Thanks.

          RAINA
  Can you stop that?

          JOSHUA
  What?

Raina nods down at that table.

          RAINA
  Writing on the table cloth.

Joshua looks down at his hand. He has got to the end of the napkin and is indeed writing on the table cloth. With what seems a little effort, he slaps the pen down on the table. He starts to reach into his pocket.

          JOSHUA
  I am so sorry. Please, let me buy the
  cloth.

Joshua puts a $50 bill on the table.

             JOSHUA
      Will that cover it?

Raina puts down the coffee jug and picks up the
$50 bill. She straightens it out and places it
on the cloth where Joshua has been writing.

             RAINA
      Not quite. You'll need something a
      little bigger if you want to get the
      whole of that last sentence. If you'd
      omitted that final sub-clause you
      might have got away with it.

Joshua laughs nervously.

             RAINA
      Look, I'll square it with Clyde, but
      you'd better be fixing to give me a
      big tip.

Raina picks up the bill and the coffee jug. She
heads towards the counter.

INT—NEW YORK—COFFEE SHOP—PM

Joshua turns the page over on his large notepad
and starts writing again. Raina returns to his
table and sits down opposite him. Joshua doesn't
notice. Raina lifts her side of the table cloth
and gives it a little tug.

             RAINA
      Shift your elbows, and I'll fold it
      up. You can take it away with you.

                    JOSHUA
Oh, thanks.

                    RAINA
Wouldn't want you to lose any of your
masterpiece.

Raina folds the table cloth and places it on top
of Joshua's large notepad, forcing him to stop
writing.

                    RAINA
There you go. Clyde was cool about it.
It's not every day we get a celebrity
in here.

                    JOSHUA
Celebrity?

                    RAINA
You are Joshua Creasey, aren't you?

                    JOSHUA
Er, yes. Yes, I am.

                    RAINA
Thought so. I love your columns.

                    JOSHUA
You like sports?

                    RAINA
Hate sports, love your column. You
have a great turn of phrase. You make
even the most mundane game sound
majestic.

                    JOSHUA
          Thanks. Er, will your boss mind you
          sitting here, chatting?

                    RAINA
          Not at all. I've just gone off duty.
          Been here since 5 a.m.

Raina reaches behind her back and unties her
waitress's apron. She lifts it over her head and
places it on top of the folded table cloth.

                    RAINA cont'd
          Don't mind chatting with me for a few
          minutes, do you?

                    JOSHUA
          Guess not. Least I can do as you
          sorted the cloth for me.

                    RAINA
          I've missed you, you know.

                    JOSHUA
          What? Have we met before?

                    RAINA
          No. Your column. I've missed reading
          you. Your locum's bunkum.

Joshua makes a note on the left notepad while
Raina's talking.

                    JOSHUA
          I've heard he's a competent writer.

                    RAINA
If you want to read about what
happened in the ball game, he is. But
who wants to do that?

                    JOSHUA
Probably 99.9% of the readership!

                    RAINA
You describe atmosphere and rivalry
and emotion and passion and love
and drama. It's often easy to forget
you're talking about sports at all. A
good thing in my book.

                    JOSHUA
I'm glad you like it.

                    RAINA
What are you working on at the moment,
aside from the table cloth that is?

                    JOSHUA
Just a few ideas. I came to Central
Park to get some inspiration, and now
I just can't seem to write down the
ideas quickly enough.

                    RAINA
Nice problem to have!

                    JOSHUA
It is, and it isn't. The ideas just
keep coming thick and fast. As soon
as I work on one idea, a new one comes
in before I've finished the first. And
so on.

                    RAINA
What's with the triple notepads?

                    JOSHUA
My attempt at trying to impose a
little order on my thoughts. This
one's my main theme—that's the one
that ended on the napkin and the
table cloth. This one's for snippets
of interesting dialogue that I hear
if people are having a conversation
near me. And this one's for jotting
down one-liners of new ideas that
suddenly come to mind.

Raina picks up the small reporter's notepad on
Joshua's left. She flips through some of the
pages.

                    RAINA
You afraid someone might take offence
to your note taking? That why you
write like that?

                    JOSHUA
Like what?

                    RAINA
Mirror writing. I can read it, but
it's certainly not easy:

          (slowly, while reading from the
          notepad)
'I've missed reading you. Your locum's
bunkum.'

Joshua takes the notepad from Raina and looks
at the writing.

                    JOSHUA
                (wistfully)
        God. I didn't know I did that.

Raina picks up the small notepad on Joshua's
right. She flicks through a few pages.

                    RAINA
        And this one's the right way round.
        Neat trick you've got there.

                    JOSHUA
        What trick?

                    RAINA
        Your ambidexterity. You do the mirror
        writing when you write with your left
        hand. Everything you write with your
        right hand is the right way round.

                    JOSHUA
        God. I didn't know I did that either.

Joshua puts both his hands on the table and
examines his palms. He then turns them over and
examines their backs. He picks up the pen with
his left hand and starts to take a few notes:

                    JOSHUA
                (speaking as he writes)
        'Your ambidexterity. You do the mirror
        writing when you write with your left
        hand.'

We see that the handwriting is identical in size
and style to that written by his right hand, but
in reverse. Joshua and Raina are both silent for
a few moments as Joshua flicks through the pages
of his various notepads.

                    RAINA
So what are you going to do with all
this stuff?

                    JOSHUA
Well, I'm trying to shape it into a
novel.

                    RAINA
Why would you want to do that when you
are so good at what you write now? I
mean, this all may never go anywhere,
but your sports stuff . . . It must
be good. You're even read by a sport-
phobic like me!

                    JOSHUA
I might be a good writer, but I'm not
a satisfied one.

                    RAINA
No?

                    JOSHUA
'Write what you know' is what my
English professor advised. So I've
written sports for the last 15 years.
But I want to try something new.
Stretch myself.

                    RAINA
You could try yoga.

                    JOSHUA
Very funny. I want to write like a
Heller or a Pynchon.

                    RAINA
Not aiming too high then!

                    JOSHUA
               (ignoring Raina)
     Or Hemmingway. That's it: I want to be
     Hemmingway.

                    RAINA
     You mean you want to move to Spain,
     take up bullfighting, and start brawls
     in bars?

Joshua laughs.

                    JOSHUA
     No. I mean I want to be a great writer.

                    RAINA
     And I want to be a famous actress on
     Broadway, but that ain't gonna happen
     any time soon.

                    JOSHUA
     You never know.

                    RAINA
     Believe me, I know.

                    JOSHUA
     How do you know?

She starts to tell him about her life. Joshua
is very attentive. He seems captivated. Every so
often he makes some notes on his left-hand pad,
but he never looks down, never takes his eyes
off her while she talks.

                    RAINA
     My mother was a single parent. She
     fled to the city to escape her abusive
     father. I had dreams of being an

actress, but missed too many lectures to earn enough credits to complete my drama degree. I was too busy holding down three jobs, trying to earn enough money to support us all.

INT—NEW YORK—JOSHUA'S APARTMENT—LATE AFTERNOON

Joshua's apartment is a mess. There are notes written on every visible scrap of paper. There are scraps of paper on every surface. There's a pile of dirty dishes piled up in the sink.

We notice that the computer is unplugged with the power cable draped over the monitor.

Joshua is kneeling on the floor writing with a thick coloured pencil on an A1-sized sheet of paper. He's wearing a baggy T-shirt, running shorts, and old running shoes. His eyes have dark rings round them. He looks like he's not slept for many days.

The DOORBELL rings. Joshua looks up. He sits back on his heels and stares at the front door. The DOORBELL rings again.

>   JOSHUA
>   Shit.
>
>   (beat)
>   Shit, shit, shit.

Joshua hurries over to the door and opens it. It's Raina.

>   JOSHUA
>   Raina! I was going to . . .

                    RAINA
Going to ask me in? Don't mind if I do.

She marches past him into the apartment.

                    RAINA
Jeez-Louise, what happened in here?
Is this how the rich and famous live?

                    JOSHUA
I've been busy.

                    RAINA
I should say. I wondered who my rival
was.

                    JOSHUA
Rival?

                    RAINA
You come in for coffee every day for
a week. Each time ten minutes before
you now know I go off duty. You chat
to me all afternoon. And then, just
when I think you might get around to
asking me out, you stop. Just like
that. Thought you might have another
woman. And here she is.

Raina lifts her hands to shoulder height and
waves them round the room.

                    RAINA
Bet her coffee's not as good as mine!

Joshua looks over the pile of dishes in the sink.

                    JOSHUA
Hmmm.

                    RAINA
So has it been worth it?

                    JOSHUA
Worth it?

                    RAINA
Is the novel finally taking shape?

                    JOSHUA
I wish. I've got ideas, plenty of them,
but I've got no idea where any of them
are going. And I need to deliver a
treatment for the novel by tomorrow.
And, . . . well, the novel and the
treatment are non-existent.

                    RAINA
Want some advice?

Joshua slumps on to the sofa, squashing several
pages of notes as he does so.

                    JOSHUA
               (imploringly)
Please.

Raina suggests excluding all distractions, and
suggests trying to bring some order to the chaos
that is his brain dump.

                    RAINA
My creative English teacher used to
advise us to write by not writing.

                    JOSHUA
Is that the Zen school of writing? And
what's the sound of one-hand clapping?

                    RAINA
In short, you're trying too hard.
The biggest obstacle to get past is
the blank sheet of paper. Go and let
inspiration come to you. Be open to
it all the time. Then write when the
story comes to you.

                    JOSHUA
Well, I've got just about as much
inspiration as I can handle right
here. But coaxing it into a usable
form is the problem.

                    RAINA
So you have an unusual, but enviable,
problem. An excess of ideas. Where
does your inspiration come from?

                    JOSHUA
Everything. Every sodding thing.
I just have to look outside, and a
new idea jumps into my head. And
I'm supposed to be coming up with a
treatment for a novel tomorrow.

                    RAINA
So let's start off by getting rid of
any external distractions.

Raina rushes around Joshua's apartment closing
his blinds. She then unplugs his TV and his
radio. She hurries over to the telephone in the
kitchen.

                    RAINA
Ever use the land line?

                    JOSHUA
          Well, not really, it's just there for
          emergencies.

Raina unplugs it from the wall.

                    RAINA
          Need the Internet right now?

                    JOSHUA
          Guess not.

Raina unplugs the router.

                    RAINA
          So. No distractions, and no leaving
          the apartment until you're done. But
          this, you do need!

Joshua looks up. Raina is holding the power
cable to the computer.

                    JOSHUA
                 (sheepishly)
          Ah. I had a bad experience with that
          a week or so ago.

                    RAINA
          And this all is a good experience?

She waves her hands around the room again.

                    JOSHUA

          Not exactly.

                    RAINA
          Your notes. Your ideas and
          inspirations are everywhere. On every

scrap of paper there's a disconnected
thought. Not surprising your novel's
struggling. It's not non-existent, it's
just fragmented. You need to organise
your thoughts better. Group them into
ideas, characters, and themes. And to
do that, you've got to start getting
it on the computer.

Raina plugs the computer's power cable back into
the wall.

>   RAINA
> You've probably got enough raw material
> for a half a dozen novels in this very
> room. You now need to shape it, to
> mould it. Become a sculptor, instead
> of a stonemason. Let the computer be
> your chisel.

Raina starts to tidy the notes for him. She
picks up a huge pile of notes.

>   RAINA
> Plot idea. Plot idea. Random twists,
> Dialogue. Dialogue. Plot idea.

She puts the scraps of paper on to four separate
piles on the dining table. Joshua starts
gathering up some of the scraps and starts
sorting them as well.

>   JOSHUA
> You know, I think this might work.

Rainer picks up one of the small reporter
notepads with real-life dialogues in it.

                    RAINA
Still doing the mirror writing I see.

                    JOSHUA
You'd never believe the rich stream of
ideas you get from a few snippets of
conversation. It's best when you can't
see the participants, so you can let
your imagination run riot.

                    RAINA
This sounds like a good one: 'He
finessed the queen. I didn't think
he'd play around like that.' What was
that about?

Joshua laughs.

                    JOSHUA
That was particularly good. That
inspired me to make my hero a closet
transvestite who's forced to out
himself after he bumps into his boss
in a gay bar.

                    RAINA
I can't imagine what they were really
talking about.

                    JOSHUA
Believe it or not, they were talking
about a cleverly played hand of
bridge.

Raina starts to laugh, but then stops suddenly.
Joshua looks up. Raina has turned a few pages
back in his book of dialogues.

RAINA
'My mother was a single parent. She'd
fled to the city to escape her abusive
father. I had dreams of being an
actress, but missed too many lectures
to earn enough credits to complete my
drama degree. I was too busy holding
down

three jobs, trying to earn enough
money to support us all.'

JOSHUA
        (under his breath)
Oh, shit.

RAINA

That's my story. I told you that in
confidence. They're my memories, not
yours for the stealing.

JOSHUA
I wrote that down when we first met.
I didn't know you then.

RAINA
What difference does that make? You
know me now. It's here for all to see.
You could have ripped that page out.

JOSHUA
But I don't throw any ideas away.

RAINA I feel violated.

JOSHUA
Oh, don't be ridiculous, I've not
violated you.

                    RAINA
          So I'm ridiculous now, am I? Is
          that why you've not been returning
          my calls? Is that why you've been
          ignoring me?

Raina rushes towards the door.

                    JOSHUA
               (yelling after Raina)
          Wait! Where are you going?

Raina storms out of the apartment, slamming the
door behind her. Joshua rushes to the door, then
looks down. He's not wearing shoes.

                    JOSHUA
          Shit.

He flings open the door, rushes out, then slides
across the landing in his socks.

                    JOSHUA
          Shit. Shit. Shit

Joshua leans over the banister. We see Raina
disappearing down the stairwell already two
floors below.

                    JOSHUA
          Raina, wait!

Raina doesn't stop. She doesn't look up. Joshua
hurries back into the apartment. We see one of
his trainers near the desk with the computer
on it. He hurries over to it, stoops down, and
picks up the trainer. He then looks up at the
computer monitor and the keyboard. We see the

cursor flashing temptingly in the middle of the screen.

Joshua hesitates. He drops the shoe and slides himself on to his chair.

> JOSHUA
> (under his breath as he types)
> She storms out of the apartment. He tries to go after too, but he's drawn to the computer. There's an invisible force dragging him away from reality and into the Second Life of his imagination.

Joshua gets up and turns off all the lights. He stumbles back through the apartment to his desk by the light of the monitor.

He again starts to type and type and type. He then stops. Something catches his eye. He hurries over to a pile of notes and picks one up.

> JOSHUA
> Distractions, distractions. Fucking distractions.

He screws up the note and throws it on the floor. Before going back to his desk, he opens the door to his closet. He rummages round until he finds a case for spectacles. He sits back in front of his computer. He opens the case and brings out a pair of dark sunglasses. He puts them on.

He carefully puts his hands over the keyboard, lifts his glasses to check the placing of his hands. Then he starts to touch-type at high speed. Faster and faster. It was as much as his fingers could do to keep up with the deluge of ideas.

INT—NEW YORK—JOSHUA'S APARTMENT—EARLY MORNING

The lights in Joshua's apartment are still off, but the blinds are now open. The room is illuminated by the pale dawn light. The notes look better ordered now, and the printer is chugging away, printing page after page.

EXT—NEW YORK—OUTSIDE SHELDON PUBLISHING HOUSE—AM

Joshua parks his white BMW M5 outside Sheldon Publishing House for a second time. This time round he slightly misjudges the turn into a parking spot and ends up with the passenger-side front wheel on the sidewalk.

He gets out quickly hurries and over to the tall building. He is wearing light chinos that look a little grubby, and the buttons on his blazer have been misaligned. His white shirt looks a little crumpled, and he's not wearing a tie.

INT—SHELDON PUBLISHING HOUSE—RECEPTION AREA—AM

Joshua exits the lift and hurries towards Paul's office. We now see sitting on Tina's desk Joshua's manuscript: The 'Wishing Well'. It looks well thumbed.

                    JOSHUA
          I'm Josh . . .

                    TINA
              (interrupting Joshua)
        Joshua Creasey. The man of the moment.

                    JOSHUA
        Did he like my manuscript?

                    TINA
        You'd better go straight through.

Joshua walks into Paul's office.

INT—SHELDON PUBLISHING HOUSE—PAUL'S OFFICE—AM

Paul hurries over to the door as Joshua walks
in. He shakes Joshua's hand heartily.

                    PAUL
        OMG, my friend. O. M. f'ing G.

                    JOSHUA
        Did you like the manuscript?

                    PAUL
        Is the Pope a Catholic? Does a bear
        go in the woods? Would a rose by any
        other name smell as sexy?

                    JOSHUA
        I think you mean sweet.

                    PAUL
        Exactly! How. Sweet. It. Is. Loved
        each and every scintilla.

                    JOSHUA
              (incredulously)
        Wow. You read it all? Overnight?

            PAUL
Of course not. Tina did. Why have a
dog and wag your own?

            TINA's VOICE
        (through an unseen speaker in Paul's
        office)
You calling me a dog now?

            PAUL
Couldn't put it down, could you, Tina?

            TINA's VOICE
Not even to go for walkies.

            PAUL
        (to Joshua)
We've got a money-maker here.

            JOSHUA
You're kidding? It's my first att—

Paul interrupts him by grabbing hold of both of
Joshua's elbows with his own perfectly manicured
hands and looking Joshua straight in the eye.

            PAUL
I never kid about money. How the ruddy
duck did ya get it out so quick?

            JOSHUA
It was in my head. I just had to get
it out.

Paul takes Joshua's head in both his hands
forcing Joshua to bend forward a little. Paul
kisses him on the forehead.

PAUL
If there's anything left in that head
of yours, this could be the start of
a beautiful partnership.

Paul release Joshua's head from his grip and
wanders back over to the window. He starts
talking into his telephone headset, already
mentally with another client.

PAUL
It's Austin, 's'up?

(beat)
Flapping in the breeze, my friend,
it's flapping in the breeze.

As before, Joshua backs out of Paul's office and
closes the door.

INT—SHELDON PUBLISHING HOUSE—RECEPTION AREA—AM

Joshua turns round. Tina gives him the thumbs
up.

JOSHUA
I feel shell-shocked!

TINA
You should. I've never seen him so
excited by an unproven writer before.

JOSHUA
(indignantly)
I wouldn't say I was unproven. I've
been doing my column for 15 years and
have had 4 awards.

                    TINA
          You're unproven as far as Sheldon
          Publishing is concerned. You've not
          even signed a contract yet.

                    JOSHUA
          Er, when would we . . .

Tina waves several pieces of paper.

                    TINA
          It's here.

Joshua takes the offered pages and starts to
read through them.

                    TINA
          Take it away with you. Read it at your
          leisure. Or . . .

Joshua looks up. Tina is holding a pen and
moving it from side to side like a metronome.

                    TINA cont'd
          . . . or you could sign it now. Your
          choice.

INT—NEW YORK—JOSHUA'S APARTMENT—PM

There seems to be more organisation to the chaos
now. The flat is still a mess as far as the
dirty plates go, but there are no longer scraps
of paper everywhere, just piles and piles of
printed paper, each marked up with post-it notes.

Joshua is finishing another long print job.
When the last page arrives on the printer,
Joshua stuffs several reams worth of paper into

a large rucksack. He heaves the rucksack on to his back. He then puts on a huge pair of cordless headphones and picks up a pair of dark sunglasses and a bandana. He walks over to the door.

We see there is a white stick near the door. He ties the bandana around his head like a blindfold and puts on the dark sunglasses.

He picks up the white stick and lets himself out of the apartment, fumbling with the doorknob and lock as he does so. He closes the door behind himself.

We now hear Joshua's FOOTSTEPS as he goes down the stairs. We also hear the CLICK, CLICK, CLICK of the white stick as he uses it to guide himself.

EXT—NEW YORK—SHADY GLEN IN CENTRAL PARK—AM

Joshua is sitting on the bench holding a handful of printed pages very close to his face. He is still wearing the dark sunglasses and the headphones. We see that the bandana is on the bench next to him alongside the white stick.

As in the past, we see a group of runners passing Joshua's bench. And as in the past, we see Slam amongst them. This time Slam runs right past Joshua. He appears not to have noticed him. He goes a hundred yards further down the path before stopping. He looks back at the figure on the bench and then returns back up the path. He sits down next to Joshua.

> SLAM
> Hey, man. Where you been?

Joshua says nothing. He doesn't look round. He seems totally absorbed in the pages that he is reading. Oblivious to everything around him.

Slam deftly removes Joshua's huge cordless headphones. Joshua cries out as if in agony. Slam puts on the headphones.

> SLAM
> Whatever this is, it better be g . . .

Slam looks at Joshua.

> SLAM cont'd
> What you playin' at, man? There's nothing playing on your headphones.

> JOSHUA
> They're not headphones. They're industrial hearing protection earmuffs. Tractor drivers and construction workers use them to block out engine noise.

> SLAM
> Question remains: What you playin' at, man?

> JOSHUA
> Actually it was Raina's idea.

> SLAM

> Who's Raina?

> JOSHUA
> She's a waitress in the coffee shop on the corner.

        SLAM
So some waitress you've been dating . . .

        JOSHUA
Not dating exactly, chatting to.

        SLAM
OK. So some waitress you vaguely
know . . .

        JOSHUA
I know her very well actually. We're
just not dating. Yet.

        SLAM
OK. So. Some crazy chick tells you to
walk around town wearing earmuffs,
and you do so. I'm guessing she's also
responsible for your dark glasses and
white stick.

        JOSHUA
Yes, and no. She suggested avoiding
distractions. The muffs, bandana,
dark glasses, and white stick were
my idea.

        SLAM
Think I'm missing something. We
spoke a while back about your
lack of inspiration. I suggested
people watching. Seemed to work.
Your imagination turned, went into
overdrive. You sure this woman even
exists?

        JOSHUA
'Course she does. Though I've not seen
her in a while.

                    SLAM
          Well, this could be your problem.

Slam covers his own eyes with Joshua's bandana.

                    SLAM cont'd
          Can't see much of anything through
          this!

                    JOSHUA
          I know it sounds nuts . . .

                    SLAM
          No kidding, it sounds nuts.

                    JOSHUA
          OK, let's play a little game. What do
          you see on the path right now?

We see a woman struggling along the path with
four Alsatians straining on the ends of short
leashes.

                    SLAM
          I see an attractive young woman
          with too many dogs. She's probably a
          professional walker. What of it?

                    JOSHUA
          And you're probably right. But I also
          ask myself: Does she have full access
          to the houses of several rich clients?
          What type of misdeeds could she get
          up to in their absence?

                    SLAM
          Classic people watching. Again, what
          of it?

                    JOSHUA
Other questions are already in my
head being asked and answered: Was
she using the properties as a front
for drug running? Perhaps she's
replacing expensive furniture and
paintings with fakes and selling the
originals? Is she entertaining groups
of people and allowing her guests to
assume that the property was hers?
In which case, what could she gain
from it?

                    SLAM
OK. So you're better at people watching
than me.

                    JOSHUA
          (talking faster and faster)
Perhaps she's not a professional
walker at all. Perhaps the dogs are
all hers. Why would she want so many
dogs? What do dogs do? Dogs poop.
Dog walkers scoop poop. Could that
be useful? What could you do with
poop? Could you use it in gardening?
Could it be used for fertiliser? What
else can you do with fertiliser?
Build bombs maybe. Perhaps she's a
terrorist.

                    SLAM
          (interrupting Joshua's stream of
          consciousness)
Now you're sounding like a conspiracy
theory nut.

                    JOSHUA
The thoughts could have gone anywhere.
I could just as easily have imagined
that her name was Delilah Doolittle,
and she was a dog obedience trainer.
A trainer who owes her extraordinary
success rate to the fact that she
can actually talk to her charges, a
talent that runs in her family.

                    SLAM
OK, so where are we going with this
all?

Joshua puts his hand on the back of the bench
and vaults over it with surprising agility. He
stands behind Slam, leans over, and puts his
hands over his eyes.

                    JOSHUA
What do you see now?

                    SLAM
Nothing, you duffus!

Joshua takes his hands from Slam's eyes.

                    JOSHUA
And now?

                    SLAM
A rather tasty rollerblader at three
o'clock.

Joshua clamps his hands over Slam's ears.

                    JOSHUA
What do you hear now?

STANLEY JACKSON AND GAVIN JACKSON

                    SLAM
Some white dude, who's seriously
trying my patience, shouting in my
ear.

Joshua vaults back over the bench.

                    JOSHUA
Same for me, but more so. When I
open my eyes, I don't just see the
here and now: I see any and every
possible otherwise. When I open my
ears, I hear conversations that tell
not just one story, but every story
imaginable. At times it's like I no
longer have control of my own mind.
And it never goes away, unless I make
it. Hence these.

Joshua picks up the earmuff/headphones, the
bandana, and the dark glasses. Both Slam and
Joshua say nothing for a few moments.

                    SLAM
So what about right now? Without your
glasses and your muffs. And you're
taking no notes.

                    JOSHUA
I'm buffering.

                    SLAM
You're what?

                    JOSHUA
Like a computer does. It's all
accumulating up here for later
download.

Joshua taps his own forehead.

>   SLAM
>   (sounding sceptical)
> For downloading?

>   JOSHUA
> Every night, overnight, I type up
> the ideas and story lines that have
> accumulated during the day.

>   SLAM
> When do you sleep? How do you sleep?

>   JOSHUA
> Seldom, and poorly. I bought myself an
> orthopaedic bed. I have an infrared
> keyboard. I prop myself up into a
> sitting position when I go to bed. I
> start to type. If I fall asleep, my
> fingers keep typing.

>   SLAM
> What's the output like?

>   JOSHUA
> Some of it's brilliant. Some of it's
> total crap. But what can you expect
> if you write when you're sleeping?

>   SLAM
> So you then have to sift the wheat
> from the chaff?

>   JOSHUA
> Exactly. That's what I'm doing here
> today.

Joshua hands Slam the papers that he was reading earlier. We see that some passages have been struck through. Some have been highlighted. Some have been marked as 'promising' and others as 'worth pursuing'.

>   SLAM
> What does Raina make of all this?

>   JOSHUA
> Well, as I said, I've not seen her in quite a while.

EXT—NEW YORK—OUTSIDE SHELDON PUBLISHING HOUSE—AM

Joshua parks his white BMW M5 outside Sheldon Publishing House a good two feet away from the kerbside and at a jaunty angle. We see his bumper is dented, and there is a scratch along the driver's side door.

He gets out quickly and hurries to the back of the car. He is wearing jeans and training shoes. He's still wearing his blazer, but this time over a baggy T-shirt. He removes two large bundles of printed paper from the boot. It takes several attempts to close the boot. He hurries over to the tall building, a large bundle in each hand.

INT—SHELDON PUBLISHING HOUSE—RECEPTION AREA—AM

The doors to the lift open. Joshua struggles out with his two large piles of paper. Tina looks up from her desk as Joshua comes round the corner. Joshua dumps the bundles on the floor on the far side of Tina's desk. We see the title of the top bundle: Fountain of Truth.

Joshua reaches into his pocket and brings out his car keys. He gently tosses them towards Tina in a low arc. Tina reaches up and catches them one-handed.

>   TINA
> Again?

>   JOSHUA
> 'Fraid so.

>   TINA
> How bad?

>   JOSHUA
> Fender bender, front and rear.

>   TINA
> Oh dear. Just you?

>   JOSHUA
> Just me and a fire hydrant.

>   TINA
> Front and rear on a single fire
> hydrant?

>   JOSHUA
> Long story.

Joshua walks into Paul's office.

>   TINA
>   (to the phone)
> Hi. CP Auto Repairs? Tina Cortéz.
> 'nother job for you.

INT—SHELDON PUBLISHING HOUSE—PAUL AUSTIN'S OFFICE—AM

Paul looks up as Joshua enters.

> PAUL
> You may be a great writer, Joshua, but you're a shit driver. You don't notice anything.

> JOSHUA
> On the contrary, Paul, I see everything. And that's the problem. Just the littlest thing catches my eye, and my imagination goes wild. Before I know it, I'm somewhere else. And just as quickly, the real world comes racing back to smack me in the face. Or in this case, in the bumper.

> PAUL
> Well, I forbid you to drive. Ever again. Ever.

> JOSHUA
> I'm touched.

> PAUL
> I'm not about to lose my prime asset.

> JOSHUA
> Your golden goose, you mean.

> PAUL
> From now on, it's cabs everywhere. It's not as if you can't afford it. Did you count the zeros on that last advance?

                    JOSHUA
          Actually, I've not had a chance.

                    PAUL
          Oh, the decadence of the man: So rich
          he doesn't know how rich he is!

INT—SHELDON PUBLISHING HOUSE—RECEPTION AREA—AM

As Joshua walks out of Paul's office, Tina hands
him a business card.

                    TINA
          They're good.

                    JOSHUA
          Thanks.

                    TINA
          I've created an account for you.

                    JOSHUA
          Of course you have.

                    TINA
          He cares as much about you as he does
          the money.

                    JOSHUA
          Really?

                    TINA
          I'm sure he does. Deep down.

                    (beat)
          Probably.

INT—NEW YORK—JOSHUA'S APARTMENT—MORNING

Joshua's apartment now resembles an incident room in the midst of a complex criminal investigation.

Joshua has moved the desk into the main living room. There is a row of 5 FLIP CHARTS between Joshua's desk and the window. They have written on them the following headings: Storyline 1, Storyline 2, Back story, Character list, and Historical events.

On each flip chart, there are multiple coloured pins. From each pin, there is a coloured thread connecting it to a pin on one of the other flip charts. The overall affect is that of a multi-coloured spider's web woven around the flip charts. There are also newspaper cuttings and pictures attached to the charts and notes written with thick marker pens.

On the dining table, there are four large piles of paper each of a different colour: light blue, light yellow, light pink, and white.

Joshua is sitting at the computer pounding away at the keyboard like crazy. He hasn't shaved for many days, and his hair is longer than before and unkempt. His fingernails are now broken, and the thumb nails are bitten to the quick. His clothes are scruffy and look unwashed. He looks a real mess.

There are piles of dirty dishes on various surfaces and take-out pizza boxes everywhere. The printer is chugging away, spewing out page after page of blue paper.

A KITCHEN TIMER alarm goes off. Joshua looks at his watch (a BREITLING NAVITIMER that looks comically out of place in the messy surroundings).

> JOSHUA
> Shit. Shit. Shit.

He picks up his mobile phone and speed-dials a number.

> JOSHUA
> (to the phone)
> Hi, Triple-A Cars? Can you send a car to . . .
>
> (beat)
> Yes, that's right: Winbourne Towers. Account in the name of . . .
>
> (beat)
> Yes, that's right, Creasey. To . . .
>
> (beat)
> Yes, that's right, Sheldon Publishers. Have we had this conversation before?
>
> (beat)
> That many, eh! Ten minutes if you can. Thanks.

The printer falls silent. Joshua grabs the latest printout and places the pages on the blue pile.

EXT—NEW YORK—OUTSIDE SHELDON PUBLISHING HOUSE—AM

A limo pulls up outside Sheldon Publishing House. The door opens, and Joshua struggles out, clutching a huge pile of blue paper held together

STANLEY JACKSON AND GAVIN JACKSON

by string. He has clearly rushed straight from his apartment without changing.

INT—SHELDON PUBLISHING HOUSE—RECEPTION AREA—AM

There is a tray on Tina's desk with a magnum of Dom-Perignon '55 and 3 champagne flutes. As Joshua walks over, Tina looks up. Joshua points towards Paul's door.

>   JOSHUA
>   May I?

>   TINA
>   You may.

INT—SHELDON PUBLISHING HOUSE—PAUL'S OFFICE—AM

Paul is standing by the window as Joshua struggles into the room with his latest mammoth manuscript: Careful What You Wish For. Tina follows him through carrying the tray of champagne.

>   PAUL
>   (eyeing the bundle that Joshua is
>   clutching)
>   Is that what I think it is?

>   JOSHUA
>   Yup. Complete first draft. I went a
>   little over this time, I'm afraid, at
>   250,000 words.

>   PAUL
>   Don't you worry about that. Tina will
>   junk the extra crap. The important

thing is that it's here and it's on time. You're a star!

Paul holds Joshua's head between both hands and kisses him on the forehead.

> PAUL
> I knew you'd be a winner as soon as I read that first book of yours, what was it? *Wishing You Well* . . .

> JOSHUA
> (crossly)
> *The Wishing Well.* As in the supernatural co-hero of the entire Central Park series.

> PAUL
> Yeah whatever. And here you are again. Novel number 5. Bang on time. Another masterpiece. Everything you touch turns into literary gold. I can't wait to read it.

> JOSHUA
> Who're you trying to kid, Paul? You've never read any of 'em.

> PAUL
> I read enough to know they're good.

> JOSHUA
> Oh yeah? Which bits have you read?

> PAUL
> The bits that say 'Pay Joshua Creasey the sum of . . .' That's good enough for me, my friend.

STANLEY JACKSON AND GAVIN JACKSON

                    (beat)
          By the way, Josh, you look like shit.

                    JOSHUA
          You've got such a great way with words.
          I am surprised you never thought of
          becoming a writer yourself, Paul.

                    PAUL
                    (ignoring Joshua's sarcasm)
          But you do. You haven't shaved. Your
          shoes have seen better days. You look
          like you've slept in that shirt. When
          was the last time your hair got even
          close to a comb, and . . .

Paul holds his nostril.

                    PAUL cont'd
          There's something rotten in the state
          of Primark. You need a shower! Have
          you forgotten about your talk to the
          Mystery Writers' Guild this evening?
          You can't go downtown looking like
          that.

Joshua says nothing.

                    PAUL
          You have, haven't you? You've
          forgotten!

                    JOSHUA
          Not forgotten, exactly, just busy
          trying to hit the deadline.

                    PAUL
          'Cept of course, you had finished it two
          weeks ago, but decided to rewrite it.

                    JOSHUA
          I thought the ending could do with a
          little work.

                    PAUL
          You rewrote the second half. That's
          more than just the ending.

                    JOSHUA
          Well, you know what it's like when
          you get a little inspiration: You just
          have to act on it.

                    PAUL
          Actually, no, I don't. But I do know
          what it's like when YOU get a 'little'
          inspiration.

Paul mimes air quotation marks with his fingers.

                    PAUL cont'd
          It's 'hold the presses, genius at
          work'. Anyway, the Mystery Writers'
          Guild will be pissed if you blow them
          off again.

                    JOSHUA
          Don't worry, I'm not going to 'blow
          them off', to use your charming
          vernacular.

Joshua mimics Paul's air quotation marks.

                    PAUL
          Yeah, but you can't go like that! Why
          don't you go down to the lobby and get
          Frankie to sort you out.

                    JOSHUA
Who's Frankie?

                    PAUL
Who's Frankie? What d'ya mean: 'Who's
Frankie?' The guy you walk past every
time you come into this office. Never
noticed everyone say 'Good morning
Frankie' whenever they walk through
the lobby? Or in reply a cheery 'Good
morning, madam' or 'Good morning,
sir'

                    JOSHUA
Not really, I'm normally a bit
distracted.

                    PAUL
Well, that's Frankie. Only the best
goddamn concierge this building's
ever had. Knows New York and Central
Park like the back of his hand. He'll
do anything for anyone. Sorts out
dry-cleaning, orders fruit, sends
condolence flowers, gets your car
filled up with gas for you if you're
running on empty (or in your case,
books the limo for you to be on the
safe side).

                    JOSHUA
Oh, is that how they always know—

                    PAUL
                (interrupting him)
D'oh! Of course it is. Frankie is
there for everyone. He picked out my
wife's Valentine's Day present for me
this year: sexy red lingerie.

                    JOSHUA
Nothing like the personal touch, eh,
Paul?

                    PAUL
              (missing the sarcasm in Joshua's
              tone)
Exactly. Now you're getting it. Take
yourself downstairs and let him sort
you out. Frankie'll get you measured
you up for a decent suit and get it
sent over. Tell him to get Carl over
too: he may be a fruitcake, but no
one cuts hair better then Carl. And
for crisp-bread's sake, get something
inside you or the Dom'll go straight
to your head. Tina, call Alfredo, the
master baker.

Joshua looks at Tina and rolls his eyes.

                    TINA
No, he really is. He used to be the
pastry chef at The Waldorf.

INT—SHELDON PUBLISHING HOUSE—RECEPTION AREA—AM

Tina and Joshua return to the reception area.

                    TINA
Be a love, and take this down to
Frankie, will you. He'll appreciate
it.

Tina hands Joshua her untouched champagne.

                    JOSHUA
Don't you want it?

TINA
I don't drink.

INT—SHELDON PUBLISHERS—LOBBY—AM

Joshua takes the elevator down to the ground
floor. As the doors slowly open, we hear a couple
of voices at the front desk.

WELL-DRESSED MAN (O.S.)
That's fantastic. Thanks, Frankie. My
wife's gonna love that!

FRANKIE (O.S.)
No problem, sir.

WELL-DRESSED MAN (O.S.)
Can I give you anything?

FRANKIE (O.S.)
Fuhgeddaboudit!

As Joshua reaches the front desk, the smartly
dressed man is heading out through the revolving
door. FRANKIE (the concierge) looks up as Joshua
approaches. Frankie is impeccably dressed in
a concierge uniform: Highly polished shoes,
dark blue trousers and jacket with gold piping,
matching cap, and a pale blue shirt. On the
breast pocket of his shirt we see he has his
name tag: Frankie Dimas.

JOSHUA
Frankie?

FRANKIE
That's right.

                    JOSHUA
          Tina thought you might like a glass.

Frankie accepts the glass and takes a sip.

                    FRANKIE
          Hmmm. '55 if I'm not mistaken. Great
          year. And how may I help you, Mr
          Creasey sir?

                    JOSHUA
          I need a suit. Is that something you
          can help me with?

                    FRANKIE
          Of course, sir.

                    JOSHUA
          For this evening.

                    FRANKIE
          Not a problem. Charcoal, single-
          breasted, light pinstripe?

                    JOSHUA
          That sounds perfect.

                    FRANKIE
          I'll call Bloomingdales. They'll send
          over something appropriate later this
          afternoon.

                    JOSHUA
          Won't they need to take my
          measurements?

                    FRANKIE
          I have them already, sir.

                    JOSHUA
You do?

                    FRANKIE
All part of the service, sir.

                    JOSHUA
I'll need a tie.

                    FRANKIE
And shirt and shoes?

                    JOSHUA
Er yes, thanks.

                    FRANKIE
Not a problem, sir. Anything else?

                    JOSHUA
Paul mentioned Carl.

                    FRANKIE
Are yes, a wizard with the blade. Best
barber north of 42nd.

                    JOSHUA
And his nail artist.

                    FRANKIE
An excellent choice. No one better in
the manicure business. Anything else
I can do for you, sir?

                    JOSHUA
No, I think that's it. When do you
think Carl will be able to come over?

                    FRANKIE
          I've booked him in for six o'clock.
          Mr Austin thought you might need his
          services.

                    JOSHUA
          Might have known. I think I'll go for
          a walk in park while I'm waiting.

                    FRANKIE
          Very good, sir.

Joshua heads towards the exit. He goes through
the revolving door. But rather than going out,
he keeps walking and comes back into the lobby
again. He walks back to the front desk.

                    JOSHUA
          Can you spare me a quarter, Frankie?

                    FRANKIE
          Certainly, sir.

Frankie hands Joshua a quarter. Joshua heads
back towards the revolving doors.

                    FRANKIE
               (calling out after Joshua)
          Be careful what you wish for!

**EXT—NEW YORK—SHADY GLEN IN CENTRAL PARK—LATE
AFTERNOON**

Joshua is walking slowly through Central Park. It
is overcast, and there are fewer people around
than on previous occasions.

Joshua stops walking. We see he has arrived at Inspiration Point. He walks down to the Wishing Well. He stares down into the water for several moments. Eventually he reaches into his pocket and brings out the quarter that Frankie gave him. He stares at it in his hand. Then he tosses it into the well and takes several steps backwards.

As before, nothing happens.

He walks back up the slope to the bench that overlooks the lake. He sits down and stares at the view. A light rain starts to fall. Picnicking couples and families playing ball with their children start to pack their belongings together. Everywhere around the shady glen people are beginning to move to more sheltered spots.

The rain gets heavier. Joshua continues to sit looking at the view. There is a CLAP OF THUNDER in the distance. This seems to prompt everyone still loitering in the glen to start hurrying out of the park.

All except one lone figure dressed in a hooded raincoat. Joshua doesn't notice the figure approaching. The figure sits down on the bench very close to Joshua. Joshua turns his head. We see the figure is Raina. She snuggles up to Joshua.

                    RAINA
        Hello, stranger. Let's start over.

                                        The end

Sample Decamot Film Screenplay

The sample screenplay in this section is the result of the Decamot writing process described in **Chapter 2**. To recap, the first two Decamot stories, **A Tale of One City** and **German Graffiti**, became a longer short story: **The Wall**. This then became the film screenplay **The Border Guard**.

THE BORDER GUARD

By

Gavin Jackson

EXT—BERLIN—OUTSIDE LEHMANN'S BOOKSTORE—MORNING

People are waiting outside Lehmann's bookstore in a huge line. The queue stretches the full length of the block, around the corner and out of sight. Most people are wearing heavy overcoats, hats, and scarves. Many are stamping their feet to keep warm.

A subtitle appears at the foot of the screen:

LEHMANN'S BOOKSTORE, BERLIN—1999

There is excited CHATTER in the line. A MAN starts to clap his hands.

>   MAN IN LINE #1
>   (shouting)
>   ERIK
>   (three quick claps)
>   ERIK
>   (three quick claps)

The man nudges his NEIGHBOUR in the line. The second man picks up the chant.

>   MAN IN LINE #2
>   ERIK
>   (three quick claps)
>   ERIK
>   (three quick claps)

Several other people pick up the chant.

At the front of the line there is a news crew interviewing the people closest to the door.

INT—BERLIN—LEHMANN'S BOOKSTORE—MORNING

ERIK FRIEDHEIMER and ARTHUR BEHRENDT are standing inside the bookstore. Both men are about 50 and are smartly dressed in suits and conservative ties.

There is a large clock over the door. It is 08:45. Erik looks at his watch.

>   ERIK
> 15 minutes to go.

>   ARTHUR
> You nervous?

>   ERIK
> Terrified would be closer.

>   ARTHUR
> Don't be. Try to enjoy the experience.

>   ERIK
> That's easy for you to say. You're used to all this.

>   ARTHUR
> You'll be fine.

>   ERIK
> What if they hate me?

>   ARTHUR
> People have been turning up since 6 a.m. The queue is stretching around the block.

                    ERIK
Is that supposed to make me feel
better?

                    ARTHUR
It should. No one would wait for 3
hours in this weather if they hated
you.

                    ERIK

I guess not.

                    ARTHUR

Listen to that noise.

Arthur holds his hand to his ear. We hear the
sound of CHANTING.

                    VOICES (O.S.)
ERIK—ERIK

                    ARTHUR
They love you.

Erik looks at his watch again.

                    ARTHUR
How's Marina?

Erik smiles.

                    ERIK
Enjoying New York immensely.

                    ARTHUR
I'm surprised she didn't want to join
you.

                    ERIK
She said she's spent enough time in
Berlin to last a lifetime. She'll be
with us on the tour in the States
though.

                    ARTHUR
That's good. Sylvia was so glad that
you guys got back together.

                    ERIK
I've got you to thank for that, as
well as so much else. I owe you
everything.

                    ARTHUR
Nonsense. Don't start getting
emotional on me.

                    ERIK
I mean it. I could never have got to
where I am now without your help.

                    ARTHUR
You helped us stay sane for all those
years. I merely helped you realise
your potential.

                              CUT TO BLACK SCREEN

A subtitle is shown in the middle of the screen:
    38 YEARS EARLIER.

                                        CUT TO

INT—THE FRIEDHEIMERS' APARTMENT IN MITTE—ERIK'S BEDROOM - EARLY MORNING

A 12-year ERIK FRIEDHEIMER is waking up. He gets out of bed and walks over to the window. He is small for his age. He opens the curtains and squints as the sunlight floods into his room.

He stands at the window admiring the view.

A subtitle appears at the foot of the screen:
    Mitte, Berlin—1961

INT—THE FRIEDHEIMERS' APARTMENT—MAIN ROOM—MORNING

It's a large room containing a dining table and six chairs, large dresser, two medium-sized sofas. The furniture and TV look new, but the decoration looks drab.

MR FRIEDHEIMER is eating his breakfast. He is wearing a smart suit, white shirt, and dark tie. His jacket is on the back of the chair. MRS FRIEDHEIMER is drinking a mug of coffee and smoking a cigarette. She is wearing a pink dressing gown, hair in rollers.

>   MRS FRIEDHEIMER
>   (loudly)
>   Come on, Erik, breakfast's ready.

>   ERIK (O.S.)
>   Coming.

Erik hurries into the room. He is dressed now and carrying a canvas knapsack. He places the knapsack on one of the sofas and sits at the table.

                    MR FRIEDHEIMER
          What are you up to today, Son?

                    ERIK
          Not much. You know, just hanging
          around.

                    MR FRIEDHEIMER
          Seeing Willem?

                    ERIK
          Yeah, I guess.

Erik picks at his breakfast. Silence for a while. Erik gets up from the table, picks up his knapsack, and heads for the door. He has hardly eaten anything.

                    MRS FRIEDHEIMER
          Don't be late home, Erik. You've got
          football tomorrow.

The sound of the front door SLAMMING is heard followed by Erik's FOOTSTEPS as he runs down the corridor.

                    MR FRIEDHEIMER
          I'd better make a move, don't want to
          be late.

Mr Friedheimer leans over the table and kisses his wife on the forehead.

                    MRS FRIEDHEIMER
          See you later, love.

Mr Friedheimer puts on his jacket and leaves the room. Mrs Friedheimer starts to clear the dishes.

EXT—BERNAUER STRASSE—CEMETERY—DAY

Twelve-year-old WILLEM SCHMIDT is sitting on the wall of the graveyard. He looks very similar to Erik, but he is a little taller and a little heavier set.

He is smoking a cigarette and idly tossing small stones at a headstone. He spots Erik as he comes trotting around the corner.

>   WILLEM
>   Late as usual, Friedheimer.

Willem jumps off the wall and puts the cigarette out with his foot.

>   ERIK
>   You sound like my mother.

>   WILLEM
>   Have you got everything?

Erik nods and points to his knapsack.

>   WILLEM
>   Hide it over there with mine.

Erik walks over to the wall and spots Willem's leather satchel tucked behind an old and neglected headstone. He carefully places his knapsack next to it.

                    WILLEM
          Come on, let's get a move on.

Willem leaps over the wall and runs off down the
road. Erik looks up and sees Willem disappearing
round the corner. He runs hard to catch up.

EXT—BY A LARGE FENCE—DAY

LAUGHTER and WATER SPLASHING can be heard coming
from the other side of the fence. Willem comes
running round the corner and stops in front of
the fence. He looks exhausted.

Erik comes running round the corner and almost
collides with Willem. Willem puts a finger to
his lips.

                    WILLEM
                 (in a whisper)
          Shhh.

Both boys stand for a few moments hunched over
with their hands on their thighs as they try to
catch their breaths.

Willem turns to face the fence. He puts his
eye to a small hole in the fence. Apparently
satisfied, he reaches up and puts both hands at
the top of the fence. He takes a firm grip and
pulls gently backwards.

                    WILLEM
          In you go.

Erik squeezes himself through the fence. He then
leans on the fence from the other side. Willem
follows him through.

EXT—IN THE GROUNDS OF A PUBLIC LIDO—DAY

Erik and Willem are standing just inside the grounds of a public lido. In front of them is a large swimming pool with a wooden diving board at one end. There are small groups of people sitting enjoying the sun, some on towels, some on sunbeds. A number of people are in the pool, including a man swimming laps.

At the far end of the pool people are waiting in line in front of a turnstile at the entrance of the lido. Each person is paying to get in.

Both boys walk quickly down the side of the pool unnoticed. Willem nonchalantly whisks a towel off of a sunbed as he passes. Both boys hurry into a single cubicle, giggling.

They emerge a few moments later, both dressed in long swimming trunks, their clothes over their arms. They toss their clothes on to an empty sunbed. Willem climbs on to the diving board and executes a perfect dive into the pool. Erik follows him off the board and makes a much less impressive entry. Water SPLASHES everywhere.

EXT—ROADSIDE—MARIENFELDE—AFTERNOON

Willem is walking along the road. His hair is wet, and he is carrying his swimming trunks over his shoulder.

As he walks past Marienfelde, a distant VOICE on a LOUDSPEAKER can be heard.

> VOICE ON THE LOUDSPEAKER
>   763, 764, and 765.

Willem approaches the fence that surrounds the area. He leans forward and peers through a gap in the fence.

EXT—MARIENFELDE—WILLEM'S POV—AFTERNOON

On the other side of the fence is a very large building that resembles an aircraft carrier. Outside the building is a line of people waiting patiently. In the doorway is a line of trestle tables with a row of officials sitting on one side. Inside the building are supplies of blankets, clothing, and food.

A small family group move from the front of the queue and stand in front of one of the officials who places several forms on the table. He asks the man some questions and makes some notes on the forms. They are too far away for Willem to make out what they are saying.

Eventually, the official hands the man in the group a pen. The man signs each of the forms and hands the pen back. The official leans over a microphone that's on the table in front of him and flicks a switch.

> VOICE ON THE LOUDSPEAKER
>   766, 767, 768, and 769

Another four people have been processed. They walk into the building where they are handed a bundle of blankets and a box of food.

EXT—ROADSIDE—MARIENFELDE

Willem walks to the other end of Marienfelde. The fence here is lower, and he can see over the top of it as he walks along.

EXT—MARIENFELDE—WILLEM'S POV

Willem can now see the other side of the building. There is a small orchard and dozens of family groups. Some are sitting on suitcases, some on the ground, some are standing, some sitting in the shade under the apple trees. The scene resembles the departure lounge of an international airport, except that everyone is outside.

As he walks by, Willem hears snippets of conversation from the various groups.

A FATHER trying to console a distraught CHILD:

> CHILD
> Where's Mummy?

> FATHER
> She'll be along soon, don't worry.

> CHILD
> I want my mummy.

> FATHER
> I know you do, sweetheart.

TWO WOMEN exchanging stories:

> WOMAN #1
> I saw a couple of railway policemen checking everyone's papers very

carefully, so I gave Paul a very hard pinch.

                WOMAN #2
Why?

                WOMAN #1
To make him cry, of course.

                WOMAN #2
What for?

                WOMAN #1
It was really hot in that carriage, and they had at least another hundred passengers to check. I thought the last thing they wanted was to cope with a screaming child.

                WOMAN #2
And that worked?

                WOMAN #1
We're here, aren't we? They just hurried us along. Barely even looked at my passport.

A YOUNG man wrapped in a blanket talking to TWO YOUNG WOMEN:

                YOUNG MAN
I looked up and realised that a guard was staring straight at me.

                YOUNG WOMAN #1
What did he do?

                YOUNG MAN
Took aim and shouted, 'Halt'.

                    YOUNG WOMAN #1
What did you do?

                    YOUNG MAN
I saw my chance and dived in the
river.

                    YOUNG WOMAN #2
Weren't you worried he might shoot at
you?

                    YOUNG MAN
He did shoot at me. But I ducked under
the water and swam as far down the
river as I could before coming up for
air.

                    YOUNG WOMAN #1
And you brought nothing with you?

                    YOUNG MAN
Nothing at all. Just the clothes I'm
wearing, literally.

Willem is now at the end of Marienfelde. He
hurries off down the road.

INT—WILLEM'S HOUSE—DINING ROOM—EVENING

Willem and his parents are eating dinner
together. A large hot pudding is placed in the
middle of the table next to a jug of custard.
All three are part-way through the course.

                    MRS SCHMIDT
Did you have a nice day, dear?

                    WILLEM
Yes, Mum.

                    MRS SCHMIDT
Did you go swimming again?

                    WILLEM
Uh huh.

                    MRS SCHMIDT
Did I give you enough money to get in?

                    WILLEM
          (smirking)
Uh huh.

                    MRS SCHMIDT
So how was, Erik?

                    WILLEM
Fine.

                    MRS SCHMIDT
How are his parents?

                    WILLEM
Dunno, didn't see them.

                    MRS SCHMIDT
Did Erik mention them?

                    WILLEM
Not really. He says they're always
arguing about leaving something,
somewhere. But he didn't know what.

                    MR SCHMIDT
Leaving, you say?

                    MRS SCHMIDT
          (to Mr Schmidt)
You don't think they'd leave East
Berlin, do you, honey?

                    MR SCHMIDT
You never know.

                    MRS SCHMIDT
Do you think they'd come here?

                    MR SCHMIDT
I don't see why not. He's got a good
job over here with the bank.

                    WILLEM
Cool. Erik could stay here, couldn't
he? He could share my room.

                    MR SCHMIDT
          (sternly)
Willem, you mustn't talk about this
outside this house, OK? Particularly
not on the other side.

                    WILLEM
Why not?

                    MR SCHMIDT
It's not safe. You don't know who you
can trust. Promise me: Not a word
outside the house, OK?

                    WILLEM
OK. I promise.

                    MR SCHMIDT
          That's good.

          Mr Schmidt helps himself to some more pudding
          and pours on a little custard.

                    MR SCHMIDT
          So, are you looking forward to the
          Herthe game?

                    WILLEM
          You bet.

                    MR SCHMIDT
          And can Erik make it?

                    WILLEM
                (beat)
          Er yeah, sure.

                    MRS SCHMIDT
          Has he asked his parents?

                    WILLEM
          'Course he has.

                (beat)
          I think.

                    MRS SCHMIDT
          Has he? Or not?

                    WILLEM
          I think he'll ask them tonight.

                (speaking more quickly now)
          But they won't mind, honest. They
          don't really care what he does. Don't

think they'd notice if he was there
or not.

          MRS SCHMIDT
I'm sure that's not true, darling.

Mrs Schmidt looks at her watch.

          MRS SCHMIDT
It's getting late, Son. You'd better
be going off to bed. You've got a late
night tomorrow.

          WILLEM
OK.

Willem stands up and walks over to his mum. He
gives her a kiss. He then walks round the table
to his dad and gives him a hug.

          MR SCHMIDT
Night, Son.

          WILLEM
Night Dad.

Willem leaves the room. They can hear his
FOOTSTEPS on the stairs and then the distant
sound of his DOOR CLOSING.

          MRS SCHMIDT
That was easy. He normally puts up
more of a struggle than that.

          MR SCHMIDT
Yup. That's certainly a first.

          MRS SCHMIDT
Hmm. Suspiciously easy.

                    MR SCHMIDT
          Probably just tired. He's had a busy
          day.

Mr Schmidt stands up and starts clearing the
table.

**INT—FRIEDHEIMERS' APARTMENT—LIVING/DINING
ROOM—EVENING**

Erik's parents are sitting at the dining table
sharing a bottle of wine. Erik's dad is wearing
the suit he was wearing earlier, but now his tie
is loosened. Mr Friedheimer takes hold of his
wife's hand.

                    MR FRIEDHEIMER
                    (quietly)
          We've got to get out.

                    MRS FRIEDHEIMER
          Get out? Get out of what? The
          apartment? Are we moving?

                    (beat)
          At last! We can finally move to
          somewhere more fitting your income.

                    MR FRIEDHEIMER
          No, not the apartment.

                    MRS FRIEDHEIMER
          What then?

Mr Friedheimer takes a sip of his wine and
carefully puts the wine glass down.

                    MR FRIEDHEIMER
          The country.

                    MRS FRIEDHEIMER

          What're you talking about?

Mr Friedheimer leans forward.

                    MR FRIEDHEIMER
                     (in a whisper)
          I'm talking about leaving the country.
          Getting out while we still can. I'm
          talking about me going to work one
          day, and not coming back. And you
          jumping on the train with nothing but
          Erik.

Mr Friedheimer takes hold of his wife's hand.

                    MR FRIEDHEIMER cont'd
          I'm talking about defecting, honey.

                    MRS FRIEDHEIMER
          Oh, for God's sake, don't let's start
          this again. You're like a broken
          record. We're not leaving the country.

                    MR FRIEDHEIMER
          Look, it's not safe to stay.

                    MRS FRIEDHEIMER
          Of course it's safe.

                    MR FRIEDHEIMER
          It's not. We've got to get out. Now.

                    MRS FRIEDHEIMER
          Where would we go?

                    MR FRIEDHEIMER
West Berlin.

                    MRS FRIEDHEIMER
And leave our apartment? Our friends?
Our family?

                    MR FRIEDHEIMER
Yes, all of it.

                    MRS FRIEDHEIMER
But I like living here.

                    MR FRIEDHEIMER
I'd be doing the same job. We'd just
be living there too.

                    MRS FRIEDHEIMER
Where would we live in West Berlin?
Apartments are so expensive there.

                    MR FRIEDHEIMER
I'm not pretending it'll be easy. It
won't be. But it's something that we've
got to do. And at least I've got a job
that I can keep doing. Stay here, and
we've got nothing.

Mrs Friedheimer pulls her hand away.

                    MRS FRIEDHEIMER
How can you say we've nothing here?
Here I feel like we're something.
It's like I'm married to a king. How
many of our neighbours earn Western
dollars? None of them. How many can
afford good clothes? None of them. How
many can afford a TV and a fridge?

She takes a sip of her wine.

> MRS FRIEDHEIMER cont'd
> There I'd just be a humble bank clerk's wife.

> MR FRIEDHEIMER
> Do you realise how many people are leaving the East? I see them everyday milling around Marienfelde. Thousands every day. They've been going all summer—it can't go on forever. The authorities must stop it eventually. And when they do, where will we be?

> MRS FRIEDHEIMER
> You're worrying over nothing. Hundreds of people live in the East and work in the West every day, just like you. Why would the authorities stop you doing that? It would be crazy. How could they stop you?

> MR FRIEDHEIMER
> There are a hundred ways. They could forbid travel, take passports away, stop trains running. The Stasi can make people disappear, ya know.
> (beat)
> What about if the Russians brought the tanks back, like they did in 1953?

> MRS FRIEDHEIMER
> You're being paranoid. The Americans, the British, and the French would never allow any of that to happen again. We're not leaving! That's final.

INT—ALAN KENDELL'S APARTMENT—STUDY—EVENING

The room is cluttered with books and newspapers piled on every surface. One wall is lined from floor to ceiling with shelves containing yet more books. On a small table in the corner is an ADN telex machine. The room is quite dark, lit only by a single overhead bulb and a table lamp. There is an open fire in the hearth, which is down to a few smouldering embers.

ALAN KENDELL is sitting at his desk typing slowly at an old manual typewriter. He leans forward and holds the top of the paper without removing it from the roller.

> ALAN
> (reading to himself from the paper in the typewriter)
> All quiet on the Eastern Front. Another 800 arrived at Marienfelde on the other side, but no incidents on this. Nothing else to report at present.

Alan looks up at the fire. He sees it's virtually gone out. He walks over to the hearth and looks inside the coal scuttle. It's empty.

> ALAN
> (under his breath)
> Sod it.

Alan goes over to the door, takes a large overcoat off the hook on the door, and puts it on. He then opens a cupboard door, takes out a carton of cigarettes, and places them inside his coat. He then leaves the room.

EXT—JURGEN'S HOUSE—AT THE FRONT DOOR—DUSK

Alan Kendell walks up to the front door and KNOCKS LOUDLY several times. The door is opened by JURGEN, a large man dressed in a khaki uniform.

>   ALAN
>   Jurgen.

Alan taps his chest.

>   ALAN cont'd
>   I have something that might be of
>   interest to you. Can I come in?

>   JURGEN
>   Of course, my friend.

Jurgen ushers him inside and quickly shuts the front door.

They walk through to the kitchen.

INT—JURGEN'S HOUSE—IN THE KITCHEN

There are various items of army kit on the table and a rifle leaning up against the wall.

>   ALAN
>   (eyeing the items in the room)
>   Up to anything interesting?

>   JURGEN
>   Just routine manoeuvres. Don't know
>   what yet. Don't know where. They just
>   told us to get some stuff together

and make sure our weapons are clean.
The factory boys like to have a little
adventure from time to time. Pretend
like we're real soldiers.

                ALAN
Sounds like fun.

Alan takes the carton of cigarettes out of his
overcoat pocket and puts it on the table.

                JURGEN
        Ah, so what can I do for my favourite
        little capitalist?

                ALAN
Thought you might have liberated a
little package for me.

                JURGEN
Whatever would the brothers say?

                ALAN
Well, let's not tell them, eh?

                JURGEN
Good plan.

Jurgen walks to the back door and goes outside.
He returns after a few moments with a bag of
coal over his shoulder. He helps Alan take the
bag and opens the front door.

                JURGEN
            (quietly as Alan walks past)
        If anyone catches you with that, you
        don't know me.

                    ALAN
          Naturally. Pleasure doing business
          with you.

EXT—ALAN'S HOUSE—AT THE FRONT DOOR—DUSK

Alan puts down the bag of coal while he fumbles
with his front door key. From somewhere in the
distance there is the SOUND OF a dustbin being
KICKED. Alan looks up and peers down the alley
running alongside his house. He sees a movement
at the end of the alley and trots into the
darkness to investigate.

EXT—ALLOTMENTS AT THE BACK OF ALAN'S HOUSE—DUSK

A group of FACTORY FIGHTERS are marching quickly
through the allotments that fill the gaps at
the back of the apartment blocks. Each factory
fighter is dressed in a black uniform and has a
rifle slung over his shoulder. As Alan watches,
he sees that one factory fighter stops at the
intersection of each alleyway. One stops several
feet in front of Alan holding his rifle across
his body.

                    ALAN
          What's goin' on?

                    FACTORY FIGHTER
                 (staring straight ahead, not looking
                  at Alan)
          Nothing for you to worry about,
          comrade.

                    ALAN
You're standing in the alley behind
my house with a gun in your hand.

                    (beat)
Of course there's something for me to
worry about.

The soldier says nothing. Keeps staring straight
ahead.

                    ALAN
Come on—tell me. What's going on?

                    FACTORY FIGHTER
I suggest you buy a newspaper. That's
all I can say.

Alan sighs and heads back up the alleyway towards
his apartment.

INT—ALAN KENDELL'S APARTMENT—STUDY—EVENING

The door opens and Alan struggles in. He places
the bag of coal next to the fireplace and
carefully opens it. He empties the coal into the
scuttle. He then picks up a pair of fire tongs
and places a few pieces on to the rapidly dying
fire. He prods the coal with a poker until a
flame appears.

The phone RINGS. Alan answers it.

                    ALAN
Kendell, Reuters News Agency, East
Berlin.

                    CALLER #1 (O.S.)
          I would advise you to not leave Berlin
          this weekend, Herr Kendell.

                    ALAN
          Hello?

                    (beat)
          Who is this please?

                    (beat)
          Hello? Hello?

The line's gone dead. Alan replaces the receiver.
He sits looking at the telephone for a few
seconds. He turns to the typewriter, removes the
paper in it, screws it into a ball, and throws
it towards the fire. He places another sheet of
paper into the typewriter and starts typing,
with more urgency than earlier. He removes the
paper from the machine and studies it carefully.

                    ALAN
                    (reading from the sheet he has just
                    typed)
          Berlin is this weekend holding its
          breath, expecting dramatic measures.
          Unrest is in the air. Police and
          military movements are afoot. Will
          keep my eye on the streets tonight.

Alan feeds the paper into the TELEX machine. He
enters a number on the key pad and presses the
send button. He then pulls on his jacket and sits
back down at the table. He looks at his watch.

                    ALAN
                    (to himself)
          Come on, come on.

He lights a cigarette and leans back apparently waiting for something.

The phone RINGS. Alan snatches up the receiver.

                    ALAN
          Kendell, Reuters News . . .

                    CALLER #2 (O.S.)
          What's going on, Kendell?

                    ALAN
          Thought that might get your attention,
          Bob.

                    CALLER #2
          Too bloody right . . . 'Berlin holding
          its breath' . . . 'unrest is in the
          air' . . . 'police and military
          movements'. You expect me to run with
          this crap?

                    ALAN
          You bet.

                    CALLER #2
          What's going on?

                    ALAN
          I don't know just yet, but it's big.

                    CALLER #2
          How do you know that?

                    ALAN
          It's a feeling I've got.

                    CALLER #2
        Goddamnit, Alan, you want me to put
        my balls on the line for a feeling
        you've got?

                    ALAN
        Uh huh. Look, man, if I'm right, there
        could be a Pulitzer in this for us.
        I've gotta go now—I'm gonna drive
        around some, flesh out some more
        details and get back to you.

                    CALLER #2
        You do that.

The line goes dead. Alan grabs his car keys and
hurries out of the apartment.

EXT—BERNAUER STRASSE—CEMETERY—NIGHT

Erik and Willem are back in the cemetery. They
are standing near the wall that they had been
at earlier in the day.

                    WILLEM
                (in a whisper)
        I told you the bags would be OK here.

Willem leans over the headstones and pulls out
the two bags that they had hidden earlier. He
hands Erik his canvas knapsack and puts his
leather satchel over his shoulder.

                    ERIK
        Let's get out of here. This place
        gives me the creeps at night.

>   WILLEM
> Not scared of a little darkness, are
> you?

>   ERIK
> No, but . . .

Willem starts walking along the footpath heading
towards the exit of the cemetery. Erik follows
closely behind. The gate creaks as Willem opens
it. Willem walks through the gateway and takes
a side alley. It is four foot wide with a tall
fence on either side. Both boys walk slowly along
the path.

EXT—APARTMENT BLOCK—BERNAUER STRASSE—NIGHT

Willem and Erik are hiding in the shadows of
a clump of trees 20 feet from a five-storey
apartment block. All the windows on the ground
floor are boarded up, as are the eight front
doors that open on to Bernauer Strasse. Some
of the windows on the upper floors have broken
panes. In several places there are pockmarks in
the brickwork—the scars of bullets fired in 1944.

>   WILLEM
>   (in a whisper)
>   There before you lies a little bit of
>   history. Abandoned for 17 years and
>   awaiting our attention.

Willem points to the side of the building.

>   WILLEM
>   We'll go in through the side entrance
>   and up to the apartments on the upper
>   floors.

Willem looks at his watch.

> WILLEM
> There should be a guard on patrol any
> minute now.

Right on cue, a soldier walks around the corner
and along the front of the building. He has a
rifle over his shoulder. He stops under a street
lamp just long enough to light a cigarette, then
continues his patrol. He reaches the far end of
the apartment block.

> WILLEM
> We've got about 25 minutes to get in
> and out before he comes back again.

Willem reaches into his satchel and removes a
stout metal pole.

> WILLEM
> Let's have us some fun.

Willem breaks cover from the trees and dashes
towards the side door. Erik follows closely
behind. In a well-rehearsed movement, Erik leans
heavily against the door with his shoulder.
Willem inserts the pole into the gap that opens.
Both boys shove the pole as hard as they can.
The door gives way, and the boys fall into a dark
inner hallway.

INT—APARTMENT BLOCK—DARK HALLWAY—NIGHT

There is a staircase only just visible at the
far end. Willem and Erik make their way slowly
towards it. The staircase is lit by the light
from a street lamp outside a high window. The

STANLEY JACKSON AND GAVIN JACKSON

boys start climbing the stairs, their pace quickening as they get used to the light. By the time they reach the fourth flight of stairs they are running.

INT—APARTMENT BLOCK—TOP CORRIDOR—NIGHT

Willem stops at the top of the last flight of stairs, out of breath. In front of them is a long corridor with doors on either side. It is lit by the moonlight from a broken window at the far end.

> WILLEM
> Come on.

Willem starts walking quickly along the corridor, pausing briefly to read out the names on each door as he passes.

> WILLEM
> Winkler
> > (beat)
> Hartmann
> > (beat)
> Freudenberg
> > (beat)
> Katz

Willem stops. He waits for Erik to catch up.

> WILLEM
> Daniel Katz. This'll do.

Willem grasps the door handle, leans back, and hits his shoulder firmly against the door. The door gives slightly, but remains closed.

                    WILLEM
          A little help would be good,
          Friedheimer.

Erik stands right behind Willem.

                    ERIK
          OK, I'm ready.

                    WILLEM
          On three. One . . . Two . . . Three.

Both boys lean back then push hard against
the door with all their might. The SOUND of
ancient wood SPLINTERING fills the corridor, and
the door flies open. Both boys fall into the
apartment and roll around for a few moments,
giggling nervously.

INT—DANIEL KATZ'S APARTMENT—INNER HALLWAY—NIGHT

Willem and Erik pick themselves up and look
around the gloomy inner hallway of Daniel Katz's
long-abandoned apartment. There are three doors:
two to the left and one to the right. Willem
points to the door on the far left.

                    WILLEM
          You take that one, I'll take the one
          on the right.

Willem walks over to the door and opens it
slowly. He walks in and looks around.

INT—DANIEL KATZ'S APARTMENT—BEDROOM—WILLEM'S POV

A little light is coming from a broken window. In the centre of the room is an unmade bed, with some covers piled on top. There is a table on one side of the bed—a lamp lays sideways on top of it. Under the window is a chest of drawers. Some of the drawers are half open.

Willem walks over and starts looking through them. Finding nothing interesting, he turns round. In front of him is a wardrobe. Both doors are open, revealing a few empty hangers. Inside the wardrobe on the left there are some shelves.

Willem hurries over and peers inside. Most of the shelves are empty, each covered in a thick layer of dust. Willem bends down and spots a small box at the back of one of the lower shelves.

He kneels down and reaches in through ancient cobwebs. Just as he starts to move the box towards himself, a large spider runs across his hand and scurries to the back of the wardrobe. Willem snatches his hand back quickly.

Willem rocks back on his heels and takes a few deep breaths. He steadies himself. Then in one quick movement he reaches into the shelf, grabs hold of the box, pulls it out of the wardrobe in a single movement, swings around, and dumps it on the bed.

Willem slumps down on the bed and stares at the box for a few moments. He leans over and blows on the lid. Dust clouds up into Willem's face causing him to sneeze for several seconds. He rubs his eyes, then looks back down at the box.

He slowly removes the lid and looks inside. He sees a package wrapped in some kind of cloth.

He removes it, places it on his lap, and starts to unwrap it.

INT—DANIEL KATZ'S APARTMENT—KITCHEN

The kitchen is as dimly lit as the rest of the apartment. Around the room cupboard doors are open. They contain plates, saucers, cups, mugs, pans, and other assorted kitchen utensils.

Erik is opening the final cupboard. Finding nothing of interest, he turns his attention to the stove. There is a saucepan on one of the rings. He picks it up, looks inside, and puts it down again.

Erik turns round. In front of him is a table with four place settings laid out. Erik sits down at one of the settings with his back to the door and picks up a plate and looks down at the table. It is covered in a thick layer of dust. There is a round hole in the dust where the plate had lain.

Erik kneels on the chair and leans into the centre of the table. He writes the letter E in the dust with his finger, then adds R I K. He leans over further and starts writing another word above the first.

Suddenly Erik feels something cold and metallic pressed against his neck and hears the SOUND of a pistol being COCKED.

> QUIET VOICE (O.S.)
> Don't move.

He freezes.

                    ERIK
                (panic in his voice)
        Please. Don't shoot. Don't shoot.

He hears LAUGHTER behind him. Erik spins around
to see Willem clutching his sides, shoulders
heaving. In his right hand is an old revolver.

                    ERIK
                (furious)
        What the fuck are you doing, you
        stupid idiot?

                    WILLEM
        You should've seen the look on your
        face. Priceless.

                    ERIK
        You frightened the life out of me.

                    WILLEM
        What were you writing?

Willem takes a couple of steps towards the table.
Erik tries to push him away, but Willem is bigger
than he is and easily pushes him aside. He puts
the gun down and leans over the table.

                    WILLEM
                (reading from the table)
        E. R. I. K. Oh, very original. Ah but
        what's this?

Willem leans lower over the table, peering in
the darkness, still holding Erik off with one
hand.

                    WILLEM cont'd
        A.

        (beat)
N.
        (beat)
N.
        (beat)
A.
        (beat)
Anna! So it's true, you do fancy her.

          ERIK
Oh, shut up.

Willem starts laughing again. He skips around
Erik, taunting him a little as he does so.

          WILLEM
Erik loves Anna. Erik loves Anna.

Willem puckers up his lips and makes a couple of
loud KISSING noises.

Erik slumps on the chair moodily.

          WILLEM
Don't be like that, I'm only messing
with you.
        (beat)
Hey, what do you think of my gun.

          ERIK
Where'd you find it?

          WILLEM
In the bedroom at the back. Think it's
a Luger. Standard army-issue from the
war. Guess Herr Katz and family didn't
want to be caught with it when they
fled.

Willem picks up the gun from the table and waves it around a little.

             ERIK
     What d'you think you're doing? Don't
     point it around like that.

             WILLEM
     It's not loaded, you sissy. Probably
     wouldn't work even if it was. Here
     look.

Willem points the gun towards the window and pulls the trigger. There is the EXPLOSION of a gunshot and a bright orange flash. He nearly drops the gun in surprise

Erik shrieks and leaps to the floor. Willem joins him on the floor and laughs nervously.

             ERIK
     What the fuck.

Willem holds his finger to his lips.

Both boys continue to lie on the floor and listen intently. There is no sound.

             ERIK
           (in a whisper)
     I don't hear anything

             WILLEM
     Shhh.
           (beat)

             ERIK
     What is it?

> WILLEM
> I think I can hear running footsteps.

Willem hurries over to the window and looks out.

EXT—OUTSIDE THE APARTMENT—WILLEM'S POV

The guard from earlier is running down the street towards the apartment block.

> WILLEM
> The guard's on his way back. He must have heard the shot. We've got to get out of here.

Willem puts the gun in his satchel and rushes to the front door of the apartment. In his haste to get out, he nearly trips over Erik, who is struggling to stand up.

INT—APARTMENT BLOCK—TOP CORRIDOR OUTSIDE DANIEL KATZ APARTMENT

Willem and Erik both come hurtling through the broken doorway. Willem pauses. Erik rushes past, turns right, and starts running towards the stairs they came up.

> WILLEM
> (hissing loudly towards Erik)
> Not that way! He'll catch you before you get to the bottom.

Willem turns left and starts running to the other end of the corridor. Erik turns and races after him. Willem stops at the end of the corridor in front of double doors. He pushes down on the bar in the middle of the door on the right and it swings outwards into the night. He hurries out on to the top of a rickety-looking fire escape.

The boys race down the four flights of stairs and dash off down the road back towards the cemetery.

EXT—BERNAUER STRASSE—CEMETERY—NIGHT

The boys are lying on their backs between the headstones, staring up at the stars overhead, their chests rising and falling rapidly.

>   WILLEM
> That was a close one.

>   ERIK
> Too close.

Suddenly a SIREN starts up in the distance. Erik looks at his watch.

>   ERIK
> Shit. That's the curfew siren—you'd
> better get a move on.

Willem gets up quickly and throws his satchel over his shoulder.

>   WILLEM
> See ya tomorrow, Friedheimer.

He runs off alongside the cemetery wall. He stops at the gate, turns round, and points his finger at Erik.

                    WILLEM
           Pow, pow. Pow, pow.

Willem turns back and runs through the gateway
and out of sight.

EXT—FRIEDRICHSTRASSE STATION—ON THE PLATFORM—NIGHT

A train is on the platform waiting to depart.
A few doors SLAM shut, a guard BLOWS a whistle,
and the train leaves the station.

As the train leaves, Willem can be seen sitting
on a bench on the platform on the other side of
the track. He is waiting for a train. He appears
tired and upset. He looks up at the board and
shakes his head. The board indicates that the
next train for Schoenberg is due at 9 p.m.; the
clock on the wall says it's already 10.30 p.m.

We hear the noise of ROWDY SINGING sweeping
into the station, slowly getting louder. There
is a SMALL GROUP OF PEOPLE walking into the
station along the tracks from the direction
that the train has just gone. Some of them are
wearing football hats and scarves. As they reach
the station platform, THIRTY RAILWAY POLICEMAN,
armed and dressed in black uniforms, appear as
if from nowhere.

Willem gets up quietly and slowly backs away.
He keeps his eyes on the commotion as he walks
backwards to the far end of the platform and
straight into Alan Kendell. Willem jumps in
shock.

STANLEY JACKSON AND GAVIN JACKSON

                    ALAN
Are you OK, son?

                    WILLEM
Yes, sir, I'm just trying to get home.

                    ALAN
How long have you been here?

                    WILLEM
About an hour. Trains keep coming
on the other platform heading for
Treptow, but none going in the other
direction to Schoenberg. I just don't
get it.

                    ALAN
Let's see if we can find out what's
going on. Come with me, son.

Alan walks towards the animated crowd and stops
about 20 feet from them. Willem follows a few
paces behind. Both stand watching a conversation
between a POLICEMAN and some of the MEN from
the crowd. Similar conversations are going on
throughout the crowd.

                    POLICEMAN
Your papers please.

The policeman holds out his hands expectantly.
The man closest to him reaches into his inside
pocket and hands over his passport and ID papers.

                    MAN #1
Where have the trains gone, Officer?

The policeman takes a cursory look at the papers
and hands them back.

                    POLICEMAN
          There are no trains tonight, sir.
          Please leave the station.

He points to the next man in the crowd.

                    POLICEMAN
          Your papers please.

                    MAN #1
          But we've got to get home, haven't we,
          lads?

                    MAN #2
          That's right.

                    POLICEMAN
          You must leave the station, now. All
          of you.

                    MAN #1
          But we always have a get-together over
          here with you lot the night before a
          game, then jump on the late train at
          Leuter Station after last orders.

                    POLICEMAN
          Not tonight, I'm afraid, sir. Now you
          must please leave the station.

The second man looks over his shoulder.

                    MAN #2
                    (to the crowd behind him)
          Looks like we'll have to walk, lads.
          We've only got one stop to go.

The man leads a group of fellow supporters who try to get back on the railway tracks. Several of the railway policemen push their way in front of them and link arms to block their path. Pushing and SHOUTING breaks out in the crowd.

There is a lone POLICEMAN standing away from the main crowd. Alan approaches him.

>   ALAN
> Can you tell me what's going on? I'm
> a reporter.

He shows him his press card.

>   POLICEMAN
> All I can tell you is that the trains
> are not running tonight. Now move
> along please. You and your son must
> leave the station immediately.

>   ALAN
>   (to Willem)
> Come along. Let's see if we can find
> out what's happening outside.

Alan takes hold of Willem's arm, and they hurry out of the station.

EXT—OUTSIDE FRIEDRICHSTRASSE STATION—NIGHT

Alan and Willem are standing together outside the station. They are at the back of a large crowd of people pushing and shoving in front of a shop. The shopkeeper is standing in front his shop fumbling with the string on a bundle of newspapers.

He eventually gets the bundle undone. Before he can turn to face the crowd and start selling the papers, the crowd surge forward. There is a free-for-all as hundreds of grabbing hands snatch at the newspapers. Slowly, people break out of the crowd reading copies of *Neues Deutschland*.

Finally, Alan manages to grab hold of one of the papers. The whole of the front page is dominated by a story entitled Communiqué From Moscow.

>   ALAN
>   (half to himself, half to Willem)
> 'The present traffic situation on the borders of West Berlin is being used by the NATO countries to undermine the economy of the GDR. In the face of the aggressive aspirations of West Germany and its NATO allies, the Warsaw Pact proposes reliable safeguards and effective control to be established around the whole of the territory of West Berlin.'
>   (beat)
> Oh my God.

>   WILLEM
> What does all that mean?

>   ALAN
> It means I'd better get you home as soon as possible.

Alan takes off at a slow trot along the road. Willem follows a few feet behind, somewhat reluctantly. Alan stops beside an old and battered Mercedes. He takes his keys from his pocket, opens the driver's door, and climbs in. He leans through the car and opens the passenger door from the inside.

                    ALAN
           (calling out to Willem)
     Come on. Get in.

Willem hesitates.

                    WILLEM
     But I don't even know who you are.

                    ALAN
     Look, kid, my name's Alan Kendell, I'm
     an American, I'm a journalist, and as
     you can see, I've got a car.
           (beat)
     I'm your best chance of getting home
     tonight. What do you say?

                    WILLEM
     I'm not supposed . . .

                    ALAN
     I'm going over to the West, by car,
     right now. You can stay here and take
     your chances with the trains if you
     like, or you can come with me. Choice
     is yours. But you've got to make up
     your mind . . . right now.

     Reluctantly Willem gets in and closes
     the door.

                    ALAN
     Where do you live? Schonberg I think
     you said.

                    WILLEM
     Yeah.

                    ALAN
          Right then, let's go.

Alan starts the engine, shoots off down the
road, and disappears around the corner.

EXT—DRIVING ON THE STREETS OF BERLIN—NIGHT

Alan is speeding along the streets of Berlin. Lots
of people are milling around, and occasionally
they drive past groups of soldiers with rifles.
They appear to be stopping people from travelling
down certain streets.

Several times Alan has to swerve to avoid
pedestrians walking along the road. Willem is
looking at the newspaper that Alan was reading
from earlier.

                    WILLEM
          What does all this stuff about NATO
          and the Warsaw Pact mean?

                    ALAN
          It means they're going to close the
          border with West Berlin.

                    WILLEM
          How am I going to get home? Mum and
          dad will kill me if they find out I've
          been out tonight.

                    ALAN
          Don't you worry about that. We'll get
          through.

                    WILLEM
          But if the border's closed.

Alan holds up his press card.

>   ALAN
>   This should help. They always let the
>   press through.

They drive along in silence for a few minutes.
They round the corner and in front of them is
the Brandenburg Gate.

EXT—BRANDENBURG GATE—ALAN'S CAR—NIGHT

As Alan nears the Brandenburg Gate a policeman
emerges from the shadows waving a red torch.
He steps in front of Alan's car, forcing him to
stop. Alan opens the window.

>   ALAN
>   Good evening. What seems to be the
>   problem?

>   POLICEMAN
>   I'm sorry, you can't proceed this way.
>   Road's closed.

Alan shows him his press pass.

>   ALAN
>   I need to get this little chap home.

>   POLICEMAN
>   Not this way. Try again tomorrow.

Alan closes the window and tosses the press pass
on to the back seat.

                    ALAN
                (to Willem)
        So much for that idea.

Alan turns the car around. He drives to Marx-
Engels-Platz, site of the old Imperial Palace.

A few moments later they spot another policeman
and another red torch. Alan stops the car about
thirty feet away.

                    WILLEM
        Look over there.

Alan turns to where Willem is pointing. A long
column of lorries is driving towards the square.
Some of the lorries are towing gun carriages.
Some of the lorries have open backs, and sitting
in the back are rows of uniformed factory
fighters.

                    ALAN
                (muttering under his breath)
        Routine manoeuvres my ass.

                    WILLEM
        What?

                    ALAN
        I think those guys mean business.

Eventually the whole column has passed.

Alan restarts the car and follows the final lorry.
He doesn't get far before another policeman with
a torch steps in front of the car and gestures
for him to turn round and drive back the way
they'd come.

                    ALAN
               (under his breath)
     Shit.

Alan turns into Leipziger Strasse, and then on
to Ebert- Strasse.

                    ALAN
     Don't worry, Willem, there are 15
     crossing points along this road. They
     can't all be blocked.

He makes a sharp turn and nearly drives straight
into a tank.

                    WILLEM
               (in panic)
     Watch out!

                    ALAN
     Perhaps not that way. Hold on tight,
     this could get hairy.

Alan puts the car into reverse and turns to look
out through the rear window. He puts his foot to
the floor, and the car shoots backwards.

At the intersection, he pulls on the handbrake
and throws the wheel hard over to the left.
The car skids round through 180 degrees as
Alan turns round quickly to face forward in the
driver's seat. The car now shoots forward.

                    WILLEM
     Jesus Christ. That was great. Where'd
     do learn how to do that?

                    ALAN
          Misspent childhood I guess.

Alan turns right, then another almost immediately
into a side alley and puts his foot down again.

For a few minutes they speed down a road that's
barely wider than the car. Then Alan slows right
down, flicks off his lights, and takes another
right turn. He then stops.

                    WILLEM
          Where are we?

                    ALAN
          Potsdamer Platz.

EXT—POTSDAMER PLATZ—ALAN'S CAR—NIGHT

Alan and Willem watch the activity going on
in the square. Factory fighters are unloading
roll after roll of barbed wire from one of the
trucks. As each roll is unloaded it is picked
up by another factory fighter who runs off into
the night with it.

In the distance the rolls of barbed wire are
being unfurled. Off to the side, figures are
milling around wearing camouflaged jackets and
holding automatic weapons.

                    ALAN
          This doesn't look too good.

                    WILLEM
          What are we going to do?

STANLEY JACKSON AND GAVIN JACKSON

                    ALAN
          There is one thing I could try. Wait
          here.

Alan gets out of the car, goes round the back,
and opens the boot. He removes several small
boxes and puts them into his coat. He then
and heads off towards the crowd of soldiers
unrolling the barbed wire.

Willem watches from the car.

As Alan gets closer, he CALLS OUT and waves at
the men working. Several gather round him. He
shows them his ID and points back towards the
car. He talks with them for a while, but he is
out of earshot.

Eventually he takes out of his coat the boxes
and starts handing around packets of cigarettes
and chocolate.

Eventually Alan runs back towards the car. He
gets back in, starts the engine, and drives
towards the soldiers. As they draw closer, the
soldiers pull back the wire to let them through.

Once through, the barbed wire barrier closes
behind them.

**EXT—ANONYMOUS STREET WEST BERLIN—ALAN'S
CAR—NIGHT**

Alan stops the car.

                    ALAN
          Ah, there's no place like home.

Alan points to a sign outside the window. It is a large sign mounted on two stout poles. It states in 4 languages: You are entering the American Sector.

EXT—WILLEM'S HOUSE—DOORSTEP—EARLY MORNING

Alan and Willem are standing on the doorstep of Willem's house. The door opens. Mr and Mrs Schmidt are standing in the hall in their dressing gowns.

> MRS SCHMIDT
> (to Willem)
> Thank God you're OK.

She bends down and hugs Willem. Tears are falling down her face.

> MR SCHMIDT
> Your mother and I have been worried sick. We noticed you'd gone about 2 hours ago.

> ALAN
> I'm sorry it's so late. We had a lot of trouble getting over the border.

> MR SCHMIDT
> Getting over the border?
> (to Willem)
> What the hell have you been up to?

> WILLEM
> I went to see Erik.

> MR SCHMIDT
> (furiously)

In the middle of the night? What the hell were you thinking?

                    WILLEM
I'm sorry, Dad. I . . .

Mr Schmidt turns his attention to Alan.

                    MR SCHMIDT
Who are you again?

                    ALAN
I should explain. My name's Alan Kendell. I work for Reuters. I was following a lead on a story when I found your son on Friedrichstrasse Station trying to get home. But they've stopped the trains from running.

                    MR SCHMIDT
Who has?

                    ALAN
The East Germans. So I offered to give Willem a lift home.

                    MR SCHMIDT
What do you mean the East Germans have stopped the trains from running?

                    ALAN
Just that. Trains are leaving West Berlin travelling East, but none are coming back. I think they may have closed the border.

                    MR SCHMIDT
Oh my God.

ALAN
There're loads of troops out on the
streets tonight.

WILLEM
And we nearly ran straight into a
tank. A big green one with a Russian
star on it . . . and Mr Kendell
drove like a maniac. It was really
cool . . . and . . .

MR SCHMIDT
That's quite enough, young man. You
go up to your room. I'll be up to give
you a good talking-to shortly.

Willem pulls a face and hurries inside.

MRS SCHMIDT
(to Alan)
Thank you so much for bringing Willem
all this way home. Please come in. Let
us get you a drink.

ALAN
That's really kind, but I must be
going. I think my working day is only
just beginning.

INT—ALAN'S APARTMENT—DAWN

Alan is once again back in his apartment. The
grey light of dawn is coming in from the window.
The fire is burning brightly in the hearth, and
the coal scuttle is half empty.

There are several mugs on the table containing
varying amounts of cold black coffee. There

is also an ashtray on the table, some of its contents spilling over on to the table. There is a lit cigarette balanced on the side of the ashtray with several centimetres of ash threatening to fall.

Amongst the clutter, Adam is typing furiously. The phone RINGS. Alan snatches up the receiver.

>   ALAN
> Hello. Alan Kendell.

>   BOB (O.S.)
> Looks like you hit the big one.

>   ALAN
> You can say that again.

>   BOB (O.S.)
> We've had confirmation from the embassy. They're walling us in.

>   ALAN
> And me out.

>   BOB (O.S.)
> Yeah, I was coming to that. We want you to stay there for the moment, and get as much as you can.

>   ALAN
> Thought you might.

>   BOB (O.S.)
> Where's Mary?

ALAN
She went to see her sister for the
weekend. She should be back sometime
tomorrow.

BOB (O.S.)
Look, Alan, I'm gonna be honest with
you. It could get ugly over there in
the next couple of weeks.

ALAN
Have you thought about an exit plan
for me?

BOB (O.S.)
Don't worry. If it gets real nasty,
we'll get you and Mary out somehow
via Prague.

ALAN
You don't fill me with much confidence,
Bob.

BOB (O.S.)
Sure I'm confident, pal. Just keep
smiling and think about that Pulitzer.
I think they award them posthumously
as well.

ALAN
Very funny.

Alan puts the phone down and goes back to his
typing.

INT—ERIK'S APARTMENT—BEDROOM—DAWN

Erik is asleep in bed. His knapsack is on a chair near his bed. His clothes are hanging over the back of it. A little light is coming through the open curtains.

Suddenly there is the sound of DRILLING coming from outside the window. Erik wakes with a start. Leans over and looks at the clock on his bedside table. 04.45 AM.

Erik throws off the covers of his bed and hurries over to the window. Confused, he watches for a while.

INT—ERIK'S APARTMENT—VIEW FROM BEDROOM WINDOW— ERIK'S POV

Some workmen appear to be clearing the ruined houses along Ebert Street. Further in the distance is a fence that was not there the previous morning.

INT—ERIK'S APARTMENT—BEDROOM—DAWN

The SOUND of someone HAMMERING on the front door causes Erik to turn round. There are FOOTSTEPS running through the hallway. There are MUFFLED VOICES and the SOUND of the front door SLAMMING.

INT—ERIK'S APARTMENT—LIVING ROOM—DAWN

Mr Friedheimer, Mrs Friedheimer, and their NEIGHBOUR are all in the living room. Their neighbour is sitting on the sofa distraught, tears streaming down her face. Mrs Friedheimer is sitting next to her, her arm around her shoulders.

>   NEIGHBOUR
>   They're shutting us out. They're
>   shutting us out.

>   MRS FRIEDHEIMER
>   Try and stay calm. I'm sure you're
>   mistaken.

The door opens and Erik enters.

>   ERIK
>   Who is shutting us out?

Nobody notices Erik.

>   NEIGHBOUR
>   They're outside right now with their
>   drills and jackhammers. Can't you
>   hear them? Go look out the window if
>   you don't believe me.

>   ERIK
>   (louder)
>   Who is shutting us out?

Still nobody notices Erik.

>   MR FRIEDHEIMER
>   I told you this would happen. I told
>   you.

>   MRS FRIEDHEIMER
>   (to her husband)
>   Will you stop with the 'I told you'?

                    MR FRIEDHEIMER
If only you'd listened to me, we
could've been out of here. We could've
been safe.

                    ERIK
          (shouting now)
Who is shutting us out?

Mrs Friedheimer suddenly notices Erik standing
in the doorway. She hurries over to him and hugs
him, holding him close to her.

                    MRS FRIEDHEIMER
Oh, Erik. It's going to be all right,
honey. Nothing to worry about.

                    MR FRIEDHEIMER
Don't lie to the boy.
          (to Erik)
Look, Son, the government have decided
to close the border to the West.

                    ERIK
Closed? For how long?

                    MR FRIEDHEIMER
It could be forever.

                    ERIK
But what about the football?

                    MR FRIEDHEIMER
Football's out, Son.

                    ERIK
What about your job? How will you get
to the bank if the border's closed?

> MR FRIEDHEIMER
> I won't be able to. I'll have to get a
> job in the East instead.

A thought suddenly strikes Erik.

> ERIK
> Willem! When will I get to see him
> again?

Tears are forming in his father's eyes.

> MR FRIEDHEIMER
> I don't know, Son. Maybe never.

EXT—BERLIN—BERNHAUER STRASSE—EARLY MORNING

There are two GROUPS OF CIVILIANS facing each other, one on the eastern side of the street and one on the western side. In the middle of the two groups are twenty or so FACTORY FIGHTERS driving giant concrete pillars into the ground. Others are unrolling barbed wire between the pillars. A LINE OF SOLDIERS armed with rifles are standing guard over the workers, keeping their eyes on the crowd on the Eastern side and long way from the construction work.

The civilians on the Western side are jeering and shouting abuse at the guards in the middle. The civilians on the Eastern side are more subdued; the line of soldiers are facing them. They are pointing their rifles directly at the crowd, silently warning them not to get too close.

Between the workers and the line of soldiers a COMMANDING OFFICER is pacing back and forth. He alternates between inspecting the work in progress and checking on the crowd gathered on the Eastern side. Occasionally, he barks out orders, urging the workers to increase their work rate.

Suddenly one of the soldiers breaks rank. He turns and runs towards the barricade being hastily erected. As he nears the barbed wire fence, he lets his rifle drop to the floor. The commanding officer suddenly notices him.

> COMMANDING OFFICER
> (shouting loudly)
> You there, halt!

The soldier ignores him and keeps running towards the low barbed wire fence. The commanding officer shouts something at the two soldiers closest to him. They both spin round, drop to their knees, take aim, and fire above the crowd.

The escaping soldier doesn't falter. He hurdles the barbed wire fence, takes a dozen more steps, and lands in the awaiting arms of a fellow German on the Western side of the Wall. LOUD CHEERS go up throughout the crowd as the soldier disappears into a sea of arms.

He reappears, now being carried shoulder high. The crowd bear him like a conquering hero further into the West and away from the Wall.

CUT TO

EXT—EAST BERLIN—DAWN AT THE WALL

The Wall now stands 12 foot tall. It is a white concrete mass topped with a pipe 4 foot in diameter that runs its length. In front of the Wall is a deserted service road. There are cracks in the tarmac with weeds growing through and strewn with rubbish. This is the death strip.

A subtitle appears at the foot of the screen:
    East Berlin—1984

The camera pans over the Wall to show the West side of the Wall.

EXT—WEST BERLIN—THE WALL—DAWN

The west side of the Wall is covered with graffiti. Much of the graffiti consists of hastily written words and simple drawings. Among the rough graffiti are works of much greater quality:

A series of skipping angels in silhouette created using a spray can over a stencil.

A humpty dumpty climbing over the Wall.

Figures resembling cave paintings that Picasso might be proud of.

A blackened section of the Wall decorated with an astronomical scene.

Many of the better works are accompanied by the tag 'Phizz' and are dated.

PHIZZ, a lean, 6-foot, 17-YEAR-OLD BOY, is standing a few feet from the Wall. He has long blond unwashed dreadlocks tied back with a leather strap. He is wearing tattered baggy jeans and a loose-fitting T-shirt. He is holding a spray can with his right hand and steadying himself against the Wall with his left.

Leaning against the Wall in front of him is an ancient satchel. Phizz bends down and opens the satchel to reveal several more spray cans of varying colours. He chooses another and goes back to work.

After a few moments he takes a few steps back to admire his latest creation. He raises his hand to shield his eyes from the sun now appearing over the Wall.

His work takes up the full height of the Wall. The pipe running across the top forms the top of a partially opened roller blind. Under the blind is an imagined scene on the far side of the Wall. The scene is of a stylised woodland clearing with mutated animals and sinister-looking trees. Beneath the picture is that same tag as seen on so many of the artworks—Phizz.

EXT—EAST SIDE OF THE BERLIN WALL—NEAR A GUARD TOWER—AFTERNOON

A 35-year-old Erik is walking on the pavement alongside the service road. He is dressed in the uniform of an EAST GERMAN BORDER GUARD, complete with greatcoat, rifle, and binoculars. He has just finished his latest patrol.

He starts climbing the steps to the guard tower twenty feet above the ground. When he reaches the platform at the top of the stairs, he turns around. With his back to the hut at the top of the tower, he raises his binoculars and looks out across no-man's-land, over the Wall, and to the checkpoint on the side.

EXT—WEST SIDE OF THE BERLIN WALL—CHECKPOINT—ERIK'S POV

There is a SOLDIER in a similar uniform standing outside the checkpoint. On his sleeve, above his rank insignia, is an American flag. He raises his binoculars and stares back at Erik. He then takes one hand off his binoculars and waves directly at Erik, his hand making several sweeps over his head.

EXT—EAST SIDE OF THE BERLIN WALL—GUARD TOWER—AFTERNOON

Erik looks around him furtively. He then waves back to the American soldier. The movement is slight, his hand moving no more than a foot from his side, but a wave nonetheless. Erik then turns and enters the hut. OTTO is already in there sitting at a table reading a newspaper.

> OTTO
> I might have to report you for that one of these days.

Erik stares at him blankly.

> OTTO
> Fraternising with the enemy.

> ERIK
> Oh that. Just being friendly.

                    OTTO
        We're not here to be friendly,
        Friedheimer. We've got a job to do.

                    ERIK
        Yeah, I know. And a very important
        job it is too.

                    OTTO
        Seriously though, you get caught
        doing that, and you'll be facing an
        espionage charge.

EXT—WEST SIDE OF THE BERLIN WALL—NEAR BRANDENBURG

A 35-year-old Willem and his wife ANNA are
taking a walk alongside the Berlin Wall. Both
are dressed for the weather: long raincoats,
hats, and scarves.

They are on a paved footpath. A small dog is
scurrying along in front of them at the end of
a long extendible lead that Willem is holding.
To their right is an avenue of trees. Beyond the
trees is open grassland stretching down to the
first row of buildings that mark the edge of
residential West Berlin.

The view on their left is broken by the Wall.
It stretches off into the distance seemingly
forever. They are nearing the familiar outline
of the Brandenburg Gate, with its triumphant
chariot and horses borne aloft.

Willem directs Anna to a bench. They both sit
down.

ANNA
Do you ever wonder what might have
happened to Erik?

WILLEM
Constantly. He's been my inspiration.

ANNA
Really? You've never mentioned that
before.

WILLEM
As a boy, I used to write to him. In
fact, I came to this very spot on
the anniversary of the building of
the Wall. It was here that I wrote my
first letter to him.

ANNA
What did you write about?

WILLEM
I just let him know what was happening
in the West. What I was doing. How
much I missed him. As I got older I
told him about what university I'd
chosen to go to, and why, and what I
was doing to bring down the Wall.

ANNA
Do you think he ever got any of the
letters?

WILLEM
No.

ANNA
How can you be so sure?

                    WILLEM
I never sent them.

                    ANNA
What? Why not?

                    WILLEM
Because I couldn't bear the thought
of not knowing whether or not he had
received them. I wanted to deliver
them to him by hand when he was once
again free.

                    ANNA
What did you do with them?

                    WILLEM
I kept them. They're all in a shoe
box in my office at the university
along with all my other paraphernalia
associated with the Wall and all its
evil.

                    ANNA
I can't believe that you've never told
me about this before.

                    WILLEM
Well, you've never mentioned him in
the twenty years we've been together.
And I've always felt a little guilty
about you and me.

                    ANNA
What do you mean?

                    WILLEM
Erik had the hots for you.

Anna LAUGHS gently.

> ANNA
> But we were just kids. And it was so
> long ago. Erik would have forgotten
> about me long since.

> WILLEM
> It's not logical I know. But he ended
> up there, and I ended up with you,
> and so mentally, I tried to keep the
> two of you apart.

They sit in silence for a while. Eventually,
Willem looks at his watch.

> WILLEM
> Well, the Board should have made their
> decision by now. We'd better make a
> move back to see what news they've
> got for me.

**EXT—EAST SIDE OF THE BERLIN WALL—GUARD
TOWER—AFTERNOON**

Erik and Otto are both in the guard hut. Otto is
cleaning his boots. Erik is sitting at the table
writing in a large notebook.

> OTTO
> How's the novel coming along?

Erik doesn't look up.

> OTTO
> (more loudly)
> Hey, Friedheimer.

This time Erik does look up.

>   OTTO
> How's the novel coming along?

>   ERIK
>   (sounding distracted)
> What novel? Oh, this—no—this is just
> a story, for the group.

>   OTTO
> So they're still meeting, are they,
> your Guild of Socialist Writers?

>   ERIK
> We're not a guild, or anything like
> that. We're just a group of people who
> like writing. And yes, we're still
> meeting.

There is a knock on the door of the hut, and a
third guard comes in.

>   OTTO
> Hey, Manfred.

>   (to Erik)
> Looks like your shift's over.

Erik quickly tidies his notes and stuffs them
in his bag.

EXT—WEST BERLIN TECHNICAL UNIVERSITY—CAR PARK— LATE AFTERNOON

Willem and Anna are getting out of a two-year-
old Audi. Willem takes off his long raincoat and
lays it over the back seat of the car. He leans

in and removes a suit jacket that's hanging behind the driver's seat.

He does up the buttons on the jacket and shuts the door firmly. He walks round to the other side of the door where his wife is waiting patiently.

>   WILLEM
>   How do I look?

Anna removes a few dog hairs and unbuttons his jacket.

>   ANNA
>   Never do up the buttons on a single-
>   breasted suit.

>   WILLEM
>   But it's cold out here.

>   ANNA
>   Believe me, you look much smarter
>   like that.

Anna leans forward and kisses her husband on the cheek.

>   ANNA
>   Good luck.

EXT—WEST BERLIN TECHNICAL UNIVERSITY—DEAN'S

Willem is sitting at a large desk across from the Dean of the West Berlin Technical University. It is a comfortable room, but sparsely decorated. On his desk he has a photograph of his family, and on the wall he has a framed Periodic Table.

DEAN

Herr Professor Schmidt, it seems like
only yesterday that you were sitting
there at the end of your graduate
years and I had the pleasure of
addressing you as Herr *Doctor* Schmidt
for the first time.

What impressed me then and still
impresses now, is your dedication and
dogged determination.

WILLEM

Thank you, Dean. You are most kind.

DEAN

You love your subject matter with a
passion almost as great as your love
of Berlin. I respect that. The Board
respects that.

WILLEM

Thank you, Dean.

DEAN

Many of your fellow students left
for Western Europe and the States,
choosing industry over studies. But
you stayed right here.

And then there are your publications.
500 political essays and theses
published in recognised publications.
I've checked back through our records
and can confirm that that's a record
in the university.

Because of that dedication and your
eminent position within the academic

world at large, I am delighted to
offer you the position of Head of
Political Science.

Both men stand up. The Dean leans over the desk
and gives Willem a hearty handshake.

> DEAN cont'd
> Congratulations, very well deserved.

INT—WORKERS' APARTMENT BLOCK, EAST BERLIN—FRANK AND SYLVIA'S LIVING ROOM

ARTHUR, KAREN, SYLVIA, FRANK, and BORIS, members
of Erik's writing group, are in a dismal-looking
apartment in East Berlin. Three are sitting
on the sofa (a tatty, threadbare affair), two
sitting on chairs by the dining table. There is
an empty chair on the other side of the table.
In the middle of the table is a half-empty
bottle of vodka. Everyone is either holding, or
is near a full glass.

Arthur looks at his watch.

> ARTHUR
> It's getting late. Maybe we should
> start.

> FRANK
> Without Erik? What would be the point?

> BORIS
> He'll be along soon. Probably just
> lost track of time.

> FRANK
> Unless he's defected of course.

Boris and Frank break into disproportionate
LAUGHTER. Frank reaches for the vodka bottle.

                    ARTHUR
          Don't you think you've had enough on
          an empty stomach.

                    FRANK
          Good point. Sylvia, got any nibbles?

                    SYLVIA
          You know where the kitchen is, you
          lazy oaf.

                    FRANK
          Of course, my love, but will it be
          worth my while venturing out there?

                    SYLVIA
          Oh for God's sake, it's all of 10 feet
          away.

Frank SIGHS, struggles to his feet, and goes into
the kitchen.

                    FRANK (O.S.)
          We have some salty biscuits, a little
          dry bread, a lump of smelly cheese,
          and a large bag of peanuts. Any
          takers?

There is a KNOCK on the front door.

Arthur stands up quickly and opens the door.

                    ARTHUR
          Erik, you made it. We were starting
          to get worried.

                    ERIK (O.S.)
          Hi, Arthur.

Erik walks in and puts a large bag on the table.

                    ERIK
          Sorry I'm late. I've been on night
          patrol this week.

                    KAREN
          I don't know how you bring yourself
          to defend that bloody Wall.

                    ERIK
          That 'bloody Wall' keeps me employed,
          and able to buy . . .

Erik reaches into the bag and brings out two
full bottles of vodka, several large packets of
crisps, a loaf of bread, a large pork pie, and
several bars of chocolate.

Frank appears at the doorway to the kitchen.

                    FRANK
          Ah ha, emergency supplies. I'll bring
          the plates.

Frank returns with the plates. Everyone helps
themselves to some food.

                    SYLVIA
          No Marina today.

                    ERIK
          No. She's doing something with Karl.

                    SYLVIA
          She doesn't mind you abandoning them
          both?

                    ERIK
          I don't think so.

                    (beat)
          So whose turn is it tonight?

No one says anything. Frank, Karen, and Boris
exchange looks.

                    ARTHUR
          We were rather hoping that you'd have
          something for us.

                    ERIK
          What, again?

                    FRANK
          Yeah, you know, something to cheer us
          up on this dark and stormy night.

                    ERIK
          But we've had a lot of my work recently.
          I don't want to dominate the group.

                    SYLVIA
          We don't mind.

                    BORIS
          Your stories are so much better than
          ours.

                    ERIK
          The more you practise, the better
          you'll get.

                    FRANK
          True. But do you have anything for us
          or not?

                    ERIK
          Well, as it happens . . . I do.

Erik reaches into his bag and brings out the
notes he was working on in the guard tower.

                    FRANK
          Thank God! I'm not drunk enough to
          hear one of Arthur's efforts.

                    ERIK
          It's really just another Politburo
          anecdote I'm afraid.

                    ARTHUR
          Taken from your rich vein of Politburo
          guffs, gaffs, and blunders.

                    ERIK
          If you've had enough of them, I can
          always treat you to something else.
          Something a little more serious, if
          you prefer.

                    FRANK
          Oh no, you can never have enough of
          your Politburo anecdotes.

                    BORIS
          What else have we got to live for in
          this God-awful city?

                    FRANK
          Of course, you've got an unfair
          advantage on the rest of us.

                    ERIK
How's that?

                    FRANK
You being tight with the secret
police.

                    ERIK
I'm just a humble border guard. I've
nothing to do with the secret police.

                    FRANK
Except when you're acting as chauffeur
to the general's mistress.

                    ERIK
Secretary . . .

                    FRANK
Whatever. Lots of pillow talk. Or how
about when you get roped in to wait at
the divisional dinner? Don't tell me
there weren't some loosened tongues
there by the end of the evening.

                    ERIK
Well, I must admit, that did provide
the source of some of my stories.
But . . .

                    FRANK
I'm not knocking you, mate. You take the
most banal of facts and occurrences
and turn them into priceless gems.

                    ARTHUR
Hear, hear!

                    FRANK
          I'm just jealous.

                    BORIS
          For God's sake, you two, let him get
          on with his story.

                    ERIK
          It's a little rough around the edges,
          and I may have to make up some of it
          as I go along.

                    BORIS
          Just get on with it, man.

**EXT—SCHOENBERG, WEST BERLIN—DRIVEWAY TO WILLEM'S
HOUSE—NIGHT**

Phizz is standing at the foot of a long drive
leading up to a large house. Willem's Audi is
parked on a newly gravelled drive. There is a
light on in a ground-floor window. Willem can be
seen sitting at a desk near the window.

Phizz hurries silently to the edge of the house.
He walks towards the front door, keeping close
to the wall to avoid the gravel. When he gets
to Willem's window, he ducks down to avoid being
seen from inside.

He reaches the front door, takes something from
his satchel, then fiddles with the lock, and
opens the door. He lets himself in and closes
the door quietly behind him.

INT—SCHOENBERG, WEST BERLIN—BEDROOM—NIGHT

The bedroom is gloomy, a little light coming in through the open curtains. It is a large bedroom—double bed, wardrobe, chest of drawers, desk by the window, and a set of shelves containing a small hi-fi, several school textbooks, and a model of the Statue of Liberty.

The door opens and Phizz walks in, closes the door behind him, leaves the light off, and places his satchel on the bed. He removes a small package wrapped in a clear plastic bag and places the satchel on top of the wardrobe, tucking it behind a large box.

He picks up the package and takes it over to the desk and sits down. He takes out an oversized Rizzla and spreads it out in front of him. From the plastic bag, he takes out a small amount of dark green grass and spreads it evenly over the cigarette paper. He rolls the paper expertly between his thumbs and forefingers, leans forward, licks along the open edge, and sticks it down.

He then opens both windows fully and positions himself and the chair so that his head is virtually out of the window and his feet are propped up on the desk. Finally, he lights the joint, takes a deep draw, holds his breath for a few seconds, and blows a single long plume of smoke out the window. He then stretches his arm, holding the joint outside the window, and stares up at the stars in a clear night sky.

Suddenly the door flies open and the lights are switched on.

                    WILLEM
                (shouting)
          Max! What the hell do you think you're
          doing?

                    PHIZZ
          Er hi, Dad, you frightened the life
          out of me.

Phizz frantically tries to place the joint on
the sill outside the window.

                    WILLEM
          Do you realise what trouble you could
          get me into?

                    PHIZZ
          What do you mean?

                    WILLEM
          This.

Willem picks up the baggie lying in plain view
on the desk in front of Phizz.

                    PHIZZ
          It's just a little weed—is all.

                    WILLEM
          It's illegal . . .
                (imitating Phizz's drawl)
          . . . is all.

                    PHIZZ
                (defensively)
          Yeah, and so's running a red light,
          dropping litter, and speeding.

                    WILLEM
Look, Max, under my roof, you'll obey
my rules—and that includes no gange.

                    PHIZZ
Gange? Man, you are so seventies.

                    WILLEM
I mean it—this goes.

Willem picks up the wastepaper basket and throws
the baggie into it.

                    PHIZZ
What is your problem? It's a lot less
harmful than your tobacco—and less
harmful to the environment than that
gas-guzzler on the drive.

                    WILLEM
You do realise that a single gram of
that stuff found on my premises could
get me sacked?

                    PHIZZ
             (quietly)
I didn't know that
(beat) I'm sorry.

                    WILLEM
I'm a teacher, for Christ's sake. I
have to command respect and set an
example. This sort of thing is highly
frowned upon.

                    PHIZZ
OK, OK, you made your point.

Willem sits down on the edge of the bed. He is still holding the wastebasket.

>   WILLEM
>   Look, Son, when are you going to sort
>   yourself out?

>   PHIZZ
>   What do you mean?

>   WILLEM
>   This . . .

He flicks at Phizz's hair.

>   WILLEM cont'd
>   . . . and this . . .

He points to a pile of clothes lying in the corner of the room.

>   PHIZZ
>   It's part of who I am.

>   WILLEM
>   You've got to think about who you
>   want to become. You've got to start
>   thinking about the next step—
>   university perhaps. Who's going to
>   take you on looking like that? Have
>   you even applied yet?

>   PHIZZ
>   Actually, yes, I have.

>   WILLEM
>   You have? Where?

                    PHIZZ
New York School of Art.

Willem SIGHS and rolls his eyes.

                    WILLEM
You need a portfolio before you can
interview for an art college.

                    PHIZZ
          (smirks)
I've got a very large portfolio.

                    WILLEM
You mean that vandalism you call art?

                    PHIZZ
          (surprised)
You know about that?

                    WILLEM
Yes, of course I do—I'm not stupid . . .
          (beat)
. . . Phizz.

                    PHIZZ
Anyway, it's not vandalism.

                    WILLEM
What would you call it?

                    PHIZZ
Freedom of expression. You of all
people should understand that.

                    WILLEM
Can't you express yourself on canvas?

                    PHIZZ
You are so bourgeois.

                    WILLEM
OK, smart-arse. Suppose I concede for
a moment that your defacements are
art: How are you going to present that
to a college entrance board?

                    PHIZZ
                  (giggling)
How about I tear down the wall and
take it over with me, brick by brick,
and reassemble in front of them?

                    WILLEM
There's no point talking to you when
you're in this state. We'll talk more
tomorrow.

Willem leaves the room, taking the wastebasket
with him.

INT—SCHOENBERG, WEST BERLIN—WILLEM'S STUDY—NIGHT

There is a large desk with a huge swivel chair
by the window. There are also two smaller angled
drawing-board-style desks. Books are open on
every available surface. There are also dozens
of photographs of the Wall in various phases of
development pinned to cork boards around the
room. And there are pictures of people who have
died at the Wall, with names and dates written
on them.

Two walls in the study are devoted to shelves
stretching from floor to ceiling. They contain
hundreds of books, piles of student papers, and

in the middle of the middle shelf, a Bang &
Olufsen hi-fi. A MOZART HORN CONCERTO is PLAYING
quietly.

Willem is sitting at the large desk and typing
at an Apple Mac computer. The door opens, and
Anna walks in. She is wearing a dressing gown
and slippers and carrying a mug. Willem doesn't
look up.

> ANNA
> Are you coming up soon?

Looks up, startled.

> WILLEM
> I didn't hear you come in.

> ANNA
> It's very late—nearly 3 a.m. I heard
> you arguing with Max, but that was
> just after midnight.
>
> (beat)
> I thought you might have taken the
> evening off work to celebrate your
> promotion.

> WILLEM
> I suddenly had a little inspiration—
> something Max said got me thinking in
> a new direction.

> ANNA
> Max inspired you?

                    WILLEM
He said something about taking down
the Wall and reassembling it in New
York.

                    ANNA
Reassemble it? I thought you just
wanted to be rid off the blessed thing.

                    WILLEM
Metaphorically reassemble it. Put
it in the faces of the Western
governments. Make it so they can't
ignore it.

                    ANNA
I think they know it's there, Willem.
The Americans and the British have
troops positioned here.

                    WILLEM
That's part of the problem. By
assigning troops to the Wall, they
are validating its existence. *Action,
not Acquiescence*—that's the title of
the piece I've started.

                    ANNA
So what do you suggest they do? Walk
away from it? Hope the Russians take
it away when we decide not to play
any more?

                    WILLEM
No, not at all. What I'm saying is,
the Americans and the British are not
applying enough pressure on the USSR
to get rid of it. They should be doing
more, not less, because the people

themselves will never bring down the Wall. There's not enough desire.

On the East, people are afraid of the Russians, and they have every right to be. They've seen the tanks on the street in '53 and '61. They don't want a Tiananmen Square in Potsdamer Platz. Attempts to cross the Wall have diminished considerably during the last 5 years. Life for them has become tolerable enough to make it not worth the risk.

On the West, people are indifferent to the Wall. It's been there for a generation. They're used to it. It's part of the scenery, figuratively and literally. If anything, they'd rather have it than not have it.

                    ANNA
Why do you say that?

                    WILLEM
Because our economy has steadily improved over the last 20 years. We have rebuilt successfully and are dominant in Europe. Many feel that any tinkering with that would be catastrophic. Open the Wall and the West would be swamped.

                    ANNA
But you don't think that?

                    WILLEM
No. I think if you take away the Politburo, you take away the reason to

leave the East. They would be free to model their economy on ours and join us in the European Union as equal members.

                ANNA
But how do you get rid of the Politburo?

                WILLEM
Good question. One thing's for sure: The USSR is not going to suddenly implode of its own accord. It's too well entrenched, too much a part of its people's psyche.

No. We have to chip away at it. We start off by getting the Yanks and the Brits to coordinate efforts with the European Union to apply sufficient diplomatic pressure on the USSR to remove their influence in East Germany. We can then work on other Soviet states.

The USSR will always remain. There'll be a hard core of states that will always remain loyal, like Belarus and Georgia. But at least it will be a smaller USSR—a more containable USSR.

INT—ERIK'S APARTMENT—LIVING/DINING ROOM—EVENING

Erik and his wife MARINA are eating dinner in virtual silence. Erik has a carton of notes on the chair next to him. Every so often he makes a note on a sheet of paper and then carries on eating.

Marina lights a cigarette.

>   ERIK
> Must you do that at the dining table?

>   MARINA
> Must you do that?

Marina points at his papers.

>   ERIK
> My habit isn't antisocial, is not
> an irritant, and is not harmful to
> health.

>   MARINA
> Antisocial . . .
>   (beat)
> yes, it is. Irritating . . . (beat)
> certainly irritates the crap out of
> me. Harmful to health . . .
>   (beat)
> you'll find out just how harmful if
> you don't fucking stop.

Erik slams his pen down on the table.

>   ERIK
> So if I stop writing, you'll stop
> smoking.

>   MARINA
> Sure, why not.

Marina grinds her cigarette into her ashtray.
Erik grudgingly puts his notebook back into
the carton. Erik and Marina continue eating in
silence.

Suddenly LOUD MUSIC starts blaring from another room in the apartment.

>   ERIK
> Oh, for God's sake!

Erik's stands up quickly, sending the chair toppling backwards.

>   MARINA
> Just leave him be. He's just being a teenager.

He storms out of the room. Marina starts to clear the dishes from the table.

INT—ERIK'S APARTMENT—KARL'S BEDROOM—EVENING

The room is very messy. There are clothes on the floor and books all over the place. KARL FRIEDHEIMER is sitting on his bed, reading a book. He is wearing scruffy jeans and a dirty T-shirt.

Erik storms in.

>   ERIK
> Will you turn this rubbish down?

>   KARL
> It's how I like to relax.

>   ERIK
> Why do you need to relax? Isn't lying around all day relaxing enough?

                    KARL
Oh, here we go. Have I started looking
for a job, have I decided what to do
with my life, have I bothered to tidy
up around here.
          (beat)
I'll save you the interrogation.
No. No.

And, no. Is that what you wanted to
know?

                    ERIK
That's pretty much it, yes. From you,
it's just take, take, take.

                    KARL
Let me guess, in a minute you're going
to say: From each according to his
ability, to each according to his
need.

                    ERIK
You could do a lot worse than at least
considering that a little. Why don't
you have any aspirations?

                    KARL
How would you know whether or not I
have aspirations? You don't know a
thing about me. When was the last
time you showed any notice of me or
my interests?

                    ERIK
What's that supposed to mean?

                    KARL
You're too busy with your stupid
friends and your stupid writing to
pay me any notice.

                    ERIK
So what are your aspirations?

                    KARL
I want something better than this.

He waves his arms around the room.

    It might be good enough for you, but
    it's not good enough for me.

                    ERIK
And you're going to achieve this . . .
whatever . . . how exactly?

                    KARL
I'll think of something, just leave
me alone.

Erik storms out, SLAMMING the door on the way
out.

INT—ERIK'S APARTMENT—KARL'S BEDROOM—NIGHT

The lights are off, and the MUSIC is turned down
low. Karl is standing at the window. From his
window, he can see row upon row of bleak grey
workers' apartment blocks. He can also see a row
of pre-war shops, complete with the hand-painted
signs of family-run businesses.

He turns round and opens the cupboard over
his wardrobe. He takes out an ancient canvas

STANLEY JACKSON AND GAVIN JACKSON

knapsack and puts it on to the bed. He gets on to his knees and rummages under his bed. He brings out a length of rope with a large hook attached and a pair of sturdy bolt cutters.

All of these he carefully packs into the knapsack.

He opens his bedroom door. The rest of the apartment is in darkness. He closes the bedroom door quietly behind himself and walks to the front door. He lets himself out of the apartment.

INT—TREPTOW—SIDE ALLEY—NIGHT

Karl walks down the deserted street. He keeps to the shadows. He spots a BORDER GUARD walking along the other side of the road and so slips into a shop doorway. He waits until he's out of sight before continuing his journey.

He rounds the corner and stops. In front of him is the East side of the Berlin Wall. Unlike the West side, this side is free from graffiti and continually guarded.

EXT—PANKOW—NEAR THE WALL—NIGHT

Karl is standing in an alley looking towards the wall.

The inner fence is 10 feet in front of him. It is six feet tall and topped with two rows of barbed wire. 50 yards beyond that is the outer wall. The outer wall is smooth white concrete, 11 feet tall, topped with a concrete sewage pipe four feet in diameter.

Between the inner fence and the outer wall is the patrol track used by East German border patrol jeeps. There is a guard tower about 100 yards to his right. One BORDER GUARD is inside.

A second guard walks along the patrol track. He passes no more than 15 feet from Karl's position, but doesn't notice him. He is heading for the guard tower. He stops at the bottom of the tower, slings his rifle over his shoulder, and starts to climb the ladder up to the tower.

Karl makes his move. He reaches into his canvas knapsack and takes out a pair of wire cutters. He runs quietly to the inner fence. He cuts the top two strands of barbed wire and pulls them wide enough apart to allow himself to squeeze through.

Karl looks over towards the guard tower. Both guards are still talking to each other. Karl takes a deep breath, places both hands on the fence, and vaults over. He lands quietly. A quick look at the guards—still in conversation. Keeping low, he runs across the death strip.

As he nears the outer wall, he stumbles. His knapsack falls to the ground with loud CLUNK. One of the guards looks up.

> GUARD #1
> You there! Stop where you are!

The second guard turns on the spotlight and points it in Karl's direction.

Karl is back on his feet and running the final few feet to the Wall.

STANLEY JACKSON AND GAVIN JACKSON

The second border guard raises his rifle and takes aim at Karl.

                    GUARD #2
          Halt, or I'll fire.

Karl reaches into his knapsack and brings out a home-made grappling iron tied to a length of rope. He starts swinging it over his head and lets go. The grappling iron catches hold of the sewage pipe on top of the Wall. Karl pulls hard on the rope and starts to climb.

The border guard fires a warning shot that strikes the Wall two feet above Karl's head. Karl continues to climb. The border guard fires two more shots; both hit Karl between the shoulders. Karl lets go of the rope and falls backwards off the wall. He lies motionless on the border patrol track.

INT—HOSPITAL—WARD—EARLY MORNING

Karl's lifeless body is lying on a hospital gurney. His body is covered with a tarpaulin. It is pulled back to expose his head and shoulders. Dried blood covers his shirt and jumper. There are some medical machines near the gurney; none are turned on.

Two NURSES and a PORTER are standing by the gurney. They are saying nothing; their faces are expressionless. Waiting. In a corner of the room a SECOND PORTER and an off-duty Otto are drinking coffee, quietly sharing a joke.

After a few moments a DOCTOR enters the room. He is shabbily dressed, has on a stained white coat, and looks like he has only just woken up.

>   OTTO
>   (in a whisper to the second porter)
>   Ah, Dr Death, I presume.

The second porter stifles a laugh.

Without any preamble, the doctor peers down at Karl. With one hand, he gently holds Karl's chin and turns his head to one side. With his index and middle fingers on his other hand, he feels Karl's neck for a pulse. He looks up at the clock on the wall.

>   DOCTOR
>   Time of death One O Two a.m.

One of the nurses picks up a clipboard and makes a note.

>   DOCTOR
>   Check his pockets for ID. If he has
>   none, put him down as September No.
>   1. Then get him out of here.

The doctor hurries out of the room.

The first nurse removes the tarpaulin completely. She removes a wallet from his pocket. Inside the wallet she finds his ID card.

>   NURSE #1
>   (to the nurse with the clipboard)
>   Karl Friedheimer.

The second nurse makes a note.

The border guard looks up quickly at the small group gathered around the gurney. He is no longer smiling.

The first porter holds up Karl's knapsack.

>   PORTER #1
>   What shall I do with this?

>   NURSE #1
>   Send it to the incinerator with the
>   body.

The porter replaces the tarpaulin over Karl's body and places the knapsack on his now-covered chest. The second porter walks over to the gurney, and together they push the gurney out of the room.

The border guard sidles over to the nurse with the clipboard.

>   BORDER GUARD
>   Did you say Friedheimer?

>   NURSE #2
>   Yes, Friedheimer, Karl Friedheimer.
>   Why?

>   BORDER GUARD
>   I've been on duty with a Friedheimer.
>   It could be his son. Where's he from?

The nurse looks at the ID card.

>   NURSE #2
>   Mitte.

BORDER GUARD
I think it's him. Can I take his ID
card to his family?

NURSE #2
I'm sorry. It has to be processed
along with the body.

EXT—ERIK'S APARTMENT—FRONT DOOR—MORNING

OTTO is standing in front Erik's front door. He
raises his hand in a fist as if to rap on the
door. He hesitates. Finally he makes three loud
RAPS.

The SOUND of several BOLTS being drawn back. The
door opens. Erik looks half asleep.

ERIK
Hi, Otto, what are you doing here?
I've not forgotten a shift, have I?

OTTO
It's nothing like that.

MARINA (O.S.)
Who is it at this time in the morning?

Erik turns his head to look back into the
apartment.

ERIK
        (to Marina somewhere in the shadows)
It's Otto.

Marina comes into view holding her dressing gown
tightly around her.

                    MARINA
Otto? What are you doing here?

                    OTTO
Can I come in?

                    ERIK
Of course.
Erik shows Otto into the living room.

                    ERIK
What is it, Otto?

                    OTTO
It's Karl.

                    MARINA

Karl? What's wrong with him? Where is
he?

                    OTTO
There was an incident at the Wall
and, well, Karl's . . .

                    MARINA
Oh my God!

She collapses on to the sofa in tears.

EXT—MITTE—OUTSIDE ERIK'S APARTMENT—EVENING

Erik parks his car outside his apartment. It
is a five-year-old red Skoda. He sits staring
straight ahead, his hands still holding the
steering wheel. He sighs and finally gets out
of his car.

He is wearing his border guard uniform; it looks like it could do with a wash. He walks slowly round to the passenger side of the car, opens the door and takes out his overcoat, and places it over his arm. He closes and locks the door.

He looks up at the plain grey concrete apartment block and starts to walk to the door. Once inside, he slowly climbs the two flights of stairs up to his apartment. He unlocks the front door and goes inside.

INT—ERIK'S APARTMENT—DINING ROOM/LIVING ROOM—EVENING

Erik is standing in the doorway looking down at the floor. In front of him are two suitcases. He looks over to the other side of the room and notices that Marina has piled all his cartons of notes to Willem on to the dining room table.

He calls out to Marina.

> ERIK
> Marina? What's all this?

Marina walks into the room. She's wearing her shoes and coat. Dressed ready to go out.

> MARINA
> I'm leaving.

> ERIK

> Where are you going?

> MARINA
> To my sister's.

                    ERIK
          When are you coming back?

                    MARINA
          I'm not, Erik. I'm leaving you.

                    ERIK
          Why?

Marina starts crying. She rushes over to Erik
and beats her fists against his chest.

                    MARINA
          Why? Our son dies at the Wall you
          protect, and you have to ask me why?

Erik tries to cuddle her, but she pulls away.

                    MARINA
          Your son dies at that fucking Wall,
          and you keep defending it.

She runs over to the table and starts emptying
Erik's cartons on the floor in the middle of the
floor.

                    ERIK
          Stop that!

                    MARINA
          Every morning you go out to work as
          if nothing has happened, and every
          night you come home and start writing
          again. Writing. Writing. Writing.

Marina gets down on to her knees in the middle
of the papers. She starts clutching them to
her as if they were bundles of money and she a

lottery winner. She throws a handful of papers into the air.

>   MARINA
>   Silly stories! Stupid poems! Plays
>   that you will never put on in any
>   theatre. Why, Erik, why?

>   ERIK
>   You know that's how I keep my memories
>   of the past alive.

>   MARINA
>   You miss the Berlin of your youth, but
>   what about your son? Your own flesh
>   and blood? He's dead. Why don't you
>   miss him? You ignored him while he
>   was alive, now he's dead and you still
>   ignore him. And you still defend that
>   damn fucking Wall that killed him.
>   (now shouting)
>   I've had enough.

Marina reaches into her pocket and brings out a box of matches.

>   ERIK
>   What are doing?

>   MARINA
>   What I should have done years ago.

Marina lights a match and tosses it on to the papers in front of her.

>   ERIK
>   (shouting imploringly)
>   NOOO . . .

Erik rushes over and throws his coat over the burning paper. Marina moves away and walks over to the door. Erik doesn't even look up as Marina picks up her suitcases.

>   MARINA
>   Goodbye, Erik.

INT—WORKERS' APARTMENT BLOCK, EAST BERLIN—FRANK AND SYLVIA'S LIVING ROOM

Arthur, Karen, Sylvia, Frank, Boris, and Erik are in Frank and Sylvia's living room. Erik and Karen are sitting on the sofa. Everyone else is sitting around the dining table.

The mood is much more sober than their previous scene together.

>   FRANK
>   We weren't expecting to see you
>   tonight.

>   BORIS
>   No, we weren't.

>   KAREN
>   Are you OK?

>   ERIK
>   I'm fine.

Karen takes a hold of Erik's arm.

>   KAREN
>   You must feel terrible.

                    ERIK
No, really. I'm fine.

                    SYLVIA
I'm sure she'll come to you.

                    FRANK
Yeah, 'course she will. After a couple
of weeks in the country with her
sister, she'll be bored and desperate
to get back.

                    BORIS
You're probably better off without
her.

                    KAREN
Boris! How can you say that?

                    BORIS
Well, he can write when he likes. Work
when he likes. Go out when he likes.
Total freedom.

                    SYLVIA
You are the epitome of unreconstructed
male chauvinism. Is it any wonder
you're still single?

                    BORIS
I'm just messin' with you.

                    ERIK
Actually, I don't miss Marina. And I
hate myself for not missing her. I know
I should miss her. We've been married
for 20 years. I've known her for 25.
But we've not really communicated for
the last five. Not since Karl died.

                    SYLVIA
At least you've still got us. We'll
always be here for you.

                    ERIK
It's not me I'm worried about, it's
her. She can't stay with her sister
forever. It's only a small cottage.
She'll then have no one.

                    KAREN
It's so sad. You used to be every bit
the perfect couple.

                    ERIK
The problem is she grew out of my
writing. The older Karl got, the less
time she had for idle contemplation.
Which, let's face it, is all we do.

                    ARTHUR
Don't put yourself down, Erik. Yes, we
as a group spend a lot of time chewing
the fat. But our writing, your work in
particular, is important.

Boris GUFFAWS.

                    BORIS
How do you work that out, Arthur?

                    ARTHUR
Because it's our way to assert ourselves
as free-thinking individuals and to
distinguish ourselves from the State.

                    BORIS
          I thought it was just a good excuse
          to get pissed.

                    ARTHUR
          That too. But any fool can do that.
          We keep the dream of freedom alive.

                                        CUT TO

EXT—CHECKPOINT CHARLIE, 1989—PARKING BAY—NIGHT

MAJOR BERNIE GODEK drives up in an army jeep and
parks outside the Allied forces observation hut.
Facing the hut is the elaborate set of buildings
that comprise the passport control of the East
Germans. Between the two sets of buildings is
a white line, about three inches thick. This is
the demarcation line that separates East and
West Berlin.

A subtitle appears at the foot of the screen:
          Checkpoint Charlie—1989

There is a lot of activity on the East German
side. There are forklift trucks and a mini
crane moving around. There is also an army
of construction workers attending to mounds of
concrete blocks and piles of wood.

Godek gets out of the jeep and watches the
construction work for a few moments. He then
walks towards the Allied forces trucks. He
notices a WAITRESS locking up Cafe Adler for
the night and waves in her direction. He then
enters the observation hut.

STANLEY JACKSON AND GAVIN JACKSON

INT—CHECKPOINT CHARLIE—MITCHELL SUITE—NIGHT

Godek enters a room in the observation hut with a brass plaque on the door bearing the legend The Mitchell Suite. It's a small and cluttered room. There are several desks with monitors on, a handful of chairs, and a TV tuned in to an American channel. Two men, SERGEANT YOUNG and MAJOR ARMSTRONG, are chatting.

> GODEK
> What's going on out there?

> ARMSTRONG
> It looks like they're building an extension to the Wall. They've been at it for several hours now.

> YOUNG
> I think it's in honour of Gorbachev's visit next week. Don't want anyone escaping whilst he's here.

> ARMSTRONG
> It really is most impressive—the speed they've been working. It should be complete in the next half an hour or so, if they stop at Hagen Koch's white line that is.

> GODEK
> That's one line they wouldn't step over.

> YOUNG
> Hey, who's that?

Young points to the monitor in front of him. On the monitor, they see a senior EAST GERMAN

OFFICER in full dress uniform walking towards the demarcation line. He stops about two feet from the line and starts inspecting the new section of Wall.

>   GODEK
>   Two can play at that game. Come along,
>   Young, you can translate for me should
>   the need arise.

Godek walks towards the door.

>   GODEK
>   Oh, and bring the video camera.

>   YOUNG
>   What for?

>   GODEK
>   It's the most powerful weapon of our
>   media age.

EXT—CHECKPOINT CHARLIE—DEMARCATION LINE—NIGHT

Godek strolls up to new section of Wall. Young follows him with the video camera placed on his shoulder. Godek stops within two feet of the Western side of the demarcation line and four feet behind the East German. The East German turns to his right and starts walking parallel to line. Godek follows suit.

Two BORDER GUARDS on the Eastern side watch impassively as Godek keeps pace with the East German officer and Young records the whole proceedings.

Godek stops, allowing the East German Officer to get a few paces ahead. The East German Officer stops, turns round, and starts walking back towards Godek. As he passes Godek, he leans over the line and intentionally bumps Godek's shoulder with his own.

> YOUNG
> (in a whisper)
> I can't believe he just did that to you.

> GODEK
> I can't believe it either.

Godek turns round and walks quickly to catch up with the East German. Now Godek bumps the East German as he passes him. The East German walks back towards the passport control buildings on the eastern side and disappears round the corner.

> YOUNG
> You do realise that we've just had a serious international incident?

> GODEK
> Yes, but let's just keep that to ourselves, shall we, Sergeant?

EXT—EAST BERLIN—NEAR A GUARD TOWER ON THE WALL—NIGHT

Erik is on patrol. He is wearing a greatcoat over his uniform, gloves, and a large Russian-style fur hat. He throws his arm around himself to keep warm.

Erik looks up at the guard tower. The lights in the turret are off.

> ERIK
> (loudly)
> Otto?

There is no reply.

> ERIK
> (more loudly)
> Otto! Are you up there?

Still no reply.

> ERIK
> Manfred?

Erik hurries up the stairs to the turret and goes inside.

INT—EAST BERLIN—GUARD TOWER TURRET—NIGHT

The hut is empty. The chairs are placed neatly around the table. The bag containing Erik's notes is hanging on a hook by the door. Otto's polish and boot-cleaning rags are piled on a shelf.

Erik leaves the hut and stands on the platform outside. He raises his binoculars to his eyes and looks out over the Wall.

EXT—WEST BERLIN—NEAR THE WALL ERIK'S POV—NIGHT

There is a steady flow of people walking towards and congregating at the Wall.

EXT—WEST BERLIN—NEAR THE WALL—NIGHT

Phizz is standing in the shadows of a clump of trees near the Wall. He has a satchel over his shoulder and looks quite agitated.

People are passing between him and the Wall. They are laughing and joking, some carrying beer cans. After they've passed, Phizz peers out from the trees. He quickly ducks back again as more people file past.

INT—BERLIN TECHNICAL OFFICE—WILLEM'S OFFICE—NIGHT

Willem is typing furiously at his Apple Mac. He has a small CD player on his desk playing a MOZART PIANO CONCERTO. Several books are piled up on the small desks. On the main desk by the printer are several sheets of notes. The title page reads:

> Culpable Negligence of the Western Economic Model.

From outside the window there are some SHOUTS from a group of people passing by. Willem stops typing and looks up. There are some more SHOUTS and some LAUGHTER.

Willem gets up and walks to the window. He peers out for a few moments. He then closes the window and shuts the blind. He returns to his desk, turns up the volume, and resumes typing.

INT—WILLEM'S HOUSE IN SCHOENBERG—LIVING ROOM—NIGHT

Anna is sitting on the sofa reading a magazine. She has a mug of coffee on the table in front of her. The TV is on, tuned into a football match, the volume low. There is a break in the commentary.

>   TV ANNOUNCER (O.S.)
> We interrupt this programme to bring
> you a very special announcement.
> In a press conference earlier this
> evening, Gunter Schabowski, Berlin
> Party Secretary, announced that all
> travel restrictions on his people have
> been lifted with immediate effect.
> The following footage is from that
> news conference.

Anna looks up from her magazine.

>   SCHABOWSKI (O.S.)
>   (in a flat monotone)
> Today new regulations have been
> drawn up to allow East Germans to
> travel. Private trips abroad can be
> applied for without questions, and
> applications will be dealt with at
> high speed. The People's Police have
> been instructed to hand out long-
> term exit visas without delay, and
> the conditions that have applied up
> until now are redundant.

>   TV ANNOUNCER (O.S.)
> Following this announcement hundreds
> of people have started to march

towards the Wall from the both the
East and the West.

Anna picks up the telephone and dials a number.

> WILLEM (O.S.)
> You have got through to the office of
> Professor Willem Schmidt. I am unable
> to take your call at the moment.
> Please leave a message after the tone,
> or try Schoenberg 128762.

> ANNA
> Willem, I hope you know the news and
> that you're out by the Wall. If not,
> turn on the TV as soon as you can,
> then go enjoy the moment. I'll put
> some champagne in the fridge for when
> you return. I'm sorry I'm gabbling—I'm
> just so excited. See you later.

INT—BERNAUER STRASSE CHECKPOINT—CANTEEN—EVENING

HARALD JAGER is in the canteen eating his evening
meal. He bites into his bratwurst sandwich and
takes a long pull on his beer. He is watching
the press conference on a large screen.

> REPORTER
> When will this policy come into
> effect?

> SCHABOWSKI
> Immediately.

Jager nearly chokes, spitting beer all over the
table.

                    JAGER
              (muttering to himself)
        Rubbish.

INT—DAHLEM DISTRICT, WEST BERLIN—GENERAL GODEK'S HOUSE—EVENING

General Godek is making a phone call. The TV is on in the background.

                    GODEK
        Something's going on, Sergeant. We
        need to get down to Charlie ASAP.

                    YOUNG
        Yes, sir.

                    GODEK
        Swing by and pick me up on the way
        through, will ya?

                    YOUNG
        Yes, sir.

Godek puts the phone down.

INT—WEST BERLIN—CAFE ADLER, NEAR CHECKPOINT CHARLIE—EVENING

The restaurant is quiet. A little gentle JAZZ is playing quietly. There are seven customers, most sitting alone. The waitress at the counter is reading a novel.

The door BURSTS open, and a photographer rushes up to the counter.

                    PHOTOGRAPHER
Ten coffees to go please.

                    WAITRESS
           (sounding surprised)
Ten?

                    PHOTOGRAPHER
Yeah, I've got a news crew out there.

                    WAITRESS
What's going on?

                    PHOTOGRAPHER
Haven't you heard? They're opening the
border.

The photographer picks up his coffees on a
cardboard tray and hurries out.

                    CUSTOMER 1
Can you believe that?

                    CUSTOMER 2
           (to the waitress)
Can we have the radio on.

                    WAITRESS
Of course.

She walks over to the hi-fi behind the counter.
She stops the tape that's playing, switches to
the radio, and turns up the volume.

                    RADIO ANNOUNCER (O.S.)
. . . 50 to a 100 people have already
gathered at the Berholmer checkpoint
and at other checkpoints throughout
city.

INT—MITTE, EAST GERMANY—LIVING ROOM—NIGHT

A woman is on the phone to her husband.

> HUSBAND (O.S.)
> Are you watching?

> WIFE
> Of course.

> HUSBAND (O.S.)
> The borders are going to open tonight.

> WIFE
> I heard that.

> HUSBAND (O.S.)
> Where's our son?

> WIFE
> He's gone to bed.

> HUSBAND (O.S.)
> Get him up! Go to Trabbi. You should
> be able to get across from there.

> WIFE
> Are you sure? He's got school tomorrow.

> HUSBAND (O.S.)
> Of course there'll be no school
> tomorrow. Tonight is the night of all
> nights. You must be a part of it.

INT—EAST BERLIN—GUARD TOWER TURRET—NIGHT

Erik is still standing watching the crowds
gathering on the West side of the Wall. Now

there are hundreds of people gathering on the East side as well as the West. A Trabant stops yards from the Wall. Erik looks into the East and sees that there is a steady stream of cars heading in his direction. Cars are choking all the side alleys that go up to the Wall.

There is the sound of doors SLAMMING as people abandon their cars and start marching towards him. The mood is good-natured, like a large crowd gathering for a football match.

> VOICE IN THE CROWD
> (shouting loudly)
> We are free! We are free!

The shout is taken up by the crowd as a CHANT.

He once again raises his binoculars and looks out over the Wall and past Checkpoint Charlie to Cafe Adler beyond.

EXT—WEST BERLIN—NEAR CHECKPOINT CHARLIE—ERIK'S POV—NIGHT

Hundreds of people have gathered around outside Cafe Adler. The door opens and two waitresses come out holding a tray bearing a bottle of champagne and several glasses. They walk to the Wall. As they cross the white line that separates East from West, border guards approach them and wave them away. As they turn back and return to the West, one of the waitresses removes the bottle from the tray and places it on the white line between East and West. A CHEER goes up in the crowd.

INT—EAST BERLIN—GUARD TOWER TURRET—NIGHT

Erik climbs down the stairs from the turret at
the top of the guard tower. He has his gun slung
over his shoulder and is carrying a large bag.
As he reaches the bottom, three men approach
him. One is carrying a camera.

>   MAN #1
>   Can we take our picture with you?

>   ERIK
>   OK.

The man with the camera arranges his two mates
on either side of Erik. He takes a few steps back
and aims. The camera FLASHES.

>   MAN #1
>   Thanks. You take the next one, Hans.

He hands the camera to his friend and stands
alongside Erik in his place.

>   MAN #1
>   Hold on, Hans.
>   (to Erik)
>   May I?

He points to Erik's rifle.

>   ERIK
>   Sure. But be careful with it. The
>   safety's on, but you never know with
>   these Russian designs.

The men LAUGH. The man on the other side of Erik
pinches Erik's cap and puts it on.

STANLEY JACKSON AND GAVIN JACKSON

                    HANS
    Are you both ready now?

                    MAN #1
    Yup, off you go, Hans.

There's a second FLASH from the camera.

                    MAN #1
    Thanks, pal.

They hand back Erik's rifle and cap and run off
towards the Wall. Erik turns and walks off in
the opposite direction.

INT—BERNAUER STRASSE CHECKPOINT—JAGER'S SUPERVISOR'S OFFICE

Harald Jager is with his SUPERVISOR speaking
on the phone to the general in charge of the
district. Jager is on an extension, listening in
to the conversation.

                    SUPERVISOR
    Comrade Jager says that the situation
    is exceptional.

                    GENERAL (O.S.)
    Is this correct? Jager: has he panicked?
    Is this a true representation of the
    situation?

                    SUPERVISOR
    I have known comrade Jager for many
    years. If he says it is so, it is so.
    Rely on it.

                    GENERAL (O.S.)
     I have my doubts.

                    JAGER
               (shouting down the phone)
     If you don't believe me, listen to the
     crowd for yourself.

     He flings the window open and holds
     the phone out.

EXT—WEST BERLIN—NEAR THE WALL—NIGHT

Cars are parked haphazardly all over the place.
CAR HORNS are being TOOTED. There is now a
large group of people gathered at the Wall. As
more people join, they greet each other with
handshakes and hugs.

A news truck turns up and parks within 20 feet
of where Phizz is still standing in the shadows.
Several people get out and start setting up
mobile TV cameras and microphones. A man with a
very professional-looking camera, complete with
extensive zoom lens, checks a light meter. He
walks towards the people, stopping every so
often to take photographs of the people, the
Wall, the cars parked along the wall, and the
border guards.

A trickle of people start to approach the wall.
A car drives right up to the Wall and parks
alongside it. The driver gets out, climbs on to
the roof, and from there springs on to the Wall.
Several border guards watch, but do nothing
to stop him. The man on the Wall has a camera
on a strap over his shoulder. He starts taking
photographs of the people on the West side of

the Wall and then starts taking pictures of the people on the far side of the death strip on the East side of the Wall.

One of the border guards approaches the Wall. He removes his rifle and lays it alongside the bottom of the Wall. He then removes his cap and flings it into the crowd. Several other guards remove and throw their caps into the crowd as well.

EXT—EAST BERLIN—BERNAUER STRASSE—NIGHT

Thousands of people are marching with unhurried, but purposeful steps. In the crowd there are men, women, and children. Some children are sitting on their fathers' shoulders, others are marching alongside. Some people are in night clothes with coats thrown hastily over. Some in the crowd are wearing slippers.

Finally, they reach the Wall at Bernauer Strasse. They can get no further—there is no checkpoint here—the Wall is blocking their path, gleaming in its whiteness. They stop about 10 feet short.

Egged on by several members of the crowd, a burly man approaches the Wall. He produces a sledgehammer from inside his long overcoat. Turning to the crowd, he holds the hammer aloft. The crowd CHEER their approval. He turns back to the Wall and smashes the hammer into the Wall with all his might, sending chippings flying through the air. He takes another strike. And another. And another.

From the crowd, other people come forward with hammers, and they too start to pound away. A group of four men move towards the Wall with a huge metal pole. A gap in the crowd opens up, and the men take a run at the Wall. The collision covers them with debris. The Wall remains standing, but badly damaged. The crowd continue their assault.

INT—WEST BERLIN TECHNICAL UNIVERSITY—COMMON ROOM—AFTERNOON

A party is in full swing in the common room. Willem walks in.

>   COLLEAGUE #1
> Congratulations, Professor Schmidt.

>   WILLEM
> Thanks, but . . .

>   COLLEAGUE #1
> It's thanks to your work, and that of those like you, that we've finally brought that accursed Wall down.

>   WILLEM
> Well, I . . .

>   COLLEAGUE #1
> A toast.

He shoves a glass of champagne into Willem's hand and raises his own.

>   COLLEAGUE #1 con't
> To the man of the moment.

The TOAST is echoed throughout the room.

                    WILLEM
          I'm really not sure that I deserve
          all this.

                    COLLEAGUE #1
          Make the most of it, man. This is your
          day.

                    COLLEAGUE #2
          You must be delighted.

                    WILLEM
          Of course.

                    COLLEAGUE #2
          A dream come true. So what's next?

                    WILLEM
          What do you mean?

                    COLLEAGUE #2
          Now that the Wall's come down, what's
          your next campaign?

                    WILLEM
          I see what you mean. I've not really
          thought about that yet. It's all been
          so quick.

                    COLLEAGUE #2
          Quick? It's been 28 years.

                    COLLEAGUE #3
          You'll have to find yourself another
          Wall to campaign against.

LAUGHTER breaks out in the room.

                    WILLEM
     Well, I confidently predict that no
     government will ever impose a wall
     upon its citizens again.

                    COLLEAGUE #3
     But if they do, you'll be able to
     offer consultancy. Right?

More LAUGHTER.

EXT—WEST SIDE OF THE BERLIN WALL—NEAR BRANDENBURG GATE

Willem is sitting alone on a bench overlooking the Brandenburg Gate. It is the same bench that he and Anna sat on before his appointment to the position the post of Head of Political Science.

Cars are flooding into the area from both the East and the West. People are gathering around and on the gate from both sides. East and West embracing other. Festivities have broken out. Restrictions no longer apply.

Tears are streaming down Willem's face.

INT—MITTE—RUN-DOWN BAR—NIGHT

The bar is heaving with people. Erik is sitting on his own at a corner table. He has a half-full glass of beer in front of him. He looks glum. A man holding a beer approaches his table.

                    MAN
     Is this chair taken?

                    ERIK
No.

                    MAN
May I join you?

                    ERIK
Go ahead.

                    MAN
You don't look so happy.

                    ERIK
I'm just in shock, I guess.

                    MAN
I know what you mean.

He takes a sip of his beer.

                    MAN
You're a border guard, huh?

                    ERIK
That's right.

                    MAN
On duty tonight?

                    ERIK
Yup.

                    MAN
You must have had a good view.

                    ERIK
You could say that. I was stuck in the
guard turret for most of the evening.
I was afraid to come down.

                    MAN
Afraid the mob might attack you?

                    ERIK
Perhaps 'afraid' is too strong a
word. Ashamed perhaps. I have become
anathema in the last 24 hours.

                    MAN
You were just guarding the establishment.
It was the establishment.

                    ERIK
Oh yeah?

                    MAN
I am, or should that be was, Passport
Control. I'm Stasi. There'll be no
place for us tomorrow.

                    ERIK
Tomorrow?

                    MAN
Well, maybe not tomorrow. But our
days are numbered. There's a momentum
building. Tonight was just a release
of pressure. More's to come, of that
I'm certain.

                    ERIK
What will you do?

                    MAN
Try to disappear into the crowd. You?

                    ERIK
        I don't know. I just don't know. Think
        I'll start by having another of these.
        Want another?

                    MAN
        Thanks.

EXT—OUTSIDE ERIK'S APARTMENT—NIGHT

Erik is fumbling with the key to his apartment.
He is very drunk. He still has his large bag
over his shoulder, but his cap and rifle are
gone. In his left hand he is carrying a full
bottle of vodka.

He finally gets the door open and stumbles
inside, holding on to the wall as he goes. He
pushes the door with his foot, but the door fails
to close.

INT—ERIK'S APARTMENT—LIVING ROOM—NIGHT

It's dark in the apartment. Erik doesn't bother
to turn the light on. He trips on something and
grabs hold of the table to steady himself. He
swings his bag off his shoulder and on to the
table. It slides across the table and on to the
floor, spilling papers everywhere.

Erik walks round the table, slips on a few of
the papers, and falls on to the sofa. He puts
the vodka on the floor beside him, lies back,
and closes his eyes.

EXT—OUTSIDE ERIK'S APARTMENT—AFTERNOON

Arthur walks along the corridor to Erik's apartment. He goes to knock but notices that the door is ajar. He pushes the door gently. It swings open.

> ARTHUR
> Erik? Are you there?

No reply.

> ARTHUR
> (louder)
> Hey, Erik, it's me, Arthur.
> (beat)
> Do you mind if I come in?

Arthur walks into Erik's apartment, closing the door behind him.

INT—ERIK'S APARTMENT—LIVING ROOM—AFTERNOON

Arthur switches on the light. The room is in chaos. Several chairs have been turned over. Empty wine and vodka bottles are lying on the floor. Erik's greatcoat is draped across the table. In the middle of the floor is a huge pile of crumpled papers.

There's a LOUD SNORE. Arthur turns quickly. Erik is sound asleep on the sofa. He looks in a bad way. He's still wearing his border guard's uniform, but it now has stains down the front. He looks like he's neither bathed nor shaved in at least a week.

Arthur crouches on the floor next to him and
shakes his arm.

> ARTHUR
> Erik. Wake up.

No response. Arthur shakes him more vigorously.

> ARTHUR
> Erik, come on, man, wake yourself up.

Erik opens his eyes.

> ERIK
> What is it?

> ARTHUR
> Are you all right?

> ERIK
> I'm fine. What time is it?

> ARTHUR
> Four o'clock.

> ERIK
> A.M. or P.M.?

> ARTHUR
> P.M.

> ERIK
> Wake me in a couple of hours, and
> we'll go out for a drink.

Erik closes his eyes again.

                    ARTHUR
          Don't go back to sleep just yet. Tell
          me, what happened here? Have you been
          burgled? Or mugged?

Erik lifts his head a little and looks around
the room.

                    ERIK
          Oh, just having a little clear-out.
          Getting rid of the rubbish.

Arthur picks up one of the many sheet of paper
strewn across the floor.

                    ARTHUR
          These are your Politburo stories.

                    ERIK
          Yup.

                    ARTHUR
          And you were thinking of throwing
          them away?

                    ERIK
          I would have burnt them last night,
          but I ran out of matches. Never seem
          to have matches around the house now
          that Marina's gone.

                    ARTHUR
          You can't throw this away. This is
          priceless.

                    ERIK
          Not much good to me now.

                    ARTHUR
     Erik, do you mind if I tidy them up a
     bit? You might feel differently about
     them tomorrow.

                    ERIK
     Whatever.

                    ARTHUR
     You look terrible, you know.

                    ERIK
     Gee, thanks. You're looking peachy
     too.

                    ARTHUR
     Why don't you get some proper sleep?
     In bed?

                    ERIK
     Good idea.

Erik struggles to his feet, then stumbles back
down again.

                    ARTHUR
     Here, let me give you a hand.

Arthur takes hold of Erik's arm and places it
around his own shoulder. He then puts his arm
around his waist and pulls Erik to his feet.
Gripping tightly, he half carries, half drags
Erik towards the bedroom.

A few minutes later Arthur returns to the living
room. He picks up the chairs and places them
back around the table. He then starts picking up
handfuls of papers, piling them on to the table,
flattening them out a little as he goes.

INT—ERIK'S APARTMENT—KITCHEN—EARLY MORNING

Arthur is sitting at the table. He has a large box next to him. There are three piles of paper neatly stacked on the table in front of him. He is reading a handwritten sheet.

Erik walks in.

> ERIK
> Oh, hi, Arthur. What you got there?

> ARTHUR
> One of your many masterpieces.

> ERIK
> Fire lighters more like.

> ARTHUR
> Nonsense. This is good stuff.

> ERIK
> If you say so.

> ARTHUR
> And you've been holding out on us.

> ERIK
> What?

> ARTHUR
> I found that second box in your cupboard. The plays and the poems.

> ERIK
> Oh yeah. Forgot about them.

> ARTHUR
> When did you write them?

ERIK
On and off over the years. Everyone
always liked the Politburo stuff so
much, I just didn't bother you with
them.

ARTHUR
Some of them are the best stuff you've
ever written.

ERIK
They're just doodles really.

ARTHUR
Seriously, Erik, I don't think you
realise quite how good you are.

Erik opens the refrigerator. It's well stocked.

ERIK
What happened here? Someone's broken
in, felt sorry for me, and filled the
fridge.

ARTHUR
I popped down to the store. Hope you
don't mind.

ERIK
Mind? Why would I? You can break in
any time you fancy. Don't suppose you
bought any aspirins, did you?

ARTHUR
Bathroom cabinet, top shelf.

Erik walks out of the room. Arthur continues
sorting through the papers. Erik returns holding
a glass of water.

>   ERIK
> What time did you get here?

>   ARTHUR
> Sometime yesterday afternoon.

>   ERIK
> Was I lucid?

>   ARTHUR
> Lucid: yes; sober: no.

Erik sits down at the table opposite Arthur.

>   ERIK
> Sorry about that. I've been overdoing
> it a little lately.

>   ARTHUR
> That's all right.

>   ERIK
> So what brought you round?

>   ARTHUR
> The writing group. We've been worried
> about you.

>   ERIK
> The writing group's still going?

>   ARTHUR
> Why wouldn't it be?

                    ERIK
I'm just surprised. Everything's
changing. I thought there'd be no
need for it now. The Wall's gone. The
government'll be next. What's left to
rebel against? We are now free.

                    ARTHUR
There'll always be a reason for
friends to meet up together.

                    ERIK
Yes. Of course you're right. I've been
a little out of sorts. Feeling sorry
for myself. Little low.

                    ARTHUR
It's not surprising.

                    ERIK
I should be out partying with everyone
else. But I just feel that the Wall
is all I've ever known. Since I was a
kid anyway. I remember life before.
That's what all this has been about.

Erik points at the pile of plays and poems.

                    ERIK con't
Reminiscences. They are my memories
of the past. Not solid fact. Glimpses.
Imperfect impressions. But my
impressions. That's why I'm secretly
pleased that everyone seemed happy
with the Politburo trash.

                    ARTHUR
It's well-written comedy.

                    ERIK
OK, it's well-written trash. But the
rest, that's much more personal.

                    ARTHUR
And much more poignant because of it.

                    ERIK
You're too kind. The problem is, Life
after the Wall is never going to be
the same as it was before the Wall.
I'm 28 years older for one thing. And
the bitterest irony is that the Wall
has paid for my rent, my food, my
clothes, everything.
          (beat)
What am I going to do now?

                    ARTHUR
You write.

                    ERIK
What?

                    ARTHUR
That's what you do. You write. You've
got a gold mine right here.

                    ERIK
This handwritten pile of garbage?

                    ARTHUR
Not in its present format obviously.
But if we tidy it up, get it on to
a computer, mess around with it a
little, I'm pretty sure we can lick
it into some sort of saleable shape.

                    ERIK
You're serious, aren't you?

                    ARTHUR
Deadly. What do you think?

                    ERIK
What the hell! It's not as if I'm
inundated with offers.

                    ARTHUR
Would you consider involving the
writing group as well? They might
come up with some useful input.

                    ERIK
You think they'd be interested?

                    ARTHUR
Are you kidding? Once they've read
this stuff, they'll be with you in a
flash.

                    ERIK
Well, I must admit, if it weren't for
them, I wouldn't have kept writing.

                    ARTHUR
So you're happy us asking them to
help?

                    ERIK
Absolutely.

                    ARTHUR
They're meeting tonight at Frank and
Karen's.

Arthur looks at his watch.

>ARTHUR cont'd
>That gives you a couple of hours to
>get yourself cleaned up a bit first.

INT—WORKERS' APARTMENT BLOCK, EAST BERLIN—FRANK AND SYLVIA'S LIVING ROOM

There is a KNOCK on the door. Frank answers it.
It's Erik and Arthur, both holding large boxes.

>FRANK
>Howdy, stranger. Good to see you back
>on feet.

>KAREN
>We've been worried about you. Haven't
>heard from you in weeks.

>BORIS
>Yeah, thought you might have taken
>off for the West and abandoned us.

>ERIK
>Nothing like that. Just loafing around
>at home. Wallowing in self-pity.

Boris helps Erik place the boxes on the table.

>BORIS
>So what do we have here?

>ARTHUR
>The complete works of Erik Friedheimer.
>To date.

>BORIS
>We're in for a good evening!

ARTHUR
We thought perhaps you'd like to help
us knock it into shape.

BORIS
You mean get the writing group to
write for change, rather than listen
to Erik's mellifluous tones?

ARTHUR
Something like that.

Arthur starts emptying the boxes on to the
dining table.

ARTHUR cont'd
What we've done so far is divide
this stuff into four categories:
the Politburo stories, other short
stories, plays and poems, and essays.

FRANK
Ye Gods, you have been busy. When
did you have time to write all this?
I never had any idea how much you'd
done.

ERIK
Lonely hours in the guard tower.

BORIS
You've been holding out on us all
these years? You've just shared with
us the tip of the iceberg.

ERIK
You only seemed to want to hear the
Politburo stories.

            BORIS
I'm only kidding, Erik. Wouldn't have
missed hearing about the affairs of
state for the world.

            FRANK
What exactly do you want to do with
this lot?

            ARTHUR
Publish it. Sell it. Make Erik a
household name.

            ERIK
Not sure I want to be a household
name.

            ARTHUR
Sure you do. Who wouldn't want to be
famous?

            ERIK
Me.

            ARTHUR
Why not?

            ERIK
I just want to blend in. Nothing more,
nothing less.

            ARTHUR
If we're going to sell this stuff,
we're going to need an author we can
sell too.

                    ERIK
How about we go with 'anonymous' for
now?

                    ARTHUR
If you like.

                    FRANK
This is all good stuff, but who's
going to publish it? It's all short
stories and poems, and a handful of
plays. Short stories are not easy to
sell.

                    ARTHUR
They do if they are by an established
author.

                    BORIS
Unless I'm missing something, Erik is
not an established author.

                    ARTHUR
He will be when we've turned his novel
into the next best-seller.

                    ERIK
Hate to point this out, but I haven't
written a novel.

                    ARTHUR
Sure you have. It's right here in
instalments, in good old-fashioned
Dickensian style.

                    SYLVIA
You mean the Politburo stories?

ARTHUR
Exactly. Might need a catchier title
though—what was it you said earlier
Boris? 'The Affairs of State'. We just
need to establish an underlying plot.
That's where you guys come in.

KAREN
Oh yeah?

ARTHUR
I thought between us we could sort
out the best stories, develop a plot
and a central theme, and then Erik
can fill in the missing details while
we try to organise the rest of his
oeuvre.

FRANK
How long do you reckon this will take?

ARTHUR
About three to six months. If we pull
our fingers out, we could hit the
anniversary of the fall the Wall,
which is also conveniently close to
Christmas.

BORIS
Six months? You're kidding, right?

KAREN
It's not like you've got much else
going on right now, is it?

BORIS
Good point. When do I start?

Arthur hands him a pile of papers.

                    ARTHUR
How about right now?

                    SYLVIA
When the novel's written, then what?

                    ARTHUR
We'll have to find a publisher.

                    BORIS
If Erik wants to stay out of the
limelight, how will you market it?

                    ARTHUR
I'll act as his literary agent.

                    BORIS
And what do we get out of all this?

                    KAREN
For God's sake, Boris, you get the
satisfaction of helping one of your
oldest pals.

                    ARTHUR
No, it's a fair question. We'll share
the proceeds among us.

                    SYLVIA
Erik should get the lion's share. He
is the genius after all.

                    ARTHUR
We can discuss proportions later.
For now, let's just get that novel
written.

                                    CUT TO

INT—LITTLE BROWN PUBLICATIONS, NEW YORK—KASPER WERNER'S OFFICE—SUMMER 1990

Arthur is sitting in front of a large oak desk. KASPER WERNER is facing him. On the desk between them is a bound 500-sheet manuscript. The title reads: *The Affairs of State* by Anon.

A subtitle appears at the foot of the screen:
      NEW YORK—1990

                    WERNER
So this guy's life's not in danger?

                    ARTHUR
Er no. No, it's not.

                    WERNER
And he wasn't a member of the Politburo or the Secret Police.

                    ARTHUR
I just wanted to get your attention.

                    WERNER
Well, you certainly did that. Phone calls at 2 in the morning. Secret meetings in Central Park. Part-complete manuscripts left in lockers.

                    ARTHUR
I thought you'd appreciate the intrigue. Make you more likely to read the book.

                    WERNER
Well, I must admit, I couldn't resist taking a peek. And then—

ARTHUR
And then you couldn't put it down.

WERNER
Something like that, yeah.
          (beat)
So why come clean now?

ARTHUR
Because I feel you're about to offer
us a contract, and I wanted everything
to be above board.

WERNER
Hey now, fella. I found the thing hard
to put down, but what makes you think
we're about to offer you a contract
to publish?

ARTHUR
Because I'm still sitting here
chatting to you, and you've put your
phone on hold.

WERNER
OK, you got me there. Before we talk
business, let's get something cleared
up. You're the author, right?

ARTHUR
Actually no. The bit about the author
wanting to stay anonymous, that bit
was true. And much of the details in
the book about the internal workings
of the Politburo, they're also true.
My friend had a unique perspective.

                    WERNER
How so?

                    ARTHUR
He was an East German Border Guard.

                    WERNER
You mean like a nightwatchman?

                    ARTHUR
Close enough.

                    WERNER
So how does a nightwatchman get to
find out all this stuff?

                    ARTHUR
Well, he's no ordinary nightwatchman.
He's really a writer. Erik passed
his Arbitur (that's the East German
qualification required to go to
university) at the end of his high
school days and was accepted at the
East Berlin Institute into the School
of Writing. With a degree from there
he would have had a job for life.

                    WERNER
But he decided not to go.

                    ARTHUR
That's right.

                    WERNER
Why?

                    ARTHUR
Because he did not want to write
what he was told to write. He felt

he would've been forced to produce
propaganda for ever and ever.

Arthur takes a sip from the glass of water on
the desk in front of him.

ARTHUR cont'd
Given the choice between being
told what to write by the State and
having a job that allowed him to
think, daydream and write what he
wanted, he chose the latter. Once
in, he was treated like all the
other guards. Just another harmless
drudge.

WERNER
You mean like part of the furniture?

ARTHUR
That's right. You'd be amazed how
candid people in power can be in
front of their menials. They just
don't see them. Effectively, they're
invisible.

WERNER
So when did he start writing again?

ARTHUR
He never stopped. But what he did
do was to found a writing club. They
were very common in East Berlin.
Most of them were part of State-run
institutions—universities, factories,
government departments, that sort of
thing. His was loosely affiliated to
his workers' apartment block. I was
one of the original members.

                    WERNER
And he wrote for the writing club?

                    ARTHUR
We all wrote for each other and read
our works out at weekly meetings. But
he was the best of all of us and wrote
and performed the most—after a little
liquid persuasion.

Werner swivels round on his chair and
stares out the window.

                    WERNER
                (to himself)
So even amongst friends he was
reluctant to take the limelight. But
deep down he was a mild-mannered
subversive, kicking against the
system from the inside.

Werner walks over to the window and stares down
at the traffic on 5th Avenue, 30 floors below.

                    WERNER
                (still talking to himself)
He sees the absurdity of the political
situation and rages against it with
his biting satire.

Reminiscent of Heller's Yossarian,
perhaps. Hmm, that could work. *The
Affairs of State*—*Catch 22* recast in
the Cold War.

Werner turns to face Erik.

OK. And this friend, it's not you?

ARTHUR

No.

WERNER

So why does he want to stay anonymous?
Did he commit some terrible crime? Is
he on the run?

ARTHUR

Oh no, nothing like that.

WERNER

Pity.

ARTHUR

He just doesn't want to be a public
figure. He's a quiet guy. Not shy
exactly, but very private.

WERNER

You realise that this manuscript is
still quite rough.

ARTHUR

Of course. It's the first one we've
ever produced.

WERNER

And there's a lot work that needs
doing on it.

ARTHUR

Of course.

                    WERNER
Here's what I'd like to do: I'll pass
it to my chief editor and get him to
give it a read through. He'll give
you some pointers as to how to fix
it up. Once you're done, we'll talk
contracts. How does that sound?

                    ARTHUR
Sounds good.

                    WERNER
How do we get in contact with your
friend?

                    ARTHUR
Entirely through me.

                    WERNER
And should it go further? If we
decide to publish, how're you going
to organise the publicity angle?

                    ARTHUR
You mean the book launch and chat
shows? That sort of thing?

                    WERNER
Exactly.

                    ARTHUR
I was thinking I could appear anywhere
the author would normally appear. I
could call myself his literary agent.

                    WERNER
Interesting gimmick. That could work.
What about a pseudonym? We really

can't go with Anon. Too cheesy. And
you can forget about A. Parody or A.
N. Other.

          ARTHUR
How about the 'Former East German
Border Guard'?

          WERNER
'Tales from an East German Border
Guard'. That could work. It'll do for
now.

WERNER stands and offers his hand. The two men
shake hands.

          WERNER
We'll be in touch. Give us about two
weeks.

                        CUT TO

EXT—SCHOENBERG, WEST BERLIN—DRIVEWAY TO WILLEM'S HOUSE—AFTERNOON

Willem's driveway looks like it could do with
re-gravelling. The same Audi is parked on the
drive; it looks older and dirtier. There is a
slight dent on one of the wings and a little rust
on the bonnet over the headlamps.

The house is showing signs of wear too. There is
paint flaking off some of the woodwork. Willem
can be seen sitting at a desk staring out the
window. The window on the floor above now has
net curtains.

A subtitle appears at the foot of the screen: SCHOENBERG—1999

INT—SCHOENBERG, WEST BERLIN—WILLEM'S STUDY—NIGHT

Willem is sitting at his desk staring out of the window. Mozart's *DON GIOVANNI* is playing loudly on the hi-fi. Anna walks in.

> ANNA
> Hi, honey. You're home early.

William makes no sign that he has heard Anna come in. Anna turns down the volume of the MUSIC.

> ANNA
> And not working either. Writers' block?

Willem remains facing the window.

> WILLEM
> They're letting me go.

> ANNA
> Letting you go where?

> WILLEM
> Letting me go from the university.

> ANNA
> They're sacking you?

> WILLEM
> Early retirement.

                    ANNA
How can the department run without
you? You are the department.

                    WILLEM
They're retiring the department too.

                    ANNA
That makes no sense.

                    WILLEM
Financial considerations—nothing
personal—it is a technical university
after all—must move with the
times—real science, not technical
science—blah-blah-blah.

Willem swivels round to face his wife. Tears are
pouring down his face.

                    WILLEM cont'd
I'm being put out to pasture.

                    ANNA
You're still young. You'll find another
position.

                    WILLEM
I'm 50 years old—I'm a fossil. I'll not
get tenure anywhere else now. It's far
too late.

                    ANNA
But you've got so much to offer, so
much experience.

                    WILLEM
I was once the world's leading expert
on the Berlin Wall. I can tell you

that the main wall was 3.6 metres high, each section weighed 2750 kg, it was 96 miles long, and it claimed 192 lives. I can even tell you the names of those who died, where they died, and when. But who cares any more? Besides, you can now find that out on the Internet anyway.

                    ANNA
You were successful—the Wall came down.

                    WILLEM
It came down despite me, not because of me. I got it wrong. The people brought the Wall down, not me. If it hadn't been for you, I wouldn't even have seen it coming down first-hand.

                    ANNA
Willem, that was 10 years ago. You've done so much since then.

                    WILLEM
I've gone from professor of political science to history teacher and now to pensioner.

                    ANNA
Why not leave academia completely? Write a book instead.

                    WILLEM
I haven't been published in a journal for 8 years. Who would publish a book by me now?

ANNA
It doesn't have to be about political
science. Why don't you write a play or
a novel? If that East German Border
Guard can write a novel, I don't see
why you can't.

WILLEM
Ah yes, 'Confessions of a Politburo
Lackey'.

ANNA
I think you'll find it's called *The
Affairs of State.*

WILLEM
Have you read it?

ANNA
Phizz sent me a copy when it came out
in New York. It's actually very good.
His use of language is extraordinary.
The inside stories about the Politburo
are a scream. If half of what he
says is true, it's amazing that East
Germany lasted as long as it did.

WILLEM
So he struck lucky. Wrote a trashy
novel that they turned into a
blockbuster film, and scurried off to
the US to enjoy his ill-gotten gains.

ANNA
Ill-gotten gains?

> WILLEM
> Why do you think he uses a pseudonym
> and gets an agent to represent him?
> He's obviously got something to hide.
> And now that he has his blood money, I
> predict we'll not see him again. In a
> year he'll disappear into obscurity.

> ANNA
> Hate to tell you this, but he's just
> published a new book.

> WILLEM
> Oh God! Let me guess, 'More Confessions
> of a Politburo Lackey'.

> ANNA
> This one's called *The Collective*. I
> think it's an anthology of his early
> work.

> WILLEM
> Scraping the barrel, in other words.
> Got nothing new to say. Presumably he
> lacked the dedication and imagination
> to complete another work of novel
> length.

> ANNA
> Why don't you read it first before
> passing judgement?

INT—BERLIN—LEHMANN'S BOOKSTORE—AFTERNOON

Copies of *The Collective* by The East German
Border Guard are piled high on the main display
counter. Willem is standing in line, waiting to

pay. He moves forward when a cashier becomes free.

                    SALES CLERK
          Ah, *The Collective*—popular choice.

                    WILLEM
          So I understand.

                    SALES CLERK
          Did you see *The Affairs of State*?

                    WILLEM
          I've not had that particular misfortune -
          thankfully.

                    SALES CLERK
               (laughing politely)
          Good one.

                    SALES CLERK cont'd
          That'll be 35 euros please.

The sales clerk puts the book into a bag.

INT—SCHOENBERG, WEST BERLIN—WILLEM'S STUDY—NIGHT

A Mozart PIANO CONCERTO is playing quietly in the background. Willem is sitting at his desk with a book open in front of him. In his right hand he is holding a pencil and a highlighter pen. He leans forward, highlights a paragraph, and writes a few notes in the margin.

INT—WILLEM'S HOUSE IN SCHOENBERG—LIVING ROOM—NIGHT

Anna is watching the TV. Willem walks in.

>   WILLEM
>   Just listen to this tripe.

Willem opens the book and prepares to read a passage.

>   ANNA
>   That's Erik, isn't it?

Willem looks up sharply.

>   WILLEM
>   What?

>   ANNA
>   On the telly. That's Erik. Erik
>   Friedheimer.

Anna points at the screen.

>   WILLEM
>   No, it's not. That's Arthur Behrendt—
>   he's the East German Border Guard's
>   agent. He's the special guest on Lorna
>   Regis's show. I noticed it was on when I
>   was reading through the paper earlier.

>   ANNA
>   No, no, no. Not on the sofa. That huge
>   poster behind him. That's Erik.

Willem takes a few paces into the room and peers at the screen.

                    WILLEM
Are you sure?

                    ANNA
Absolutely.

                    WILLEM
But how can you possibly be? It's been
nearly 40 years since you last saw
him.

                    ANNA
He looks just the same to me. Same
hair - white now, rather than blond.
Same shy boyish smile. Same nose,
large and slightly crooked from when
he broke it when you two were larking
around.
          (beat)
I tell you, that's Erik.

                    WILLEM
I don't bloody believe it. What's he
doing on a New York chat show?

Willem joins his wife on the sofa. Both now
hooked on the programme.

INT—NEW YORK CHAT SHOW—EVENING

Arthur is sitting on the set of an American
chat show. He is about to be interviewed by the
host LORNA REGIS. The SIGNATURE TUNE to the show
finishes, and the audience APPLAUDS.

                    LORNA
Good evening. On tonight's show we
have Arthur Behrendt—agent to the
mysterious East German Border Guard.

                    ARTHUR
Good evening.

                    LORNA
The last time you were on the show in
March of this year I was congratulating
you on the Oscar that your client won
for his screenplay for the movie *The
Affairs of State*, based on his own
novel of the same name. And this time
last year we were talking about the
amazing success of the novel itself.
It's been quite a year. How has this
success affected you?

                    ARTHUR
Life's certainly become hectic. The
publishing company own my calendar,
and I get sent around the country
all the time. On the plus side, it's
easier to get a table in a restaurant
now.

A few CHUCKLES in the audience.

                    LORNA
So tell us about the new book. Not a
novel this time?

                    ARTHUR
No, that's right. It's a collection of
his works written between 1961 and
1989. Works inspired by the Berlin
Wall. There're 10 short stories, a

STANLEY JACKSON AND GAVIN JACKSON

handful of poems, and one of his many previously unpublished plays.

                LORNA
Why did he decide to publish his early works?

                ARTHUR
Public demand. A small sample appeared on a web site over the summer. The number of hits it got was so huge and the blogs have been so complimentary that we decided it was well worth risking publishing the work in a more conventional format.

                LORNA
I understand that you have a big announcement for us tonight.

                ARTHUR
That's right. After 5 years of anonymity, the East German Border Guard has decided to step forward and reveal himself. To coincide with the launch of his new book, he will be attending book signings and readings across the country.

The audience GASPS.

                LORNA
You heard it here first, ladies and gentlemen—the East German Border Guard will be coming out of hiding on Thursday this week.

A huge round of APPLAUSE breaks out in the audience.

                    LORNA
What can you tell us about him?

                    ARTHUR
His name is Erik Friedheimer, and he
comes from Mitte in former East Berlin.

                    LORNA
What's he like? Until now, we didn't
even know his name.

                    ARTHUR
That's him behind us.

Arthur points to one of the many posters of Erik
that surround the set.

                    LORNA
So why is Erik willing to come into
the limelight now—and in such a
dramatic fashion?

                    ARTHUR
Gratitude mainly. He wants to thank
his many readers for their support.
But also to please me. I've been
attempting to persuade him to come
forward for a while now because I
feel he deserves to be recognised.

                    LORNA
Will he keep writing?

                    ARTHUR
No one would ever be able to stop Erik
from writing. He's currently working
on a satirical novel based on the
US judicial system, which Michael

Douglas has already expressed an interest in.

APPLAUSE and a small CHEER from the audience.

>LORNA
Many thanks, Arthur.

Turns to camera.

>LORNA cont'd
The Collective by Erik Friedheimer, better known as the Former East German Border Guard, was published here in New York last week by Little Brown Publications and is available in all good bookstores. Erik Friedheimer will be at various locations across the country for book signings starting next week on his return from Berlin.

More APPLAUSE from the audience.

>LORNA cont'd
After the break: Designer babies— should America demand genetic perfection?

INT—WILLEM'S HOUSE IN SCHOENBERG—LIVING ROOM—NIGHT

Willem looks down at the book he's still holding. He turns it around several times in his hands.

He stands up slowly and walks out of the room without saying a word.

ANNA
(calling out after him)
Willem, are you all right?

INT—SCHOENBERG, WEST BERLIN—WILLEM'S STUDY—EARLY MORNING

Willem is standing by the desk dressed in a long overcoat and hat. He has an ancient leather satchel over his shoulder. His now dog-eared copy of *The Collective* is on the desk. He picks it up, puts it in the satchel, and leaves the room.

We hear the SOUND of the front door CLOSING, the car STARTING, and GRAVEL as the car pulls away.

EXT—BERLIN—OUTSIDE LEHMANN'S BOOKSTORE—MORNING

The queue outside the bookstore stretches the full length of the block and around the corner. There is excited CHATTER as opening time approaches. Some people are CHANTING: ERIK.

Willem is in the queue. There are about 30 people between him and the door. Like many people around him, he is stamping his feet to keep warm.

At the front of the queue there is a news crew interviewing the people closest to the door. A REPORTER is doing a piece for the camera.

REPORTER
We're coming to you live from Berlin awaiting a unique literary event. We're

outside Lehmann's bookstore, just a few moments away from witnessing the first ever public appearance of Erik Friedheimer, better known as the Former East German Border Guard.

Friedheimer, now an American citizen, returns to his hometown to meet his fans face to face for the first time as he attends this eagerly awaited book signing.

As you can see behind me, there is a huge turn out on this cold Berlin morning.

INT—BERLIN—LEHMANN'S BOOKSTORE—MORNING

Erik and Arthur are standing in the bookstore waiting for the book signing to start. There is a large clock over the door. It is 08.59.

Erik looks at his watch.

> ARTHUR
> Ready?

Erik nods.

> ERIK ARTHUR
> Guess so. Let's do it.

Arthur nods towards the two security guards. They walk towards the door.

EXT—BERLIN—OUTSIDE LEHMANN'S BOOKSTORE—MORNING

The reporter faces the camera again.

> REPORTER
> It's nine o'clock now, and it looks
> like they are preparing to open up.

The reporter turns to face the bookstore. The camera pans in on the door.

INT—LEHMANN'S BOOKSTORE, DOORWAY—CAMERAMAN'S POV

The blinds on the windows on either side of the door open. The people waiting in line take a few steps forward. Two security guards inside the store unlock and open the doors. A CHEER breaks out in the crowd.

The crowd remains orderly as one of the guards beckons them forward. The first people are now in the store. In front of them is a large counter piled high with copies of Erik's anthology, *The Collective*. There are also piles of his novel *The Affairs of State* and his screenplay written for the movie. Erik and Arthur are standing behind the counter flanked on either side by members of Lehmann's staff.

Suddenly there is a SHOUT in the CROWD outside.

> VOICE (O.S.)
> Hey, buddy, there's no need to push.
> We've all been here for hours, a few
> more minutes isn't going to kill you.

A MAN pushes past the camera and into the store.

                    REPORTER
                  (chuckling)
        Looks like the thought of meeting his
        hero has gotten the better of that
        fan.

One of the SECURITY GUARDS guides the man back
outside, and someone good-naturedly lets him
back in the line.

INT—LEHMANN'S BOOKSTORE—BOOK SIGNING DESK

Erik takes the book offered to him by the first
person in the line. He opens the front cover
and looks up.

                    FIRST PERSON IN LINE
        It's such a pleasure to finally meet
        you.

                    ERIK
        Many thanks for buying my book. I do
        hope you enjoy it. Who would you like
        me to write it to?

                    FIRST PERSON IN LINE
        To Howard please.

EXT—BERLIN—OUTSIDE LEHMANN'S BOOKSTORE—MORNING

The reporter turns to one of the people in the
crowd.

                    REPORTER
        How long have you been waiting in line?

                    PERSON IN LINE #1
We got here shortly after 6 this
morning.

                    REPORTER
Wow! So you've been here for nearly 3
hours.

                    PERSON IN LINE #1
That's right.

                    REPORTER
And do you think it'll be worth the
wait?

                    PERSON IN LINE #1
Absolutely. I've been wanting to meet
him ever since *The Affairs of State*
first came out. I've seen the movie 8
times. I think he's awesome.

EXT—OUTSIDE LEHMANN'S BOOKSTORE

Willem has moved forward in the line. There are
now about 5 people between him and the inside
of the store.

EXT—BERLIN—OUTSIDE LEHMANN'S BOOKSTORE—MORNING

                    REPORTER
                 (to the next person in line)
How far have you come to meet Erik
Friedheimer?

                    PERSON IN LINE #2
New York city.

                    REPORTER
New York city?

                    PERSON IN LINE #2
That's right.

                    REPORTER
Even though he starts his American
book signing tour in New York next
week?

                    PERSON IN LINE #2
We figured it'd be neat to meet the
guy in his old hometown and then meet
him again in his new hometown.

                    REPORTER
Will you get to see much of Berlin
while you're here?

                    PERSON IN LINE #2
We hope to see the Wall museum this
afternoon and go on a tour of the
remains of the Wall tomorrow.

EXT—INSIDE LEHMANN'S BOOKSTORE

Willem is now inside the bookstore. There are
just 2 people ahead of him.

EXT—BERLIN—OUTSIDE LEHMANN'S BOOKSTORE—MORNING

The reporter moves on to the next person in the
line.

                    REPORTER
Are you excited to finally be meeting
Erik Friedheimer?

                    PERSON IN LINE #3
You bet. He's been an inspiration to
me.

                    REPORTER
How so?

                    PERSON IN LINE #3
I left school early, got bogged down
in a dead end job, and was feeling
pretty low. I then found Erik on the
Internet.

                    REPORTER
On the Internet?

                    PERSON IN LINE #3
Yeah. Some of his friends, I think
it was his old East German writing
group, started to publish some of
Erik's early work quite a while back.
That's where I discovered him—it
couldn't have been a moment too soon.

                    REPORTER
Thank you.

**INT—LEHMANN'S BOOKSTORE—BOOK SIGNING
DESK—MORNING**

Willem is now standing in front of Erik. He
reaches into his satchel and removes his dog-
eared copy of *The Collective* and places it on
the table.

                    ERIK
This one looks well read. That's
always nice to see.

He looks up and smiles at the next person in the line. It's Willem.

            ERIK cont'd
My God! It's Professor Willem Schmidt, isn't it?

            WILLEM
            (visibly shocked)
Er yes . . . yes, it is.

            ERIK
I was holed up in this bookshop for 3 hours before it opened. I was browsing in the Political Theory section when the name Willem Schmidt just leapt out at me. I thought maybe it was a different Willem Schmidt, but I opened the cover and there was your photo in the inside jacket.

Erik reaches behind him and picks up a book that he shows Willem.

            ERIK
And now here you are, I can't believe it. I've read about half the book already. I love the papers you wrote on the Wall.

            WILLEM
You do?

            ERIK
It's brilliant work. Your arguments are so cogent. You're Berlin's Noam Chomsky. I had no idea that anyone

on the West cared. You're an amazing
man.

        WILLEM
I'm speechless. I don't know what to
say.

        ERIK
Hey, is that the satchel?

Erik points to the SATCHEL slung over Willem's
shoulder.

        WILLEM
Er yes, it's the same one. I couldn't
bear to let it go.

        ERIK
And is that what I think it is?

Before Willem can stop him, Erik leans over the
table and reaches into the satchel and brings
out a well-oiled, but ancient-looking handgun.

        VOICE IN THE CROWD (O.S.)
            (shouting)
Oh my God, he's got a gun!

A YOUNG MAN breaks out of the line and runs
straight into the store. He grabs hold of Willem
and wrestles him to the ground, knocking over
the book signing table as he does so. A SECURITY
GUARD hurries over.

        ERIK
            (remaining calm)
Don't panic, folks, everything's all
right. This is my old buddy from
Schoneberg, my partner in crime from

my juvenile housebreaking days. And this . . .

Erik holds the gun above his head.

> ERIK cont'd
> . . . is one of our spoils of war. It's a World War II Luger. We liberated it back in '61, and don't worry, it's not loaded!
>
> The professor here just wanted to relive old times.

Erik takes aim at a light fitting above everyone's heads and pulls the trigger of the Luger. The revolver's hammer falls on to an empty chamber and makes a LOUD CLICK, but no bullet is fired.

Suddenly there is an EXPLOSION of CAMERA FLASHES. The TV CREW and several PHOTOGRAPHERS are now crowding round Erik and the overturned table, and the piles of Erik's books are now scattered everywhere. Willem is still lying on the floor with the YOUNG MAN from the line on top of him.

CUT TO

INT—TV STUDIO—CNN NEWS—AFTERNOON

EVA SULLIVAN is reading the news. She is looking into the camera and has a monitor over her left shoulder showing a picture of Erik Friedheimer.

> EVA SULLIVAN
> . . . and finally, today nearly saw an international incident at a book signing in Berlin, Germany. Erik

Friedheimer, famous for his book *The Affairs of State,* which was made into an Oscar-winning film, was launching his latest work *The Collective*, his unique collection of writings inspired by the Berlin Wall (the barrier that once divided East and West Berlin). Suddenly a man standing in line for a signature appeared to pull a gun on him.

It turned out that the man, a retired professor, little known outside the world of German academia, was, in fact, Willem Schmidt, the hero of many of Erik's earliest works, and the man that Friedheimer refers to in The *Collective* as his muse.

The two men had not seen each other for nearly 40 years. The professor, wanting to surprise his old school friend, nearly got a lot more than he bargained for. One of Erik's loyal fans took the law into his own hands and wrestled him to the ground.

But Erik managed to save the day. They were later seen together heading over to Cafe Adler to relive old times.

Coming up after the break: Are rats ticklish? We talk to a cognitive scientist who has just completed his doctorate to address that very question.

ERIK, WILLEM, ARTHUR BEHRENDT, and ANNA SCHMIDT are sitting around a table in the corner of the cafe. They are drinking coffee and eating desserts. The SECURITY GUARD from the earlier book signing is standing by the door to the cafe making sure that no one disturbs the four of them.

          ARTHUR
Erik's right. You've got a great story to tell.

          WILLEM
Who'd be interested in reading about a washed-up teacher of political history?

          ARTHUR
Are you kidding? Your story's got everything: friendship, action, separation, lost youth, betrayal, jealousy, and revenge. It's even got a femme fatale.

Arthur looks at Anna and winks.

          ANNA
What are you insinuating?

          ARTHUR
I'm not insinuating anything. I'm guessing that you're the famous Anna of the skinny ankles, the object of the young Erik's dreams.

Erik blushes and looks a little flustered.

                    ARTHUR
And wasn't it you who recognised Erik
first?

                    ANNA
Well, yes, but we were all kids back
then.

                    ERIK
And I'm happily reunited with Marina
now.

                    ARTHUR
I'm just teasing. We're here to
persuade Willem to write his book.
Look, why don't you at least come over
to New York, and I'll put you in front
of Erik's publisher. What do you say?
It's not as if you've got anything
else on right now, is it?

                    WILLEM
Well, no . . . OK, why not?

Anna throws her arms around her husband, and
the couple kiss while Erik and Arthur look on
smiling broadly.

                                        FADE OUT

                CLOSING TITLES

STANLEY JACKSON AND GAVIN JACKSON

Printed in the United States
By Bookmasters